PUNE - TRADITION TO MARKET

PUNE - TRADITION TO MARKET

A Study of Changing Trends in Consumption with Special Reference to Service Sector in Hotel Industry

Dr. Jasmine Y. Damle

KALPAZ

Pune - Tradition to Market

ISBN: 978-81-7835-895-6

Published in 2011 in India by
Kalpaz Publications
C-30, Satyawati Nagar,
Delhi-110052
E-mail: kalpaz@hotmail.com
Phone : 9212729499

Laser Type Setting by: Rudra Computer Graphics, Delhi
Printed at : Chawla Offset Printers, Delhi

I dedicate my book
In Loving Memory of Daddy
(Late Prof. Y.B. Damle and
Aai Late Smt. Rekha Y. Damle)

Contents

Foreword

The present book by Dr. Jasmine Y. Damle is an innovative and meticulous study of the emergent 'new economy" and its social and cultural interface with the aspects of the changing social structures, ideologies and value systems in the city of Pune known for its past intellectual pre-eminence and roots in tradition. It offers an insight into the state of hotel industry in the city, and various restaurants and analyses their cultural, social and economic outcome in the changing backdrop of the history, tradition, family structure and social composition of the city. The data for this study have been generated through observation of various types of restaurants, interviews of hoteliers, members of clubs and business and software executives. In addition, historical records and published material have been meticulously used. The book demonstrates a new sensitivity in its theoretical constructs and methodological operationalization. According to the author, the new economy which is triggered primarily by the growth in the service sector comprising 'sophisticated industrial developments'. The development in the spheres of information technology, medical and management education, and net-working with the multinational concerns in various economic enterprises has contributed to the unprecedented growth of a new professional middle class in the city. This class by its nature is highly mobile, cosmopolitan and oriented to a lifestyle which celebrates quality consumption, entertainment and sophisticated style of life. The immigrant segment in this class is quite substantial, and it adds to the city's new cosmopolitan ethos in the realms of culture, consumption pattern and social life. Its cosmopolitanism contributes to the diversification in tastes and demands for cuisine of various regions from India and abroad. The result is a spurt in hotel and restaurant industries which have a multiplier effect in creation of jobs, income generation and providing reinforcement to the new style of life.

The book makes some meaningful theoretical contributions. Conceptually a distinction is drawn between "consumption" and "consumerism". A broadening of and incremental growth in the consumption behaviour of people with additional income is a normal process. Consumerism, on the other hand, as the author rightly suggests, is linked to the notion of "conspicuous waste", a concept that Veblen introduced to diagnose the malfunctioning of the consumer economy. To an extent, there is a link between wasteful consumption, or throw away culture in consumption, and perpetual demand created to sustain the capitalist production economy. The essence of this linkage between capitalist enterprise and cultural style of consumption cannot be grasped, according to the author, by a simplistic economic reductionism which the classical Marxist theories have posited to understand the economic behaviour of actors in the new economy. The new economy, particularly in the sphere of consumption, offers its participants a wide variety of choices which are guided by voluntarism and not by the determinism of the product. Its social and cultural dynamics is based upon social mobility, voluntary choices and intercultural negotiations and adaptive responses. The chain of the multiplier effect of its growth and spread begins with empowerment by education, particularly professional education. Services and not commodity, production, brands, and not the materiality of the commodity, define its standards and excellence.

Dr. Damle's book makes basic contribution to sociology of urban culture in the new economic setting. There are not many studies in this area, and her contribution would have a pioneering impact upon future researches in this field in Indian sociology. I am sure this book would be read widely by sociologists, economists and urban policy planners in India and abroad.

25th December, 2010

Yogendra Singh
Professor Emeritus
Jawaharlal Nehru University
New Delhi - 110067

Preface

The present book is evolved from my post-doctoral project completed about a decade ago. The project mainly dealt with the service sector associated with food industry which, in turn, was facilitated by the industrial development in Pune.

Prima facie the case of industrial and economic development looks self sustaining. However, in case of Pune, this development has been made possible by socio-structural and socio-cultural support by way of changing family structure, changes in the institute of marriage, higher education and professional careers of both men and women, and of course the loosening of the traditional shackles of family, caste, kinship; and slowly dissolving regional, linguistic differences, not to say prejudices. There is thus a snow-balling process of the continuous interaction between economic development, *per say*, and socio-cultural changes.

The present study focuses on socio-cultural changes as well as socio-economic development, and the interaction between the two. The primary hypothesis of this study is based on the inert-relationship between industrialization, economic development and socio-cultural support.

When one starts an enquiry with the help of some concepts, it would be unrealistic to expect a neat package of theory which guides such an enquiry. That is why many research designs imply serendipity pattern though it is not necessary that altogether the unexpected variables emerge, having explanatory power. Nevertheless, a change is characterized by various permutations and combinations of the relationship envisaged between different variables. In this study certain prime movers like industrialization of a sophisticated type which generates a level of income so as to facilitate spending adequate amount on consumption of food and various other amenities such as leisure and entertainment are taken into account. The focus is not on an economy producing goods for direct consumption, but on industrialization that is sophisticated enough to help people afford spending beyond their basic needs. This means proliferation of service economy which has deeper sociological significance. Availability of various amenities such as hotels, restaurants and different types of eating places, therefore, forms an essential part of this phenomenon.

It is also a common experience for a researcher to borrow from other disciplines and improvise a theoretical framework for conducting one's enquiry. Similarly, instead of relying on a textbook of methodology, it is both necessary and fruitful to tailor methodology to the needs of a particular work. So I have borrowed from the science of Economics and have also made use of specific tools such as interview schedule for hoteliers, restaurant owners, business executives, and club managers; and observation schedule for street food vendors. This enquiry is based primarily on secondary data, historical material, observation and a few interviews as mentioned. I interviewed about 20 hoteliers and club members, and 13 executives from software companies and other business establishments. The material provided is thus more of an illustrative type. It does not conform to the usual sampling survey, but it is collected through the use of non-probability purposive sampling and snowball technique. So it gives a fairly good idea regarding the providers of consumption as well as the consumers. Hotels have been categorized from 5 stars to no star status. Restaurants belong to various grades like A grade, B grade, and so on. The material obtained bears out the working hypothesis of relationship between industrialization, economic development, and socio-cultural ethos, particularly in the sense of making a deliberate choice of consumption as against the traditional restraints on consumption.

For long Pune had taken pride in observing the traditional restraints thereby debunking consumption. Today the same Pune has found an alternate ideological basis for consumption. Eating out, entertaining, etc. have become important features in the modern style of living. However, such desire to debunk taboos and restrictions, instead of consumption, is facilitated by appropriate changes in the socio-cultural syndrome which is amply reflected in the brief historical review of Marathi literature. That is why when consumption patterns change, something more than price and income may have changed.

Pierre Bourdieu has drawn our attention to the insights of Veblen regarding the qualitative differences in the consumption choices and how they symbolize various segments of class structure. Bourdieu is not simply talking about differentiation but rather class based means of maintaining class differences and boundaries, which vary across societies in their intensity. This approach suggests an entirely new line of research on food ways and other items of material culture.

The economic multiplier effect unleashed by service sector and the spiral growth of the hotel industry are interdependent on each other. But again, one must not forget that this would not be possible without the support of the cultural milieu sustained by changing structural arrangements like family, caste, region, nation etc. Economic prosperity and socio-cultural change, or transition, go hand in hand and therefore, both the processes have to work in unison, thus substituting a modern system for the traditional one. It should also be remembered that education also undergoes a change with the changing times. While analytical, theoretical and academic education provides the basic foundation of any education system, it needs to be strengthened by the requisite professional and technical education so as to provide the appropriate skills for handling the continuously changing system.

It is important to note that the industrially developed Pune not only generated employment and income, but also provided a margin for spending on something much more than the bare necessities of life; and hence the growing importance of consumption items of leisure, recreation, entertainment, and in general enjoying a better standard of living. This margin due to the new levels of rising income is a very crucial variable for this study.

In this work, my brief introduction to the work is followed by the detailed discussion of theoretical perspectives on which this study is based. The theory comprises three concepts – those of Service Sector, Economic Multiplier and Consumption. The Second chapter traces in brief, the historical background and the traditional ethos of Pune, the pensioner's paradise in the past. The third chapter unfolds the gradual metamorphosis of this paradise into a cyber city, an industrial hub, though still retaining its title 'Oxford of the east'. In chapter four, we can see how Pune's industries developed faster because of the academic support they got from different institutions, and how, in turn, a variety of new professional courses were started to cater to the growing demand for highly sophisticated job-market in the city.

The nexus between industries and hotels, and the hotel industry itself is an important economic and employment multiplier and forms the basis of a few other chapters that follow. Also incorporated in these chapters is the concept and classification of hotels. There is also a section on the contribution of immigrants to hotel industry, and how the mosaic of the changing diaspora has transformed the socio-cultural fabric of the city.

Lastly, I have included two, rather lengthy chapters, to fortify my analysis and observation. The first one is Pune as seen in Marathi literature. It is said that literature is a mirror to society, so the survey of relevant contemporary Marathi literature corroborates the entire history in a very interesting way. The other chapter focuses on the newspaper articles and magazines of the period.

The final section comprises appendices including the interviews, list of large industries in Pune and the bibliography.

As mentioned at the beginning of the Preface, this book is based on my post-doctoral project completed at the turn of the century. Thereafter the data has not been updated. However, this does not directly affect the relevance of the main statement this book has tried to make. This is so because to this date, in general, it is a rising curve for every aspect dealt with in the book. New and larger industries are being set up, even if a couple of earlier ones are closed down. The number of software companies is ever on the rise; and so is that of automobile manufacturing units, or electronic ones for that matter. There is also no looking back for the Street Food stalls, the latest addition being the concentration of street food vendors in Model colony off Fergusson Road. 'Service apartment' is a comparatively recent addition enriching the already active service sector associated with food industry. The city itself is bulging at the seams. Every year new professional colleges or institutions open up and more and more international students throng the city.

In short, the developments and changes the last decade has seen are so many that they could provide the matter for another separate study, with different dimensions perhaps. Nevertheless, it would not be out of place to add here that all social research is necessarily a mental experimentation. Even though empirical material is used for illustration, there is no proving in the sense of QED, Therefore, any future study, armed with the most updated statistical data, will still need to take cognizance of this work, and herein lies the rationale for the book. It is also necessary to point out that many times a decade has to pass for a transition to sink in

April, 2011 **Jasmine Y. Damle**

Acknowledgements

I dedicate this book in memory of my mother (Aai) Late Smt. Rekha Yeshwant Damle and daddy, the Late Prof. Y.B. Damle, for their constant encouragement and unflinching support in my endeavour. I am also grateful to my elder sister (Tai) Smt. Anita Girish Joglekar (USA) for her constant encouragement.

I am deeply indebted to Prof. S.M. Dahiwale, Co-ordinator, DSA programme, Department of Sociology, University of Pune for allowing me to do this project. His constant encouragement and guidance helped me to pursue my work.

I also owe my sincere thanks to Prof. Sujata Patel, the then Head, Department of Sociology, as well as the faculty members Dr. Sattoor and Dr. Swati Shirwadkar for their encouragement.

Dr. B.V. Bhosale gave me very valuable information regarding my topic on Street Food Vending. Prof. R.N. Sharma's report on Mumbai Street Food Vendors and Hawkers (TISS report) also helped me.

I am also deeply indebted to Prof. Kejriwal (Director of Adult and Continuing Education, University of Pune) and Late Prof. M.V. Namjoshi (Noted economist) for their constant guidance and valuable suggestions. It is extremely unfortunate that I am unable to show Prof. Namjoshi my final work in this book form.

I will be failing in my duty if I fail to remember Prof. U.B. Bhoite, Prof. Rath and Prof. Chitre for sparing their precious time for suggestions and guidance.

The office staff of the Department of Sociology, as well as the librarians Mr. Pawar and Mrs. Ashtekar were also extremely helpful.

Several libraries have contributed immensely to my study– Jaykar Library, Gokhale Institute Library, SNDT Library, Akshar Library and Maratha Chamber Of Commerce Library (especial thanks to Mrs. Panse,

Secretary Maratha Chamber of Commerce), Pune Shasakiya Granthalaya and TISS Sir Dorabjee Trust Library.

Special thanks are also due to Dr. A.P. Kulkarni, Director, C.S.S. Pune and Dr. Sabade, Director of Institute of Small industries, Prof. Ehsan-Ul Haq (JNU, New Delhi) for their valuable guidance.

I am deeply indebted to Mr. Ajeya Bhave without whose help I would not have been able to interview the hoteliers and also to Talib Uncle and Nargis Aunty (Khambattas), especially for the interviews in the Cantonment area.

I owe my heart felt thanks to Dr. G..B. Kolhatkar who introduced me to quite a few hoteliers and Dr. Sudhir Rashingkar (Ex. Governor, Rotary Club) through whom I was able to meet and interview businessmen as well as software executives. I am deeply indebted to all the interviewers who spared their precious time and gave me all the information. Dr. Chandkar (Chief Health Office. PMC) gave me all valuable information regarding hotel graduation and licensing. The Women's Study Centre's Director Dr. Vidyut Bhagwat, and Dr. Sharmila Rege also helped me a lot. Mrs Swati Dahedroy suggested a couple of important historical readings in Marathi – with respect to the concept of a Khanawal (Community Kitchen).

I must express my deeply felt thanks to Mr. E. Farida Master (Editor of Citadel Magazine), Mr. Asif and Corriane Manuel and many others who went out of their way to help me. Mrs. Vinita Deshmukh of *Indian Express* gave me access to *Citizen magazines,* and the *Times of India* group (Midday) publication. The list is endless but towards the end I must remember with gratitude all those who extended clerical help to me for typing, photocopying, proof-reading etc. Last but not the least the Street Food Vendors at KNP park must also not be forgotten.

April, 2011 **Jasmine Y. Damle**

Introduction

"Old Order changes, yielding place to new"
- Tennyson in 'Locksley Hall'

The strength of an economy depends on its capacity to provide and generate employment and income. This is particularly important for a country like India where 70 per cent of the population has been dependent on agriculture.

During British rule India's handicrafts and other traditional industries declined, thereby drying up the source of both employment and income generation. In addition, imposition of various goods from abroad, particularly Britain, added to the problems of the people. The unequal terms of trade imposed by the British rulers further compounded to the misery. The standard of living became abysmally low. While it may be argued that as a result of modern education, a few positions were available to Indians, their proportion was very small, and the payment also poor. In their own interest, the foreign rulers had established a few industries, but even here the same story was repeated, leaving hardly any margin for decent living. The income was just enough to take care of the basic necessities of life.

At the same time as a result of foreign rule, India had become exposed to a different economic system and technology. The standard of living of the ruling class was so high that the comparison was inevitable, and the contrast glaring.

That is why industrialization became the watchword for the nationalist movement as a whole. It was felt that unless a mechanism was provided to generate employment and income, the situation would not improve. Even after independence, the attempts at industrialization continued. In fact, in post independent India, industrialization became a major national priority for all leaders and thinkers. Mumbai was the first to experience rapid industrialization, followed by Kanpur and Ahmedabad; while Pune remained 'the pensioners' paradise' for quite some time. However, the post 1960s witnessed the setting up of a number of industrial units in and around Pune. At this juncture, it is necessary to point out why Pune was chosen for this study.

For a long time Pune has been regarded as the citadel of tradition, and though there are a few pockets which still live up to this reputation, in general there is vast difference between the pre-industrialized Pune and post-industrialized one. Prior to industrialization, Pune had already enjoyed the reputation as a educational and cultural centre. In addition to being a hub of nationalist movement, the city also nurtured various reform movements. However, for want of industrialization Pune had remained economically stagnant. Pune people's traditional ideals of frugality, simplicity and austerity which were elevated to a philosophy of life were partly due to the economic condition. Shri Bal Gangadhar Tilak had very pertinently observed that the difference between Pune (then 'Poona') and Mumbai (then 'Bombay') lay in the fact that there were no workers, no producers in Pune; there were people who would deal only in ideas and propagate them. But these ideas had no significance for economic development. That is why industrialization, and that too of a sophisticated type, was required. Pune already had (and still has) an Ammunition factory, but it was not an Employment Multiplier like other industrial units which were set up in the last quarter of the twentieth century.

It is necessary to emphasize both the quantity (volume) and quality of this industrialization in order to properly evaluate its contribution to the growing economy of the city, and the country as a whole. While the quantitative rise provides greater employment, a qualitative change in the nature of industrialization demands expertise and specialization in the higher force as well as ever increasing skill and competence in the lower work force. The nature of industrialization in Pune was such as to offer sufficiently large pay-packets to the highly skilled and specialized staff, and consequently a substantial rise in the emoluments paid to the other work-force also. The setting up of sophisticated type of industries created a variety of jobs and careers due to the nature of specialization and technological advancement. This attracted a large number of personnel from various regions of India, and even from foreign countries to Pune. As a cascading effect, this situation created a demand for hotel industry which could provide modern and satisfactory amenities and services to its clients. Hotels and clubs were necessary to house the visiting experts, consultants, specialists as well as collaborators and partners of multinational companies. Such demand was further augmented by a relatively continuous traffic of experts and consultants even within the country. Likewise several restaurants and eateries also came up to cater to the changing and sophisticated demands of the consumers. In fact, it was Shri S.L.Kirloskar, a pioneer of industrialization in Pune, who could foresee such a demand and so established the first five-star hotel 'Blue Diamond' in the city in 1969.

Apart from the sophisticated nature of new industries, there were a few other factors which gave an additional impetus to hotel industry. While Pune has always been known as 'Oxford of the East', now the traditional streams of learning such as linguistics, anthropology, classical languages and pure sciences were not enough to train the personnel required for new industries. The need for specialized, technical, professional and managerial staff called for new kinds of training institutions. This in turn generated employment. It also meant an inflow of students from different parts of India and abroad. The diversity of specialized upper echelons of industrial units as well as that of students called for a variety of food or cuisine.

Such development naturally created demand for other professional services such as doctors on call, maintenance and service engineers. lawyers, architects, landscape gardeners, accountants, professionals from the hospitality industry, tax consultants, software consultants, pest control professionals, lift maintenance units and many more. Service sectors such as transport, communication and banking also received a boost. This entire gamut of employment opportunities generated further demand for consumption. Broadly speaking the Employment Multiplier boosted the economy in diverse ways. The setting up of such industries in Pune had far reaching consequences in the sense that it had implications for a host of institutions ranging from education to family and also the changing diaspora of the city.

The economic consequences are fairly obvious, in the sense of higher income brackets and the capacity to spend on leisure, travel, recreation etc. The rise in the income provided a margin for spending on items of consumption not thought of earlier. Rise in status and higher income brackets is being reflected in the ever expanding middle class all over India, but especially in Pune which has experienced both quantitative and qualitative change in the nature of industrialization. Wider contacts and interactions due to changing diasporas resulted in exposure to new ideas about standard of living. Emancipation of people from the grip of traditional taboos also helped. For example, eating at the then famous Iranian restaurant Lucky situated in prestigious Deccan area was a strict 'no-no'. Another thing never done was women visiting a restaurant. One can also get ample examples of such restrictions and constraints from the contemporary Marathi fiction. However, expanding base of women's education, their economic independence and the shrinking structure of joint family gradually changed the situation. Women's eating in restaurants was no longer considered improper or indecent and as T.Veblem says, the odours associated; with certain foods, non-veg for example, were mitigated, if not completely neutralized. Changing ideas about caste and dietary restrictions also helped. Now playing host to guests outside the home, in a club or a restaurant has been an accepted trend. Various events such as birthdays and anniversaries are now celebrated in restaurants and hotels.

In the field of education also, the earlier preferences started being replaced by new requirements. As already mentioned, earlier kind of education had academic and civilization orientation. Though extremely relevant from a wider perspective, it was not of much utility to sustain the new industrial economy. Market needs required professional, technical and managerial skills. Education had to be performance oriented, and productive. It was wedded to Market Economy. Therefore, several institutes catering to such demands came up, and with them the new faculty, available from all corners of the country and even abroad. This in turn necessitated hotels, housing, hostels and a host of services. Naturally, the phenomenon of multiplier effects came into play. New reference groups were developed giving impetus to spending on consumption. Standard of living rose and with it thrived the service sector. Such multiplier effect continued cascading down, stage by stage. Consumption also promoted investment, modifying relationship between income, saving and investment. The trend of businessmen, managers and software professionals treating their partners and clients to dinners or luncheons at expensive hotels gave boost not only to consumption, but also to investment, as well as business deals.

Thus, the period under study, (1989 – 1999), was a period of rapid transition for Pune's social, cultural and economic fabric.

It is said that culture has its 'economic logic'(Bourdieu). This is so because consumption also requires cultural support. Without changing ideas and values about standard of living, and social approval for a certain kind of behaviour, eating out in this case, consumption cannot thrive.

Here it will not be out of place to clarify some of the misconceptions about consumption, since increase in consumption is being equated with consumerism and as such, it is given a pejorative connotation. In this study, consumption is looked upon as a positive feature, and a pre-requisite for economic development and socio-cultural change. Enhancement of income through employment multiplier and the consequent consumption supported by socio-cultural trends towards higher standard of living constitute the central focus of this study.

In short, this is a study of the dynamics of relationship between tradition and market, as reflected in all its ramifications, with special reference to consumption of food in all its manifestation and types. An attempt is made to depict the intertwining of economic development, and the requisite socio-cultural support. This study also raises a few questions regarding the dynamics between economic growth and socio-cultural institutions. It is a humble effort to analyze and appreciate the role of consumption; both as an indicator and promoter of economic development as well as social transformation.

This study has been confined to Pune, but it has a universal implication in showing how the process of development is invariably linked with change. The choice of the locale is illustrative of the dialectics of economical and sociological milieu.

1

Theoretical Perspectives Used in the Study

Serendipity Pattern

Every empirical inquiry is not necessarily guided or determined by a neat theoretical package. At times, it is after the completion of such an inquiry that a tentative theoretical frame emerges. Under certain conditions, a research finding gives rise to social theory. Fruitful empirical research not only tests theoretically derived hypothesis, but also gives rise to new hypothesis. Any research design which deals with the basic components and their interrelationship obviously implies some theoretical concerns. However, after conducting an inquiry several new insights may develop. This is what Robert Merton (Social Theory and Social Structure, 1949) has famously characterized as Serendipity Pattern. Thus, 'Serendipity' component of research is the discovery by chance of valid results which were not sought for. In Robert Merton's words, 'the unanticipated anomalies, strategies and datum exert pressure for initiating a theory.'

Thus, many times new perspectives evolve as a result of which the earlier relationship between variables gets questioned. (For example, the importance of culture in influencing institutional framework.) It is not for nothing that Talcott Parsons devoted considerable attention to cultural system with reference to social system. He did emphasize the autonomy of the two systems, but at the same time he was aware of the mutuality of the interaction between the two, and their capacity to influence each other.

In the case of this study also economy, culture and society have acquired a lot of significance. Both industrialization and socio-cultural change act as facilitators as well as beneficiaries of economic development.

The Three-fold Theoretical Base

Theoretically, this study encompasses three interdependent concepts / notions which operate simultaneously, each exerting its impact on the others, and in turn being influenced by them. These three are:

(i) the concept of Service Sector

(ii) the concept of Employment Multiplier

(iii) the concept of Consumption

(i) The Concept of Service Sector

One of the comprehensive definitions of Service Sector is attempted by J.K.Galbraith. According to him "Service Sector includes wholesale and retail trade, finance, insurance, real estate, and several other services including professional, personal, business and repair services". As against this, the industry sector is defined to include mining contract, construction, manufacturing, transport, communication and public utilities as well as government enterprises.

There are two principal hypothesis put forward to explain the growth of the Service Sector. One is 'a more rapid growth of the final demand for services', and the second is 'a relative increase in the intermediate demand for services'. The first explanation involves a relation between spending patterns and the level of income. "As the income rises, the prosperity to spend on recreation services like good restaurants rises. As national income rises, the demand for goods tends to rise less rapidly than that for services; hence the importance of services in the economy rises". (Daniel Bell, 'The Coming of the Post Industrial Society,' 1974).

Adam Smith in '*Wealth of Nations*' has stated that "the desire for food is limited for every man by the narrow capacity of his stomach". However, today it is not only the quantity of food, but often the desire for variety as well as quality of different types of food which spins the service sector into action. This is especially true of hotel and restaurant industry catering to various demands of people.

In this context, I would also like to slightly modify the concept of demand and supply as formulated by the noted economist Alfred Marshall. According to him the two factors that tend to influence the quality demanded of a good service are (1) Price of goods and (2) Price of related goods (complimentary). In the purely economic sense, the demand generates supply. However, in this study, especially with reference to Street Food Vending, it is often the supply that generates demand; this demand depends on the availability of a variety of food ranging from simple *bhelpuri* to pizzas and burgers.

This is not to refute the basic foundation of the demand supply theory – the premises of utility maximization as well as the prosperity of a person to spend, in turn depending on his income and the price of the goods. But today we find that it is equally important to take into consideration the tastes, habits, status, class, prestige, power and preferences of the people which tend to influence their demand; and not just their income or price of goods. Therefore, related to the core principal of demand and supply is also the ability of the manufacturer to cater to the changing demands of the consumers. This is especially true of food and hotel industry.

Here it will be worth-while to look at the Schumpeterian theory of entrepreneurship which rests upon four cardinal points:

1. Entrepreneur's will power 2. Innovation
3. Profit making 4. Risk taking

An entrepreneur must possess a sustained will-power to break the subconscious fixed habits of consumer's thoughts and energy, and should have the innovative mind and the foresight it implies. This means the ability to foresee the possibilities of new combinations. In case of hotel industry, we may take the example of Mr. Jagannath Shetty who started the famous restaurant Vaishali on Fergusson College Road in Pune in 1951-52, selling only South Indian dishes – dosas, idlies and Uttappams, but later expanded into realms of pizzas and burgers. Here, we find the principle of foresight coupled with keen observation of what people really want.

Next, introducing a new product involves two things – risk taking coupled with uncertainty and opening up of untapped market resulting into larger profit margins. The pioneering efforts of Mr. Joshi (Joshi Wadewale) in 1988 presents a good case to illustrate this further. He introduced 'Wada-Pav' which has now been considered a national favourite food, a mini-meal in itself, especially for poor wage earners, students and working people from outside Pune (whose families have yet to shift to Pune). Vada-Pav comprises two bread buns and two 'batata wadas' sandwiched between them.

It used to be Rs 1/- (only one) way back in 1988. Then in 1990s, the price rose to Rs 3.50/- each and today it is sold for Rs. 5/- to 7/-. Thus, Mr. Joshi tapped open an untapped market, took the risk, but today he is reaping the benefit of his innovative approach, with several outlets across the length and breadth of the city. His steady supply has also generated demand which he could foresee with keen observation.

For Mr. Joshi, it is not merely profit making, but also the satisfaction of his customers which keeps boosting him to further divulge into new avenues like starting '*Gauri Mastani House*' serving 'Mastani' (i.e. mango milk shake and ice-cream). Mr Omprakash Hardeyal's '*Manmeet*', a house of Lucknowi Chat, is the result of a similar zeal to explore and take risks. 'Lucknowi Chat' was a totally unknown food stuff in Pune, especially in Deccan Gymkhana area.

According to Alfred Knight, an American Economist, "All life is characterized by change and some portion of that change is unpredictable". In short, the pulse of the people's habits, tastes, and food preferences is a clear indicator of not only socio-cultural changes, but is also related to economic development. This is further endorsed by Yogendra Singh in one of his major books, *'Culture and Change in India'*(2000). He says, " After all, globalization in a nutshell means changes sweeping the market form of economy and its rapid expansion".

This entire story of entrepreneurship also has another strong sociological perspective as indicated by Max Weber in his pioneering work, '*Protestant Ethics and the Spirit of Capitalism*'. Professor Hagen explains Weber's theory in terms of a lower status groups seeking to overcome their social grievances by means of economic activities. There are historical cases from the UK, Japan and Russia where it has been observed that an entrepreneur always comes from a sub-dominant group, the groups seeking redressal. A classic example of this in hotel industry would be the entry of Udipis (lower caste OBC's from South Karnataka, who traditionally were the assistants of 'Pujaris' in temples). Today the *Udipi* joints (selling idli-dosa) have pervaded the food-landscape everywhere.

Therefore, in Parsonian terms it is the change (mobility) from ascriptive status to achieved status, an attempt to do away with the social stigma attached to lower castes.

(Talcott Parsons and his Concept of Pattern Variables – Achievement Vs Ascriptive status).

As Yogendra Singh has stated, "a change is related to shift in occupation, which occurs in a very substantial manner. There no longer exists a link between caste / community and hereditary occupation, especially in urban areas; thereby challenging the 'Theory of Karma and Rebirth'.

After discussing the socio-cultural dimension of this basic economic activity of demand-supply, releted to the Service Sector, let us further delve into the theory of Service as an economic activity. According to Professor Hill (1977), "A Service represents a transformation of the user (in the case of services involving persons) or the users of goods (in the case of services involving goods) as a result of the voluntary intervention by the producer of services." Hill also points out that services occur between different economic agents. Thus, the term service implies the presence of an economic organization or 'market structure'. The noted economist Jagdish Bhagwati cites an example of demand for ducks in Chinese restaurants. This is so because duck is necessary for a Chinese dish. In Hill's words, the restaurant gives us service, and this service occurs simultaneously with its provision by the producer of the service, and its users. This is a useful criterion for services in general.

In his article in 'The World Economy' (1982), Jagdish Bhagwati states: "Basically one has to draw a distinction between services as embodied in the supplies of services requiring the physical presence of the service-agents wherever the user happens to be; and the ones which can be disembodied from the suppliers and provided without their physical presence being necessary". For example, the suppliers' presence is not at all necessary once the delivery of chicken and eggs is made to the restaurants. Similarly, Hill's concept of the services is that they must be used and there must be providers of services, (or producer of goods such as cars, trucks). In case of goods, the service provider does not have to be present when the service is being used by the person, whereas in the case of services to persons, physical proximity is more useful. For example, when a person visits a hotel, and the manager/owner is present.

In his work '*Future of Service Employment*', the noted economist J.J.Gershury has stressed upon the direct contact with the customer He further explains that service is a commodity which we use more or less at the same time it is produced. Examples are: the food ordered in a restaurant; or going to a theatre and watching a movie; or buying a bus ticket and travelling. Sometimes services are short lived and in this third sense they are labour intensive production activities, very often having the producer face to face with the final consumer, for example, a street food vendor selling bhel-puri or maize cob to a customer. Again if food in hotel X is good one, the consumer often compliments the manager for it before leaving the hotel, or often gets tips about the delicacies being served there. This has also been reiterated by J.Bhagwati. The growth of the service sector can be explained with the help of the theory of three stages of economic growth. This concept of Primary – Secondary – Tertiary sectors was initially formulated by G.D. Fisher (1939) and was later developed by Clarke (1940), Fontaine (1949), and finally reformulated by W.W. Rostow (1953) in his famous work on *'Stages of Growth'*.

The theory is based on straight forward assumptions about production and consumption in order to link economic growth to the development of service economy. As far as production is concerned, productive gains (production or added value per head) are assumed to be higher in industry than in the service sector. As far as consumption is concerned, the income and the elasticity of demand for services have to be greater than the demand for goods.

However, these propositions explain only the forms rather than the uses of economic growth. From the experience of developed economies from 1970-1980, one can conclude that a slow down in growth has no effect upon the development of the service sector. The rise in service economy, therefore, should not be identified with an affluent society blessed with full employment. A critique of the proposition underplaying the standard model can aid in the identification of positive and negative aspects of service sector both in terms of growth and in terms of quality of life. Many western thinkers/intellectuals feel that a western society is blessed not only with full employment but also with a great growth of service sector. This thought needs careful examination from two central propositions (W.W. Rostow) viz hotel industry and street food vending in the third world countries.

In their famous book *'Second India Studies'* (1976) Hannan Ezeikel and Madhav Pavaskar have stated that tertiary or service sector occupies the place of pride not only in all developed countries but also in less developed countries (LDC). For example, in India, the only difference is that of degree. The contribution of service sector to both total national income and employment is the highest among all sectors in developed economies, whereas in LDCs it is less compared to that from primary sector. But even in LDCs the contribution of tertiary sector to national income is the highest, though it is the primary sector that generates more employment than the tertiary one.

It is this fact that distinguishes tertiary sector in LDCs from what is termed as "Service Sector". The transformation of service sector into industrial sector is indeed a function of economic development. The demand for service stands to increase more rapidly than demand for goods. Daniel Bell states "As economic development gathers momentum with the growth of primary and secondary sectors, and structural changes are brought about in them by such growth, services needed by the two sectors multiply not only in numbers, but also in a variety of ways, and with the rise in per capita income people tend to make use of better services in education, health, marketing, housing; as well as more and more services for recreation and other experiences such as leisure, including hotels, restaurants and tourism. In his book *'Future shock, Emergence of Leisure and Recreation'*, a noted American Sociologist Alwin Toffler calls such services Experience Industries. This suggests the changes in the life-style when people opt for one or more special services in the field of education, entertainment, health, tourism, etc. Another factor that encourages rapid growth of service sector is the slow growth of technology in it, even when the pace of economic development is more. Technology plays a relatively less important role in service sector than in primary sector. Development, therefore, brings in its wake a rapid rise in the employment in service sector. Thus, the income generation effect of this sector mainly stems from rapid growth in employment. It is for this reason that the contribution of service sector to income and employment is not only the highest among all sectors in developed economies, but also rises rapidly as economy marches towards its development peak

Here in this context, it will be worthwhile to take note of the prognostication made by Madhav Pavaskar and Hannan Ezekiel in their book, *'Second India Studies'* Hill (1977), that the total employment in tertiary sector including utilities in 'Second India' would be at 90 million on the assumption of 5 per cent annual growth in GDP by 2000 AD. In 1970s, the percentage of employment in utilities was 1.3 of total employment in services. According to the authors' prognosis this was to rise to 3 per cent in 'Second India'. The aggregate employment in Second India was estimated at 87.3 million as against 32.3 million in 1971. Today we can see that the development has taken place as predicted by the authors.

In short, in terms of both employment and income, tertiary sector is becoming larger than primary sector. Tertiary sector of Second India is on the way to become service sector of 'Third India'.

According to Pavaskar and Ezeikel, next to agriculture, the tertiary sector is also the single biggest contributor to India's GDP. In 1970's, India was still in the Pre-industrial stage of economic development. However, in spite of the dominance of service sector in post-industrial societies, the difference between post and pre industrial tertiary sector is not quantitative but essentially qualitative. It is the relative importance of service sector vis a vis not only industry but also agriculture that determines as to whether an economy is in its pre-industrial or post-industrial stage. Therefore, it is only when labour force engaged in agriculture is about 20 per cent, or even less, the economy could be deemed to have reached the stage of service economy.

Moreover, the tertiary sector is the second most crowded sector not only in an industrial economy but also in pre-industrial society, for example, in the past even in the agriculture economy like India, services such as those of public administration, defence, trade, transport and credit were necessary. With the pace of economic development, there is a steady shift in employment away from agriculture and towards industry as well as service utilities. In an industrial society economic stages, vital infrastructure for industrial development may grow even more rapidly than industries in terms of both employment and income. This is because growth of industries itself depends on growth of the infrastructure. Transport and Communication, education, health, housing and other services are pre-requisites for rapid urban development. That is why a commercial revolution usually precedes an industrial revolution. Only upon a strong foundation of trade and commerce and auxiliary services can the edifice of industrial development be built. Services included in tertiary sector also aim at social welfare fields such as health, parks and sanitation. As already indicated earlier, service sector does not grow only in volume, but becomes more comprehensive, encompassing mass communication media, trade and transport, repairs and maintenance. It also becomes more labour intensive, requiring higher technical and professional skills which are not easily available in developing economies.

In India, in 1971, the white collar jobs exceeded blue collar ones there were 33 million engaged in services and utilities at the growth rate of 9% in GDP. The labour force engaged in tertiary sector claims a relatively high return for its services as compared to agriculture industry. As economic development takes place, industry and service sector run neck to neck; but one has to ascertain whether industry overtakes tertiary sector or vice versa. Industry overtakes tertiary sector as the productivity per worker in industry rises more rapidly than in tertiary sector. This happens as industry uses mass production techniques to maximize production and profits. Such rapid development of technology is due to automation. After studying economies of many countries, Hollis Chenery and Simmon Kuznets (*Economic Growth Review*, 1960 September) have established that there is a relationship between level of economic development and structure of an economy.

In more developed countries the labour force is low in primary sector, but high in tertiary sector. In developing countries, opposite is the case. The share of primary sector in economic growth is inversely related to the level of income, while that of secondary and tertiary sector is positively related to it. Economic growth of a country is associated with decline in the primary sector (in terms of engagement of labour and subsequent income generation).

The reasons attributed to the continued growth of tertiary sector are many. First of all there is a higher stage of industrial development resulting in the rise in per capita income. Consequently the demand for services such as transport and communication also rises at a rapid pace because highly capital intensive production on a continuous basis in the secondary sector needs an elaborate system of transportation to move raw materials and finished goods. It also needs efficient wholesale and retail trade network. Thus, only a strong tertiary sector can provide vital services to industry.

Secondly, there is increase in disposable income and subsequently a demand for certain goods and services such as consumer durables, entertainment and recreation. These goods and services have high income elasticity. The increasing demand for TVs, cars, radios and mobiles generate the demand for services related to their maintenance. Urbanization is one more factor contributing to the growth of tertiary sector. The number of towns with over 1,00,000 population has increased in post-independence period. In his book *'The Coming of the Post-Industrial Society'* (1968), Daniel Bell had prognosticated the spurt in service sector. According to him the word service disguises itself in various ways, thus encompassing in its range the white collared employment in the fields of finance, real estate and insurance. In the last stage of economic growth, when a country moves from industrial economy to super-industrial economy, tertiary economy occupies the place of pride.

(ii) The Concept of Employment Multiplier

Agricultural activities provide the main foundation of economic activities in India. But this agriculture is mainly for domestic, consumption.

This is not so in case of industrial production which is basically export oriented and therefore provides an economic base. It also has deeper and wider ramifications as it initiates chain reaction. Thus, many components which go to shape the final industrial product are brought from outside a given industrial plant. Without enquiring into primary and secondary industrial products, it must be mentioned that there is a large portion of tertiary (ancillary) industries.

The concept of 'Employment Multiplier' (EM) finds its genesis in the very process of industrial production. For example, the very fact that workers have to attend the factory during a specified period of time necessitates a meaningful transport service to move them back and forth. In addition, there are a myriad of facilities and services which have to be provided to keep the industrial machine going on such as canteen (food), health services, safety precaution, etc. Nowadays labour legislation requires even the availability of crèches for the children of working women. Similarly, social welfare services such as personnel (HRD) and labour office have also to be provided. Furthermore, any complex industrial product requires buying parts from outside and to that extent there is hardly any industrial product which is not assembled. Therefore, almost every single industry is an economic multiplier. There is also an extension of this activity of Employment Multiplier outside a given industry. In a nutshell, the concept of multiplier deals with the processes. It enables one to quantify both at an aggregate level as well as at a disaggregate level, contribution made by all basic units to total employment. A.P. Kulkarni's *'Employment Multiplier (EM) in Pune City'* explains this further.

While a student of economics would be more concerned with computing the aggregate and disaggregate efforts and consequences of such multiplier effects, the interest of the present study is mainly confined to examine and understand the socio cultural dimension of multiplier effect; to be more specific, the multiplier effect in the hotel industry.

Hotel Industry as an Important Employment Multiplier

Hotels play a very vital role as a major source of employment. One hotel room alone is estimated to create three direct and nine indirect jobs. This makes hotel a labour intensive industry. The staff in the hotel is of three types:

1. Those who are in direct touch with the tourists or customers.
2. Those who are in semi-contact with them.
3. Those who have no contact with the guests.

Those who are in immediate contact with guests are security officers, reception staff, guest relationship officers, lobby managers, stewards, hostesses, waiters, operators, room service attendants, bell boys, etc. Some of those who are in semi-contact with customers are cocktail bar-drink makers (bartenders), cleaners, accountants and cashiers. However, some main staff, though important, does not need to have any contact with the guests. These employees ensure proper functioning of hot/cold water, climate control, air conditioning, food supply, gas supply, boilers, toilet facilities, etc. Thus, a specialized trained class of servants has come about right from desk management to bell-boy. Acquisitions of language skills, sophisticated behaviour and structured courtesy have become functional pre-requisites. The entire upholstery / drapery, interior decoration, and amenities like sauna bath, health spa and Jacuzzi, gymnasium and beauty parlours increase the demand for trained class of personnel.

"Wanted smart, energetic, young, dynamic aerobic instructor for a Five star hotel" – such advertisements are not a novelty now. Moreover, whatever the scale, all hotels and restaurants require specialized services of income-tax experts, chartered accountants, auditors, landscape architects etc, hired from outside. The hardware for fridge, air conditioners, lifts, swimming pools and their filter plants call for maintenance or service engineers. Besides these, there has to be a permanent cadre of experts for pest control, PEECOP, lawn maintenance, illumination, and so on.

Of late, the latest addition to the employment market is that of Event Management. More and more people opt for professional event management team for various functions. Some hotels also offer event-management among their several other services. The idea is to let the customers have one-point contact as many functions of entertaining the guests are now held in the hotels.

In this way the employment generation by hotel industry certainly augments economic development in its turn. Its multiplier effect is through types of sub-contracting and a continuous demand for professional services as described above.

The direct contribution of hotels and restaurants also lies in a huge volume of purchases of material. Apart from the bulk purchase of fruits, vegetables, meat, milk, flowers, eggs, fish etc; hotels also create market for newspapers, tooth picks, soaps, tooth pastes, bulbs, furniture, ball pens, kitchen gadgets, air conditioners, refrigerators etc. In turn, the prosperity of the industry producing these items depends on growth and development of hotels to a large extent. Another tremendous gain of hotel industry is its link with business establishments. Many conventions, conferences and other business events are held in Five star hotels. Several top officers' training programmes are conducted in good hotels. This necessitates new skills to manage modern communication, such as specialized facility of video conferencing.

The other type of indirect employment is through the multiplier effect of foreign tourists' spending. A specific item of expenditure incurred by a foreigner into convertible currency results in the multiplication of demand, and therefore further employment.

Thus, the hotel industry creates myriads of jobs, unleashing the employment multiplier effect in the society, both expanding and altering the social base.

(iii) The Concept of Consumption

Every economic system has four major goals to attain, such as production, distribution, exchange, and consumption. There is no gainsaying the fact that production forms the starting point of an economic activity. It is a prime mover, but the purpose of productive activity is to address itself to the basic need for consumption. Further still, consumption is both related to and dependent on exchange and distribution. That is why the primacy of consumption has major implications for social structure and culture. Consumption is simply not a matter of money and economics, nor only a matter of style. It is also a matter of social practice and social division; political policy and political implication in society. It is a matter of consumer society (Tim Edwards, 2000: 3)

Therefore, consumption has to be properly appreciated in its wider social context, because changing consumption patterns signify social changes in general. But again, such social change would not be thinkable in the absence of the requisite institutional and cultural support (Tim Edwards, 2000, Theoretical Perspective).

Certain Misconceptions about Consumption

In order to study consumption from the right perspective, it is necessary to clear certain misconceptions about it. Appropriate thinking about consumption is very significant for the material presented and the argument offered in this book.

Some misconceptions about consumption stem from the Marxian analysis of capitalism and its insidious impact on life, definitely the economic and social aspects of life. In fact, Marx regards capitalism as a major instrument of dominating the thinking of people, particularly consumption, since everything is geared to the market economy and whatever is produced (of course for profit / benefit etc.) has to be sold to the clients who become willy-nilly victims of the process of production. They do not have a choice over what they consume; they are manipulated to consume whatever is made available. This is one of the main reasons why consumption has been treated as an instrument of domination and imposition on the unsuspecting customers or consumers.

Naturally, it follows that consumers have no choice whatsoever but are compelled, if not condemned, to buy whatever is made available by forces which control the process of production of commodities. Taking a clue from this framework, several authors have tried to harp on the same note, completely denying the fact of voluntary choice and freedom of the consumer. Moreover, the marketing campaign by the clever manipulation and utilization of media is further stressed to point out helplessness of the consumers who fall a prey to such campaign, and buy certain commodities. However, the discretion of the consumer is completely forgotten or ignored and that is why the purely Marxian formulation does not hold true in reality. Then again in the Indian context we have the effect of Gandhian philosophy which advocated simplicity and curtailment of wants so as to curb consumption. A similar strand can be noticed in the ideology generated by deprivation and poverty at large which certainly creates a disdain about those who indulge in consumption. Veblen particularly emphasized conspicuous consumption as wastage, and several others have toed the line. It is often forgotten that economic development has to facilitate change in the quality of life of the people, which requires availability of resources to enhance both the quantity and quality of goods and services, and as such would necessarily mean or signify a transition from denial and abstinence to a situation of fulfillment of pent-up wants and also new wants such as education, housing, change in the standard of living, and so on. There is no doubt that the dimension of time is also involved to bring about such a transition.

And what a significant transition it has been-from an entirely negative approach towards consumption to the positive one. As stated earlier, the negative one has been the outcome of Marxian analysis and is being toed by Veblen and several others. We have also seen how in the Indian context this attitude is further complicated by Gandhian ideology and traditional philosophy of eulogizing thrift, frugality and denial – simple living and high thinking. At times this view is stretched to the point of total denial of materialistic pleasures.

Another point to remember here is that consumption is extremely limited if there is no margin in income to spend on anything beyond the basic necessities. On the other hand, the increasingly sophisticated nature of industry and the enhanced economic capacity, facilitated by highly trained and specialized professional personnel who cut across boundaries of language, region, state and nation, result in amplification of a margin in income which can help enhance both the quantity and quality of consumption. This is reflected in the development of service economy which again has a snowballing effect.

The advent of service economy reflects changing patterns of consumption and the efforts made to enhance the satisfaction of such demand. For example, with reference to the hotel industry the creation of posts like Desk manager, receptionists and entertainers reflect the inroads made by service economy. In fact, there is an organic link between service economy and hotel industry. That is how the phenomena of multiplier effect and its dynamics come into the play. Together with it, the entire approach and social attitude towards consumption undergoes a remarkable transformation, (which forms a major concern of the present study.)

The economic interpretation of Karl Marx reduces a consumer to be a mere passive agent, which is not true.

In this context one can cite the example of the famous controversy between agent v/s structures. The consumer is not just the victim of imperialism: he also exerts his choice because of the rising income and changing world views. Though the relative power of the consumer is largely confined to the Western affluent societies, it is still unmistakably true of Urban India; especially in relation to food industry. Consumption of food is nowadays no more a homogenous entity. 'Food as necessity to food as luxury' (Bourdieu, 1987) is the beginning of the mechanism for differentiation, of social distancing, and social stratification. One may even postulate a continuum (linear or dialectic) between food for necessity, taste, luxury, status, assertion, exclusion etc. In this sense food is also associated with the desire to move up and gain social ascendancy, social mobility.

Some important factors such as education, occupation, income, status and social recognition contribute to such a development. George Retizer (2001) adds another factor, 'fashion', but in a derogatory sense; while Bourdieu very aptly stresses: " when consumption patterns change, something more than price and income may have changed". Thus, food becomes a cuisine in the specific context of this study. That is why it should be emphasized that there is also such a thing as voluntary consumption, exerting choice in respect of consumption. Along with Marxist proposition that it is production or rather a kind of production geared to profit making under the functioning of the capitalist system which manipulates and decides consumption, the freedom or autonomy to choose cannot be neglected. Those who consume also exert their choice of what is produced for consumption (especially food, clothing and other items). That is why, instead of subscribing to the Marxian straight jacket theory, we need to introduce the element of voluntary choice. Only then the possibility and fact of a positive aspect of consumption can emerge. Otherwise consumption will always be associated with consumerism.

Larry Ray and Andrew Sayer (1999:2) also discuss how consumption has been rescued from often dismissive and negative treatment it received at the hands of Marxist, by change in society, culture and politics at large. But why has there been a cultural turn? It could be construed as largely endogenous to academia, but it would be surprising if it bore no relation to changes in society, culture and politics at large. Sayer and Ray in their masterpiece edited work *'Culture and Economy After the Cultural Turn'* (1999:8, 9) state that 'A stronger argument for fusion of culture and economy could be drawn from Bourdieu who analyses culture as having an economic logic (1977, 1986). Bourdieu sees almost every act either in explicitly economic terms or as instrumental to economy. In the latter case, pursuit of honour, or status expressions of good will, especially gift giving, are seen as disguised strategies of exchange through symbolic acts wherein social or cultural capital is accumulated. Lash and Urry (1994:64) put it very succinctly: "culture is more and more economically reflected, and economy is increasingly culturally inflected." Thus, the inextricable intertwining between economy and culture as affecting and facilitating consumption precedes a key theoretical consideration. Unless a given society discards the language of thrift in favour of expenditure on consumption, it cannot develop economically.

Alex Mac Intosh (1996-47, 48) discusses about life style resources, class distinctions and status striving conspicuous consumption. Life style resources are not used to extend life or make it more comfortable, but instead to achieve distinction from others. In some societies, simply having food on a predictable basis may serve exceedingly well as means to distinguish one's self from others, (Bourdieu, 1984).

Mac Intosh (1996 pg. 48,49) further argues that consumption of goods in modern Western Societies is driven less by human needs than by socially defined needs. Further, these wants frequently consist of what other persons of high status already possess. This point of view has been supported by other sociologists such as C. Mukerjee (1983), McCracken (1988) and Bell (1976); and has been described as "conspicuous consumption" or "the consumption ethic". Some writers claim that the consumption ethic was a precursor to capitalist production Mukherji (1983). Others argue that it was a result of the break down of the very Protestant ethic that led to capitalist production (Bell 1976).

The desire to appear of higher status implies that lower income group will attempt to consume beyond their means George Ritzer (2001), *Explorations in the Sociology of Consumption.* Bell also discusses the role of the installment plan (1976) for mobility, and mechanism of exclusion. With dress code and the recent development in instant credit system, a person can rise above his status even if momentarily. A common mechanism of momentary status change is the restaurant. A person does not have to belong to an exclusive club to dine on high cuisine. They only have to have the means (cash credit) to do so. Many exclusive restaurants restrict access, thus increasing their desirability, by limiting the number of patrons they serve. Others do so simply by elevating their prices. The diners gain both the cuisine and the elevated status to characterize like everyday lives of those with higher social status. Feldstein's (1989) classification of restaurants aptly demonstrates that their owners realize that dining out is for public display, and that image may be more important than the taste of the food served. Merton's concept of Reference Group Behaviour is also very apt in this context. It refers to a case of reference group emulating the outer group, those with higher social status. This is the transition Bourdieu mentions – from taste of necessity to taste of luxury.

Michael Lamont's work on *Money, Morals and Manners* (1992:3) contrasts the upper middle class culture of France and USA, finding that cultivated dispositions and the ability to display an adequate command of high culture was less important in USA than in France where it drew boundaries on the basis of sophistication. Bourdieu (1984: Distinction) attempts to disentangle the class system in France through his analysis of taste. Tastes represent internalized ideas regarding where the person fits in the social structure, what is his relationship to others. Taste permits individuals' ways of distinguishing their own class membership from that of others, and this taste becomes a social weapon to maintain class boundaries. Part of the taste is acquired within the family, but much is acquired from the educational system. The educational system produces cultural capital in that it provides individual with a sense of what matters most in life and how these things ought to be viewed and discussed. To produce such a taste differentiation, the educational system must be stratified. Food plays a major part in Bourdieu's work. He describes food as an 'archetype of all taste' for it reflects directly back to the oldest and deepest experiences (Bourdieu, 1984 : 79). Furthermore, practices and goods associated with different classes are organized in accordance with the structures of opportunity. Those with taste of necessity are considered to be people who don't know how to live. Thus, taste in food also depended on class.

McCracken (1988) stated that consumer goods serve as bridges, especially prior to the ownership, between an individual's cultural circumstances and idealized life. As obtaining an object eliminated the bridge, desire for newer objects occurred. Producers draw the consumers' attention by using fantasy to entertain, while at the same time they make a connection between the fantasy worlds the consumer finds desirable, and their goods. Therefore, Vaccatone beer connects the consumer with places filled with happy young beautiful people (George Ritzer, 2001). Buying the product brings that fantasy world to the consumer. Relying on Campbell, Gronow (1991: 49) states that food consumers can change their preferences dramatically within short periods of time, e.g. going vegetarian overnight.

Bourdieu (1984) has stated that occupation is the chief source of prestige. It may well be an important determinant of life style beyond the dictates of income or education because expenditure on consumption is required in business relations. Thus, Bourdieu uses occupation as a key marker of class positions, but argues that building up and maintenance of occupational status depend on both economic and cultural capital. He argues that objective conditions of class positions generate systems of social practices. Taste is thus the source of the system of distinctive features which cannot fail to be perceived as systematic expressions of a particular class or conditions of existence, i.e. as distinctive life style, by anyone who possesses practical knowledge of the relationship between distinctive signs and positions (Bourdieu. 1984 : 75). That practices and tastes are internalized through the life time of socialization is of particular interest. Bourdieu's (1984) differentiates between tastes of necessity and taste of luxury. Taste of necessity consists of those practices and perceptions that result from one's limited class circumstances. However, such taste is not defined by its possessors as that of necessity, because socialization has left the individual with the perception that such necessities are in fact virtues (language of thrift).

Those in dominant positions view dominant practices associated with taste of necessity as vulgar because they are both easy and common, others portray their own tastes and life style in more ascetic terms (Bourdieu 1984 . 174). Thus, taste classifies the classifier (Bourdieu, 1984 : 6).

Several qualitative studies have examined class differences in food behaviour using both occupations and income as indicators of class background. Factors facilitating such development have to be located in the quantum jump, in the kind of industrialization necessitating a highly trained super specialized manpower which is recruited irrespective of region, state and country. This is supported by appropriate changes in the institutions of family, marriage and status of women. The changing worldview signified a shift in the earlier emphasis on restricting, if not changing, expenditure on items of consumption. This is the focus of the present inquiry. The changes set in motion, the process of mobility, i.e. educational, economic, social, and cultural; mobility-spatial, intergenerational as well as vertical, have become the keywords of new philosophy.

Paradigm Shift

The foregoing discussion indicates a significant development promoting a Paradigm shift (T. Kuhn, 1970 – pg 104) in consumption, reflecting a clear attempt to bypass traditional (negative) attitude towards consumption. Apart from the attitudinal shift, the emerging basis of both national and international economic relations makes me suggest a modification of Keynsian proposition regarding income, saving and investment. Here I would like to introduce and insert the variable of consumption instead of saving, which plays a crucial role in investment by creating employment so as to help the economy to rise. Therefore, I would like to round up this discussion by referring once again to Bourdieu's trenchant observation that culture has an economic logic. There has been a shift in the type of education, much of which is now more relevant to the needs of various industries-utilitarian rather than liberal (or along with liberal).

2

Pune – Historical Background and Ethos

Historically Pune has been known as a centre of cultural and educational activities, Oxford of the east. During the glorious golden rule of Peshwas and the Maratha empire, it occupied the position of central importance and became its capital in the 18th century. After the fall of the Maratha empire in 1818, Pune lost its status of the capital, but its importance in the fields of educational and cultural activities continued to grow. Gradually it also became a hub of political activities due to the awareness of some of its illustrious citizens.

During 19th century, Pune saw the establishment of some of the finest academic educational centers which became renowned for excellence throughout the country. Among them were Fergusson College (1885) and Deccan College (1857). Pune also contributed significantly to the independence movement and provided leaders like Lokmanya Tilak. Through his fiery writings in local Marathi daily, '*Kesari*', Tilak created mass political consciousness. In 1906 he gave the country its four-fold resolution, 'Poorna Swaraj' (complete independence), 'Swadeshi' (indigenous goods), Boycott of foreign goods and National education. His pioneering efforts, along with his colleagues Agarkar and Chiplunkar, in setting up of good schools in Pune were remarkable. No wonder that people spontaneously bestowed upon him the title 'Lokmanya' (approved of and accepted by the people). The other stalwarts were M.G.. Ranade, who wrote a masterpiece *'The Rise of the Maratha Power'*; and Gopal

Krishna Gokhale who set up the famous 'Servants of Indian Society'. Pune also had its contribution in the field of social reforms in the form of pioneering efforts of two visionaries – Maharshi Karve and Jyotirao Phule. Their Pune was a very orthodox city where girls' education and widow remarriages were not only unheard of, but also unthinkable. Against such a background, Karve dared to marry a young widow for which he was socially ostracized. He then had to live on the outskirts of Pune, in Hingane where he set up the first school for girls, widows and other women, known as Hingane Stree Shikshan Sanstha. Today his sapling has grown into a huge banyan tree, and Hingane has come to be known as Karve Nagar, a thriving suburb of Pune.

Jyotirao Phule set up 'Satyashodhak Samaj (Society in search of truth) and started an orphanage-home for destitute widows and their babies. He also educated his wife Savitribai Phule so that girls could be educated because Pune parents of that period would not have entrusted their daughters to a male teacher. Thus, the Phules devoted their entire life to uplift the poor and downtrodden. It was a swim against the current all the way. These distinguished men were indeed men of thought and action, who initiated social and political revolution by dealing with several knotty issues such as widow remarriage, women's right to education, ban on child marriage, and ban on tonsuring of young widows. Thus, Pune has a very rich legacy of social reformers, pioneers in education and freedom fighters.

Social Fabric and Family Structure

During the Peshwa period and even as late as in the 1930s and onward, the joint family was the norm in Pune, as in several other places of India. The smallest unit of society was the patriarchal Hindu Joint family. A male elder patriarch (mostly grandfather or great grandfather) controlled the affairs of the family. Very often three to four generations lived together under one roof – in the famous 'waadas' of Pune. A noted sociologist and anthropologist Iravati Karve has written extensively about a common kitchen, ancestors' common property and a common place of worship. Married sons, their wives, children, nephews, orphans, widows, uncles, aunts, unmarried nieces, all lived in composite joint family. All were taken care of. At times relatives of daughters-in-laws were also accommodated. For example, a daughter-in-law's brother often stayed for higher education and he too became every child's uncle ('mama'). It was a kind of free lodging and boarding for dear and near ones. Even in case of some tenants occupying a corner of a 'waada', the landlord was a father figure, not just a person collecting rent. The Max Weberian notion of a householder very aptly fits such a situation.

Most of the male members worked. They had either their own business and shops or their agricultural common land holdings. Girl's education barely went beyond first two standards. All females were expected to be good cooks and sewing experts, good housewives in short. They seldom went out except to temples and for religious and marriage functions. All shopping was done by male members. A traditional culture prevailed, heavily steeped in religious rituals and ceremonies. Very strong notions of sacredness, purity and pollution guided the people. P.K. Atre's book '*Karheche Pani*' draws a vivid picture of the ethos in such joint families.

Outside the family unit, the contemporary society at large was caste-ridden. Caste-wise hereditary occupations were strictly followed. Brahmins were either religious priests or school teachers.

Changing Family Structure

Traces of caste-wise occupations are still found in certain pockets of Pune. But by and large the link between caste/community and occupation, especially in urban areas, started becoming weak as the education spread. The very theory of karma and rebirth was being challenged by new generations. Even the old taboos and notions of purity were changing. For example, among many non-meat eating castes, especially Brahmins in Pune (once known to be a highly orthodox place), the use of alcohol and non-vegetarian food was on the rise. Partly it was also the impact of westernization. Earlier eating out was also looked down upon, if not altogether a taboo. That is why when the Parsees and Iranis were opening their bakeries and 'café restaurants' in the beginning of the 20th century, the Maharashtrians were running 'Khanavalis' (mess) for either the immigrants from villages, students, bachelors or the factory labourers. Later on with the advent of college education, middle class local youths also felt the need for tea-shops and small eateries which could cater to all. 'Upahargrihas' (Refreshment houses) were set up to fulfill this need; and they served typical Maharashtrian food at reasonable price. Multi-cuisine restaurants and modern hotels were still unheard of. Whatever hotels existed were essentially for middle and lower class (e.g. Poona Guest House)

But all this had to change gradually. With growing industrialization, place of house and work became different. Men started going out of their houses, when jobs like clerks in military accounts department were introduced. With the advent of the British rule in India, several other aspects of life had started changing. For example, modern education had opened up new vistas for educated people. New occupations were beckoning – army, ICS, medical and engineering. After Charles Wood dispatch in 1854, English became the *lingua franca (Macaulay Minutes)* of India. English medium schools and colleges sprang up side by side with vernacular medium of instructions-for example, Fergusson college in 1885. A new broadening of the horizons in the citadel of tradition and orthodoxy was taking place; the end result of which was the entry of girls in the institutes of higher learning, even if they were outside the towns. Modern ideas and values of freedom and liberty started exerting their influence on people. Shri Chiplunkar often called English the tigress's milk.

Then followed Mahatma Gandhi's call to join freedom struggle, women 'folk' discarded their safe and secure place in home and hearth, and joined their male counterparts to participate in various freedom activities. The 1930s – 1940s also saw the entry of more and more women in nursing, teaching and clerical jobs. Several girls started joining medical profession. More and more urban women became graduates. The period of 1960-70s saw the birth of a modern educated girl who no longer wanted to be dominated at home, especially by mother-in-law. Women no longer wanted to be confined to the four walls of the house, to child bearing, and to bringing up children.

As a result, conflicting set of values and ideologies started sharpening the hiatus between two generations. It gradually led to the breakdown of the Joint family (1970s – 80s). The newly-wed girl wanted her independence. Her idea of a happy home was 'She and husband and children only'. The seeds of nuclear family gradually started being sown. The trend persisted even in the 1980s-90s. In old *waadas* of Pune one often found 2-3 partitions i.e. married sons living separately. The 1990s – 2000 saw a rapid change in the family structure; from a household of 25-30 people to a family of 4-5 i.e. husband wife and children, at the most the grandfather or mother. As women began working outside, acute need was felt to look after home, especially small children. This contributed to role strain, at times even to role-conflict. The crèches as well as the number of old age homes in Pune increased. The concept of eating out or buying food from outside took roots. The husbands in the nuclear families today are doing domestic chores, even making tea or cooking, and bathing children. This was once a forbidden zone for men. Today readymade food is available e.g. Dominos - pizza, Mc Donalds etc. The notion of purity and pollution regarding food has almost disappeared except for the four months of *chaturmas*; (the rainy season). A wide variety of food ranging from street food to hotel food is now available. Working women often buy supplementary food from outside to save time. This is the impact of modern education, new set of values, professions, rapid urbanization coupled with westernization, and reference group behaviour. It has also affected caste system. Casteism too is disappearing. Now many upper caste people cannot afford to worry as to who cooks their food when it comes from outside. Food is often ordered from outside if more guests are coming. Convenience and necessity are more important than the notions of purity of food.

These changes in the patterns of family and structure of authority have been facilitated by the simultaneous operation of three variables - (1) education, (2) occupation (3) income. If a son acquires higher education than that of the father, it results in pursuit of an occupation which carries higher status or prestige and subsequent rise in income. This in turn changes ideas about standard of living, social mobility and career moves. Among the young generation, very often son stays separately in a bigger flat. Running parallel to this development are two more factors – the changing age of marriage and a measure of choice of partners. Higher education of women has created a demand for independence and autonomy from the patriarchal tutelage. The result is – conflict of values, modern education and ideas of the new daughter-in-law vs traditional mother-in-law. This distancing is further accentuated by physically moving away from the family of orientation to a better physical environmental conditions e.g. setting up a house, an apartment, if not a bungalow. In its turn the unit of family which had so moved away introduces new items of food of variety and choice and there is consequent rise in expenditure on items of food at home or outside. A new routine of eating out starts occasionally or even weekly. Thus, the family as a unit, its different family members e.g. school / college going sons / daughters have given a boost to the demand for hotel food which is very clearly reflected in the proliferation of eating places all over Pune.

A parallel development to the breaking down of joint families is now the growth of caterers who deliver home-made tiffin at the door-steps of senior citizens, especially single ones, who are too old and weak to cook. Instead of hiring domestic help they prefer this arrangement, often on monthly basis, as it is fairly reliable. Such caterers have limited business and a fix number of customers. So the quality and hygiene of food are maintained.

3

Pune – Industrialisation

The Seeds of Industrialisation

Before the advent of the British, the process of industrialisation in Pune was initiated on a very modest scale under the rule of Peshawa Bajirao II. It was he who invited the silk weavers from Nasik and Paithan to Pune in the beginning of the 19th century. His rule also saw the entry of many artisans such as potters and other craftsmen from different parts, even from Andhra Pradesh, into Pune. Today's Kumbharwada in Pune, the 'separate settlement of potters', bears a testimony to it.

However, with the downfall of the Maratha Empire, the weavers' industry declined, though the introduction of railway line between Bombay and Pune in 1856, gave a fillip to the traditional brass and copper industry. It provided employment to about 2300 to 2400 persons engaged in its manufacturing and trade in 1884. Even in today's modern Pune we find certain localities, in the heart of the city, named as *'tambatalis'* ('ali' means a small lane/ by lane, and 'tamba' is copper), or *'Sutaralis'* (i.e. carpenters' localities). Surnames like *Pitale* ('Pital' means brass), Tambe and Sutar are still common. They are reminiscent of the caste-wise occupations. Other such lanes were 'daneali' (occupied by grain merchants) and 'Bohriali' (dominated by Bohri Muslims dealing in hardware). Sir Charles Metcalfe's description of Indian villages and townships as 'little republics' is aptly applicable to this historical Pune, especially so as the 'Balutedari'-barter system of economy-was prevalent.

Pune, the Growing Industrial City

Pune is one of the those few places, like Bangalore, in India where the climate seems to have blended ideally with its people to produce an ethos which has built up, on one hand, probably the best in Indian culture and education, and on the other a vital part of the country's growing industry. The city has been building up modern industry against the back drop of its old tradition of learning and administration. The renaissance in education and industry started together in the eighties of the 19th century. Today the city is being recognised as one of our new industrial cities, but its eminence as an educational centre has not diminished.

Pune's industrial growth barely spans over five decades. Earlier the city had no local tradition of large scale trade or commerce, nor were there any organised industries. The population comprised typical middle class community. Hence none of its leading entrepreneurs today claim a textile background which has been a chief ingredient in the success formula of many prominent business houses in other parts of India.

Nevertheless, attempts were made as early as in the last quarter of the 19th century to start industries in the vicinity of Pune. Deccan Paper Mills was founded by Sardar Dorabjee and Sardar Nowrosjee Pudumjee in 1888. An attempt was made by Shri Anantrao Bhau Godambe to undertake large scale production of brass and copperware with the aid of machinery. After running for twenty years, the factory was sold to its wholesale selling agents, Messrs Hukamchand Ishwardas, and was renamed as 'Gujarat Metal Factory'. In 1983, Seth Hindumal Balmukund, one of the leading traders, started Raja Bahadur Motilal Poona Mills in Pune. Lokmanya Tilak had written a special editorial in 'Kesari' welcoming this new venture of the Pune industrialist. With the blessing of Lokmanya Tilak, an industrial fund named the 'Paisa Fund' was started to give boost to Swadeshi industries. The fund financed a glass factory at Talegaon in 1908. It provided blowers to other glass factories in the country. In 1886 the famous artist Raja Ravi Varma started a litho press at Malavali near Lonavala. Some of these factories are still running and have recorded considerable progress during all these years.

Apart from these private efforts, the government set up its defence factories near Pune because of its favourable climate and proximity to Bombay. In 1869, Ammunition Factory was started at Khadki and during the First and Second World War considerable expansion took place at this factory. It gave a real impetus to the organized industry and creation of factory labour. In 1940, High Explosive Factory also went into production at Khadki.

However, for about forty years after this, beyond defence production and a few household industries, manufacturing activities did not increase manifold. The small scale industries continued producing a variety of consumer articles such as *bidis*, bricks, coarse cloth, brass and copper utensils, stationery, perfumes, soap, etc. Yet it was only after the Second World War that the first major manufacturing unit, Kirloskar Oil Engines Ltd (1945), was set up by Shri Shantanurao Laxmanrao Kirloskar. Before that in 1940, High Explosive Factory had also gone into production in Khadki. But it was not an economic multiplier in the true sense of the term, nor was it associated with service economy. Kirloskar Oil Engines marked the beginning of industrial development in Pune. It gave an impetus to the setting up of a number of small scale units, serving as feeders to the large scale units. Starting with the main purpose of manufacturing indigenous diesel engines in India, it is a sister concern of Kirloskar Brothers Ltd that manufactures agricultural implements at Kirloskarwadi, about 150 kms south of Pune.

As a result of the partition of the country immediately after independence, there was influx of refugees from Pakistan. In 1948 a separate township at Pimpri near Pune was created for their resettlement. With active support from the government the migrated population soon got engaged in manufacturing and service activities. The entrepreneurial talent of this community was later picked up by the native population. Later on with the expansion of refugee township, Pimpri-Chinchwad area expanded, gradually emerging as the largest industrial area housing small, medium and large scale industries manufacturing variety of products.

The period 1950 onwards witnessed establishment of several large scale units on the periphery of Pune *viz.* old Pune-Bombay Road, which incidentally runs parallel to Pune-Bombay railway line. Most of these units were engineering units. There were also several foreign collaborations (technical or financial or both). Kirloskar Oil Engines Ltd (KOEL) entered into the first technical collaboration with a foreign manufacturer Cummins as a deliberate policy of diversification. It was then known as Kirloskar Cummins Ltd. Large scale factories, like Ruston & Hornsby, Cooper Engineering, Buckau Wolf, K.S.B. Pumps, Bajaj Auto, Bajaj Tempo and TELCO were started and this gave further fillip to the growth of small scale ancillary units in Pune.

In 1954, Ruston and Hornsby (India) Ltd., the first factory in Greaves Cotton Group was set up at Chinchwad. Greaves Foseco, another factory in the same group was also set up in the same premises at Chinchwad in 1957. In 1955 Hindustan Antibiotics Ltd., a public sector project was set up at Pimpri near Pune. The setting up of these manufacturing units encouraged considerable industrial development near about these factories in the Bombay Pune rail road corridor in the Pimpri Chinchwad area. This growth was further accelerated mainly because of the proximity and easy accessibility of this area to Bombay and also owing to restrictions imposed by the State Government on the industrial expansion in Greater Bombay. The other factors such as salubrious climate, availability of skilled personnel, necessary infrastructural facilities such as water, transport, etc. also played a major role in attracting industries to Pune. The establishment of Hadapsar Industrial Estate (eastern outskirts of city) in 1956 by Pune Municipal Corporation and the exemption of octroi duty on the raw material and machinery of the units located in this Estate also attracted a few new industries to Pune.

In 1960 the Maharashtra Industrial Development Corporation (MIDC) undertook development of a large industrial area of 4000 acres at Bhosari in the Pimpri Chinchwad Industrial Complex. A large number of industries, both large scale and small scale, were already established in the area and the development of this area by the MIDC further helped the process of industrialization in Pune. Now Pimpri Chinchwad Bhosari Industrial Complex is one of the largest industrial complexes in the state.

The 1970s witnessed a phenomenal growth in number of large industrial units surrounding Pune city. They are everywhere, dotting Pune-Solapur Road and Pune - Ahmednagar Road to the south; Pune-Nasik Road to the east and Pune-Mumbai Road to the north-west. Later, some units also came up on Pune-Bangalore Highway. Bhor, Lonavala, Talegaon, Saswad, Pirangut, Sanaswadi, and Chakan are a few other towns around Pune where we find concentration of several industrial units.

Apart from the outskirts, several small scale industrial units are now promoted by MCCAI (Maharashtra Chamber of Commerce, Agriculture and Industries, earlier only MCC), and they are located in the city areas such as Shankar Sheth Road, Parvati, Gultekdi, etc. In fact they have created some problems of civic amenities and residential accommodation, not to mention the financial burden on Municipal Corporation.

The result was that by the turn of the century there were more than 7000 units both large scale and small scale in and around Pune. Pune's Industrial status is now established and where once cattle grazed and farmers chatted under the cool shade of the banyan trees, there have sprung up new industrial areas at Khadki-Pimpri-Chinchwad-Bhosari, Kothrud and Hadapsar, and on both sides of Pune Nagar Road. During night time, they provide a spectacle of lights, well-lighted factories with their neon-signed hoardings, and with their modern architectural designs showing prominently in their lights. This is a radical transformation of a quiet city – from Pune, the pensioners' paradise to Pune, an industrial hub.

Changing Nature of Industrialization in Pune

The industrial activities in the second half of the 19th century Pune, and the ones started in the mid-twentieth century after a lull of about 40 years, were different in more than one way.

First of all, the second phase of industrialization in Pune was much more capital intensive and necessitated recruitment of highly skilled and professional personnel from all over India, if not immediately from abroad. This in turn gradually led to establishment of advanced professional educational institutes catering to technical and managerial needs of growing industries. Both these factors had a direct link to the development of hotel industry in Pune. International collaboration in business and industrial fields also gave additional impetus to this link between industrialization of Pune on one hand, and food industry on the other. The second phase industries also paved the way for service economy.

Urbanization and Pune's March towards Super Industrial Status

During the Second World War, because of the establishment of defence industries, Pune's population increased considerably. Thereafter several other factors converged to pave the way to Pune's rapid urbanization and growing super industrial status. We have already mentioned the resettlement of the refugees in Pimpri near Pune. Then in 1950 the Pune City Municipality and the Pune Suburban Municipalities were merged together and the Pune Municipal Corporation was formed. As a result of all these developments, in one decade, i.e. from 1941 to 1951, the population of Pune city suddenly increased from about 2.37 lakhs to about 4.81 lakhs, by almost 100 per cent.

A few other developments which have helped Pune to grow are the establishment of National Defence Academy, The National Chemical Laboratory, University of Poona, a number of defence related institutes, as well as Central Water and Power Research Station. The Panshet floods in 1961 affected a large number of families living in the areas near the river banks. Hence new residential colonies sprang up and the city expanded further in all directions. In 1962, the boundaries of Pune Municipal Corporation were again extended to include certain new areas.

Pune, the Nucleus city of Industrial Expansion

As it is already mentioned, a noteworthy feature of the industrial development of Pune metropolitan region has been the development of large industrial areas around a radius of 50 kms with Pune city as nucleus centre for expansion. This has been because of the progressive policy of industrial dispersal of the State Government, formally incorporated in the package scheme of incentives. The Government also announced 64 growth centres at the taluka places and mini townships in Maharashtra with no industrial background so far. This incentive aimed at decentralization of industries and a more balanced regional development of the State. This was the force behind development of such rural centers as Bhima-Koregaon-Sanaswadi, Shikrapur, Shirwal, Khed-Shivapur, Saswad, Bhor, Chakan, Pirangut, Kanhe, Nasrapur and Bebedohol near Talegaon. The significance of this development is that Pune is now surrounded from all sides by developing industrial areas. This also signifies an all round development of the local population in terms of job opportunities, scope for starting ancillaries and an increase in the standard of living. The State Government has been giving multiple benefits to such units under its package scheme of incentives. The 1983 package scheme in this series was especially effective in terms of dispersal of industries. Another package scheme of incentive announced in 1988 gave further impetus to such dispersal of industries.

In all package schemes of incentives announced by the State Government after 1979, no incentives are offered to any new industrial units starting newly in the Pune Metropolitan Region (PMR). Exception is made only in respect of electronic industries which are allowed to grow in PMR area. On the contrary, attractive incentives are offered to units starting in developing regions outside PMR as well as outside Pune District. The result is development of such district places as Satara and Ahmednagar into new industrial townships. This is clearly a spillover of the industrial development of Pune. MIDC (Maharashtra Industrial Development Corporation) has set up industrial estates at Ahmednagar and Satara, and while some local entrepreneurs have started their own units there, a number of units from Pune have also installed additional manufacturing capacities either at Ahmednagar / Satara or in Pune district but outside PMR. Thus, location-wise, industries in Pune are well distributed over the entire region, creating well demarcated pockets of factories and workshops.

Along with the state support for industries, the technical, engineering skills of the trained personnel have also contributed to this industrial growth. There is always demand for such expertise, and in turn for the goods manufactured by experts. There is a ready market for such supplies of goods. The forces of demand and supply are very well balanced in such situations.

The twin process of modernization and globalization has further enhanced this chain process of demand and supply, thereby generating the demand for skilled manpower and generating employment at the same time. The goods being manufactured by these skilled professionals have an international demand and subsequently an ever increasing market is created. In a nutshell, it is demand that generates supply.

Pune's Super Industrial Status

Export orientation

The peculiarity of industrialization of Pune is that there is no concentration of any particular industry at the cost of some other.(see Appendix...........). Size wise also there are large scale and heavy industries, small scale industrial units working as ancillaries to these large scale ones, and also a variety of medium scale industries.

Among all these, electronic industry in Pune is mainly export oriented. The growth of electronic industry has resulted in growing demand for electronic goods. Hence indigenous home production has resulted in decrease of import of electronic goods from abroad. During the last few years, Pune has developed into a center for electronic industry. Starting from basic transistors and other semi conductor devices, TV sets, VCR, Electronic Telex Machines, EPABX's and components of all types are manufactured in the electronic industries in Pune. The small and medium scale equipment manufacturers are also specialized in different lines of instrumentation, such as digital equipment, process control equipment, industrial equipment, consumer equipment, communication equipment, etc. All these equipments are produced in Pune. Most of the raw materials and electronics and components of various types of hardware are also manufactured in Pune. No city other than Pune has such a unique group of electronic manufacturers. In addition, in Pune we have a large number of research laboratories and other government establishments wherein continuous research and development in the field of electronics takes place. The government has also established a testing and development center in electronics in Pune.

In 1987, MIDC built three multistoried buildings in MIDC Bhosari, especially to house electronic industries. About 45 units engaged in electronic industries have set up their manufacturing establishments in these buildings. There is one 100 per cent software exporting unit in one of these buildings, occupying an entire floor. Satellite communication facilities with a large disc antenna are also set up in one of the buildings. In addition to this, a separate electronic zone is developed by MIDC in cooperation with the department of electronics. The industrial zones of Pune are now dotted with several Technology Parks too. All this has helped the development of electronic industries in Pune area.

An Emerging Centre of Advanced Technology

Pune Metropolitan area has a variety of industries ranging from rather simple fabrication workshops to companies engaged in high tech areas like Electronics, Computer manufacturing, etc. The IMTEX 89 exhibition held at Bombay as far back as in February 1989 clearly demonstrated the fact that Pune city is emerging as a center of advanced technology. The IMTEX 89 attracted over 650 machine tools manufacturers from India and abroad. As many as 72 industries from Pune participated in the IMTEX 89 exhibition thereby earning reputation of sending maximum number of participants from a single city. Further more, out of ten awards declared by the IMTEX organizers; five were bagged by the industries from Pune, thereby earning recognition for their excellent performance in high techniques like CNC machines and EDM testing equipments.

Software Technology Parks at Pune

By creating international market for software development, Government is gaining lots of revenue and foreign exchange through export of software. Creation of NASSCOM and Computer Society of India bear testimony to it.

During the last few years, a large number of Software Developers have established their centres in Pune area and many more are coming. Therefore, very rightly the Department of Electronics (DOE), Govt. of India has selected Pune as one of the three centers for promoting software exports through direct satellite link, provided to the exporters connecting Pune and Boston, and thereby enabling them to have speedy communication with the software users in U.S.A. The project has a 100 PER CENT export orientation. Already Talawade and Hinjawadi villages, about 20 km from Pune but in different directions, have been developed into Infotech parks. A special electronic zone is also created in MIDC Bhosari. The software park here provides multiple opportunities not only for the electronic industries but also for computer and software allied industries in this region. With the commissioning of this park Pune has emerged as a leading software export center in the country, a cyber city next to Bangalore.

4

Academic and Institutional Support

A trained manpower is one of the largest assets for any industry- its social overhead capital. Therefore, while writing about Pune's super industrial status, one must not forget the tacit support these industries have got, and keep getting, from the academic institutions and research centres of the city. They provide the continuous upgrading of knowledge and skills to keep pace with new challenges and demands.

One such institution is C-DAC, the Center for Development of Advanced Computing, presently located on the Pune University campus. The C-DAC project under DOE ministry has been initiated by the Govt. as India's strategic initiative for development of advanced computing based on parallel processing architecture. The Govt. has selected Pune as the location because of the availability of trained technical manpower in the area. The major milestone of the project is development of super computer-'Param'-developed with peak computing power of 1000 mega floppies. Over the years C-DAC has also generated a whole range of commercial products such as VLSI chip set for P.Cs, advanced card level products, parallel processing and AI work stations, software products, etc. The spin offs from such advanced technology development efforts have been very beneficial to the entrepreneurs in this region.The National Information Centre (NIC) is another feather in Pune's cap. It not only serves as a storage bank, but also disseminates information, for example census operation with the help of the super computer. Thus, Pune's growth of service sector is partly due to such information technology.

Educational Institutions

Pune's complex of educational institutions is another great support that the city's industries get.

Some of these are the College of Engineering Pune (COEP), Maharashtra Institute of Technology (MIT), Maharashtra Association for Cultivation of Science (MACS), Government Polytechnic, Sir Cusrow Wadia Institute of Technology, Automotive Research Association of India (ARAI), Central Institute of Road Transport, Indian Drug Research Institute, several industrial training institutes and an Institute in Paints Technology. The National Chemical Laboratory – one of the 26 national laboratories – is also located in Pune. Moreover, the State Government has put up its industrial research laboratory at Pune. For small scale industries there is an extension center of Small Industries Service Institute which offers some common service facilities. We have already mentioned about C-DAC, National Information Centre, and Electronic Test. In addition, the University of Pune has very well equipped Departments of Physics, Chemistry, Energy, Electronics, Botany, Zoology, Computer Science, etc which also help industries in their R&D activities. Then there are R&D institutions connected with defence such as R&D Engineers, Armament Research and Development Establishment, Explosive Research and Development Laboratory, which also indirectly help industries in designing and developing products required by them. Institutions catering to various careers like those of Company Secretaries, Cost Accountants, Tax Consultants as well as various types of Financial Consultancies contribute to ever expanding knowledge, skills and competence. This industrial development in turn has resulted in the development of several professional organizations like Poona Management Association, Institution of Engineers, Indian Institute of Materials Management, Institute of Cost Accountants, National Institute of Personnel Management, Institute of Industrial Engineers, and so on. Inputs from management institutions also acquire crucial importance for industries; and fortunately Pune has several such institutions.

Apart from these there are other institutions around Pune such as National Institute of Virology, Deccan Sugar Research Institute, Central Water and Power Research Station, Indian Institute of Meteorology, Institute of Computer Science, Astro Physics Research Centre, National Institute of Bank Management, Central Mechanical Engineering Research Institute, and Bhartiya Agro Research Foundation which also make technically trained manpower in a variety of disciplines available. The possibility of credit is equally important for the smooth functioning and development of industries. The city has several financial services catering to this need.

To sum up, Education and Research are two main industries of Pune City. These activities provide a large number of technically trained manpower which in turn is helping local industries in their regular production, growth and expansion.

Mahratta Chamber of Commerce, Agriculture and Industries

Mahratta Chamber of Commerce, Agriculture and industries (MCCAI) is an apex body that acts as a facilitator for business community, and also as an advisory body. It has made considerable efforts to promote and develop trade and industry in the Pune region. It was founded in 1934 to spearhead the Swadeshi movement and particularly to give impetus to the growth of local enterprise. In 1935 it promoted the Bank of Maharashtra. This Bank is one of the leading regional banks and has played a very useful role in financing industry and trade, and more particularly, local small scale industries in Maharashtra State. This Bank was nationalized along with 13 other banks in 1969. The chamber also made an attempt to start a financial institution for providing medium and long term finance to industries. But this experiment, because of the apathy of the then Government, could not succeed. Some of the office bearers of the Chamber also made an attempt to develop an industrial estate called Pimpri Udyogpur at Pimpri, but the conditions then were rather unfavourable and the scheme met with failure. The Chamber has also promoted two industrial estates, one exclusively for small electronic industries and the other for all types of small scale industries. In all about 300 industrial units were helped by the Chamber. In 1983 a Stock Exchange was established at Pune. All preliminary work to organize this Exchange was done by the Chamber.

In 1953 the Chamber submitted detailed proposals for the proper development of Hadapsar Industrial Estate and requested the Corporation to exempt the industries in the Estate from the payment of octroi levy. In 1961 when a large number of industries in the city were affected by Panshet floods, the Chamber took considerable efforts to rehabilitate the flood affected units. Emergency arrangements for their raw materials, machinery, finance, and accommodation were made with the active assistance of the State Directorate of industries. Present Parvati Industrial Estate is an outcome of these efforts. The Chamber then promoted Maharashtra Commerce and Industries Rehabilitation Society as a guarantee organization for the finance of banks to such flood affected units. In 1962 the Chamber worked out a detailed scheme of Functional Electronic Estate and submitted it to Maharashtra Industrial Development Corporation. The scheme of this estate was accepted and the Estate was established in Bhosari. The problems of regional development of Pimpri Chinchwad area such as over bridge at Chinchwad Railway Station, introduction of EMU coaches, water supply, uninterrupted power supply, police outpost and telegraph facilities, transport facilities, formation of civic authority in the area, etc. were taken up by the Chamber from time to time with authorities concerned. Some of these problems have been solved and some are still waiting solution. The Chamber was also closely associated with the work of Pune Metropolitan Regional Planning Board and assisted the Board in the preparation of the Regional plan. Now it is assisting a similar plan for Pimpri Chinchwad area.

The voluntary role of MCCAI cannot ever be overlooked. It is indeed a body of dedicated people, for the people and by the people. In short, it acts not only as a server to the business community but also as an advisory body to several groups. Thus, it offers labour advisory services, engineering services, group telex services, translation services, Xerox copying service, import-export and excise consultancy service; and has organized an excellent commercial reference library along with an audio visual library. It also collects statistics, undertakes publications, and organizes training programmes, industrial tours and exhibitions, issues certificates of origin and price certificates. As mentioned earlier it has set up two industrial estates and has organized many professional committees to look after day to day problems of business and industry.

All this proves that MCCAI is not merely a grievance ventilating body, as is the common concept of any Chamber of Commerce, but during the course of years it is evolved as a common service agency – rendering important services to the business community.

Education – Industries Nexus

Pune also has a large number of Management institutions offering a variety of long and short duration management courses. All these organizations are rendering special services to industries in Pune region. Such nexus between educational institutions and industries indicates a paradigm shift in the nature of professional education in Pune.

It was feared that the rapid pace of industrial development would destroy 'Oxford of the East' and its educational and intellectual atmosphere, people's zest for learning and the rich cultural ethos of traditional Pune. Some people were disturbed that Pune, once an idyllic

'Pensioners' Paradise' would have to gear itself to a fast pace of work with no time for leisure, in short for dehumanization. Kuhn's 'Paradigm shift' was not easily acceptable to many. However, all these fears have been laid to rest by the course of events. In Pune's case tradition and modernity are not polarities. (Arthur Gusfield, 1960, *American Sociological Review)* The industrial transformation of the city has made education all the more indispensable as a highroad to employment. There is not only more education in Pune now, but education in many more fields then before. There has been no lowering of standards either. Pune still holds its position as one of the best places to bring up school going children, as well as for college going teens. Commerce colleges, management institutions, engineering colleges, colleges for nurses and polytechnics have sprouted up. Periodically, new courses in business management and in other fields are introduced to fulfill the needs of the time.

5

Hotel Industry

As indicated in the Introduction to this book, the hotel industries in and around Pune are mainly linked to industrialization of the city. Hotels, especially star hotels, have come up mainly to cater to the special demand for sophisticated places, clubs, and dining halls, thereby extending hospitality to a fraternity of executives both from within the country and from abroad. But the spurt in the number of hotels and restaurants in Pune is a product of industrialization as well as urbanization, heterogeneity of the society and ever increasing student population from all directions. Moreover, infrastructural facilities such as gas, electricity, water supply, construction business, railways, roadways, airways, banking, insurance and trade have also led to the development of hotels. All these facilities are complimentary to the growth of hotel industry which basically is indeed a service sector where the quality of the service is very important.

Concept of a Hotel

Today there has been a boom in the hotel industry. But originally the concept or idea of a hotel is a Western concept, and it is the emulation of western culture that has brought about a distinctive quantitative as well as qualitative change in the structure of hotels and their services. Sociologically speaking, this is a good example of 'Reference Group Behaviour', to use Robert Merton's term. Hotel or Inn is defined by British Laws as 'a place where a bonafide traveler can receive food and shelter, provided he is in a position to pay for it and is in a fit condition to be received. Hence hotel has to provide food and lodging to the travelers on payment and has in turn the right to refuse if traveler is drunk, disorderly or is not in position to pay for the services.

Webster English Dictionary defines hotel as 'a building or institution providing lodging, meals and service to people.' From the point of view of users, a hotel is an institution of commercial hospitality. It offers its facilities and services for sale individually or in various combinations. As a product for sale, a hotel consists of the following elements. Together they determine its saleability and price.

(a) Location – which implies accessibility and convenience to the clients.

(b) Facilities – refer to quality of bedrooms, other rooms, restaurants, bars, transport and other facilities.

(c) Services – Comprises speed, efficiency, degree of personal attention.

(d) Image – It is the way in which a hotel portrays itself, depending upon the above factors. It also depends on atmosphere, ambience, appearance, its goodwill, name of the hotel and its association with type of people who patronize it; in short the brand.

(e) Price – It is determined by all the elements mentioned above. It is the value given by the hotel through its service, reputation and the general satisfaction of its patrons. Therefore, hotel can include a restaurant but not vice-versa.

A Brief History of Hotel Industry

The Hotel industry is perhaps one of the oldest commercial endeavours in the world. When man started traveling on horse or foot, he wanted to stay where he and his horse got food, hence the need to stay, in a place to stay and eat. In England the first inns date back to the 6th century BC and were product of the urge to travel which began with the invention of the wheel. The earliest inns were ventures by husband and wife teams who provided large halls for travelers to make their own beds and sleep on the floor. They also provided modest wholesome food and thirst quenchers like wine. Entertainment or recreation was provided by the host's wife or a woman member. The entire cooking services and recreation were provided by husband and wife and the family. These conditions prevailed for a hundred years. The industrial revolution in England brought new ideas and progress in the business of inn keeping.

The Development of railways and steam engine made traveling more prominent. The industrial revolution also changed the nature of travel from travels for social purpose or government duty to business travels. There was a need for quick and clean service. The lead in hotel keeping was taken by the emerging nations of Europe, especially Switzerland. It was in Europe that hotels got recognition as organized industry. Initially they were small and provided a variety of services. In early England public houses were normally called inns or taverns. Normally the name inn was reserved for finer establishment, catering to noble persons and ministers of Christian Church. The houses visited by commoners were known as taverns. In France, a similar distinction was made with finer establishment owners known as 'hoteliers' and the small houses called as 'cabarets'. The word hotel was used in England in about 1760. In America lodging houses were called inns or coffee houses.

The real growth of modern hotel industry took place in USA beginning with opening of Facility Hotel in New York in 1794. It was the first building erected specially for hotel purposes. This led to a great competition between different cities and resulted in big hotel buildings Some of the finest hotels of USA were built in this era; e.g. Waldorf Austorai, but the real boom in hotel building came in the early 20th century. The outbreak of Second World War gave a tremendous lift. This prosperity continued through war years into the 1950s when new concepts emerged, that of motels, and international chain operations. Today hotels cater to all needs and wishes of the guests and the future holds promises for further progress of modern hotels.

Ancient India had the concept of a Dharmashala – Sarai. They were usually enroute to the places of pilgrimage. Books written by Hunyatsen (626 – 645 A.D), and Marco Polo (1271 AD) bear testimony to this. Around 18th century more number of Dharmashalas were built as the need for accommodation plus eating kept on increasing, hence now this was considered to be an occupation. – Earning money by serving people – providing them food and shelter. In England, after the industrial revolution, manufacturers had to appoint distributors, who had to stay away from home, hence hotels were started. Later industrialists, enthusiastic tourists, and others needed a place to stay. Post-industrial phase saw a number of new occupations, one of them being hostelling. In refreshment houses food and drinks were served. The need for novelty of items was felt by merchants. For example, in London city alone there were three thousand coffee houses.

In India, by the beginning of the 19th Century there were many eateries – 'Khanavalis', as they were called in Pune. As soon as Transport and Communication increased in big cities, a number of Khanavalis (community kitchens) and Dharamashalas increased. They were of two types – catering to the rich, and the middle class.

With the advent of the British rule these eateries got converted into western type of hotels. In big cities like Bombay, Calcutta, and Delhi such hotels were started. Even though Dharmashalas remained popular, many foreigners who came to India often stayed in Western, British style of hotels. In Bombay, Tajmahal type hotels were started by the British and Swiss ownership with all facilities / amenities like Billiards table. Lunch, dinner, breakfast, tea, coffee was served. Travelers, or tourists, traveled by sea route, so boating facilities were also provided. Even separate cars, taxis, for tourists were arranged. In 1840 – in Bombay – a Parsi gentleman, Mr. Penalji Pestonji, built a British type hotel. He was the first man to build such a hotel which was very well managed, well equipped, and also included a beer bar. Later he started a hotel near Fort area in Bombay (1871). John Walsk started Esplanade hotel. He himself designed the building. For hotel management, he hired British people. The Hotel had 130 rooms. In 1886 with a capital of Rs. 10 lacs was started 'Great Eastern Hotel'. In India there were very few hotels before the 2nd World war. In 1940 number of hotels / restaurants in big cities increased because foreign tourists came here, but even then there number was limited. After independence, the total number of hotels with licenses and government approval was 186. In 1962-63 star hotels classification started. Along with that the number of non authorized hotels had also increased.

The Taj hotel was started in Bombay by Jamshedji Tata on 1st April 1902. Capital invested was Rs. 30 lakhs. He had visited many European countries and tried to build such type of hotels. 'Taj' is rated as the tenth best hotel in the world, a fully equipped Five star hotel. Later on old palaces were converted to Taj Hotels e.g Lake Palace – Udaipur. A lot of foreign tourists come here. Hence these hotels have contributed a lot of foreign exchange to India.

Later on, the chain of hotels also started, for example, Ritz group of hotels in Bombay, Calcutta and Hyderabad; Bombay group of hotels, Oberoi hotels, etc. All these hotels are associated with the Hotels India Ltd. Raybahadur Mohansing Oberoi was a great hotelier and entrepreneur. He was a clerk who had a dream and passion to own a hotel. In 1943, he started his own Grand Hotel in Calcutta. Then he started his own company in partnership – Associated Hotels of India.

Very soon he expanded the chain to Peshawar, Lahore and Delhi, and to Srinagar also (1946). Then came Bombay Centaur Hotel, ITC (Welcome Group) and Maurya Continental. In 1979 Oberoi collaborated with international Sheraton – group and Oberoi Sheraton group was born. Until now hotels were only limited to private sector but after ITDC started functioning – the Central Government (Ministry of Tourism) has promoted development of ITDC hotels all over India – Ashoka Group (ITDC) hotels are all over India - especially near airports. ITDC also has forest houses and tourists bungalows all over India.

A Brief History of Hotels in Pune

Food industry in Pune has been a fallout effect of industrialization. It has emerged as a very strong and durable service economy due to the patronage offered to it by varied and ever expanding cosmopolitan population in Pune. This population comprises factory workers at one end, the top business executives on the other, and the whole gamut of different groups of community in between. Earlier in Pune only Maharashtrian men owned hotels - these were family enterprises known as 'Khanavalis'. Some of them also had provision for temporary accommodation. But after industrialization many people from other regions started coming to Pune and set up their own establishments such as Iranis – cafes, and Udipi restaurants. Today in Pune there are many Udipis, settled for about 50 years. Mr. Gundraj Shetty – owner of Modern Café is settled in Pune for 45 years. After Udipis, Chinese , Punjabi, Gujarati and continental fast food are gaining a lot of importance.

Apart from such refreshment houses and eateries, the early nineteen seventies saw a number of proper hotels being set up. Thus, there were 24 hotels in Pune in 1972. by 1990, the number increased to 147 – almost six-fold within 18 years; and there is no looking back to this date. Now the city also boasts of several hotels which can be categorized as star hotels. They are spacious and have plenty of rooms. For example in 1987 Blue Diamond had 92 rooms, Hotel Amir had 52, Gulmohor had 32, and Sanman had 22. All these are star hotels.

Characteristics of Star Hotels

Five Star Hotels:

Good clean environment, car park, minimum 25 rooms with attached toilets, hot and cold water in bathrooms, window curtains, good lighting, furniture – interior designing by well known interior decorators, AC rooms, good quality carpets, buildings more than 2 storied, swimming pool, are some of the facilities associated with Five star hotels. There are Reception desk, Cash counter and enquiry counter near the entrance, along with a spacious visitors' lobby. Persons employed here are highly educated, experienced and skilled. Conference room, laundry service, a bookstore, beauty parlour, an authorized travel agency, a bank, a cosmetic shop, and a medicine shop are some of the othercommon features. Each room has a telephone and TV. Business hotels also have internet facilities. Besides all these facilities, they have entertainment – song, dance, music, music systems, channel piped music, etc. There are separate dining halls with elegant furniture, along with bar and coffee shop. Food is national and international type. Excellent quality, skilled cooks and helpers add to their value.

Modest, polite and courteous staff in clean uniform have knowledge of foreign languages and good command over English and Hindi. Exterior is also posh and elegant

4 Star Hotels:

4 star hotels have many of the above mentioned features. May be their quality of blankets and pillows is a bit lower; or the upholstery and curtains are not exactly of the top-most grade. But by and large they too are comfortable and suit the needs of many clients, including the ones from the business world.

3 Star Hotels:

3 star hotels have lesser facilities than 4 star ones. For example, may be 50% of their rooms have AC. But otherwise they are quiet decent and comfortable for a short sojourn.

Hotel Industry of India

The travel and hospitality industry continues to be the sector, which has largely profited from the fast growing economy of India. This has largely been due to the 4.4 m tourist arrivals in Financial Year 2007 (13% growth) over the previous period. The compounded growth in tourist inflow over the last ten years (FY97 -FY07) has been 4.3%, while in the last five years, growth stands at 11.6% per annum. The hotel industry went through a rough patch between FY00 to FY04 owing to factors like the Asian financial crisis, Afghan war, Middle East unrest, September 11 attacks, SARS and domestic riots India occupies the forty-sixth position among the sixty tourist destinations in the world. The flourishing economy helped boost the demand for the industry. Also, efforts to diversify tourist attractions by offering new products such as adventure tourism, wellness tourism, medical tourism and golf tourism are expected to have a positive effect on both foreign tourist arriv als and domestic tourism. As per the 2004 findings, the total number of approved rooms by the Government of India stands at around 99,000 (estimated). These rooms are further classified into various segments out of which, Five star and Five Star Deluxe hotels account for around 27% of the total capacity, three star hotels (22%), four star (8%), two star (9%), one star and Heritage hotels (2% each) and the rest is divided between unclassified and unapproved hotels The five star hotel segments have grown the fastest during the last five years at a CAGR of 12%. Further this segment can be divided into 3 sub-segments namely Luxury, Business and Leisure. The growth in this segment indicates the genre of travelers coming into the country. Over the last few years the country has witnessed a large influx of business travelers in the country owing to relaxation of the government's stand on Foreign Direct Investments (FDI) for most of the sectors in the country.

Hotels in India are Setting their Marks in Providing Luxury Facilities to Tourists

India is probably the only country that offers various categories of tourism. These include history tourism, snow-peaked mountains, beautiful landscape, exotic wildlife, adventure tourism, medical tourism (ayurveda and other forms of Indian medications), spiritual tourism, beach tourism (India has the longest coastline in the East) etc. all these attractions of India magnetizes the tourist from all over the world. Now India became a major tourist country. Huge number of tourists visits this county every year. Hotels in India are increased due to this. Hotels in India competing each other to provide the best accommodation and luxury facilities to the tourists.

Each hotel in India has their own characteristics in facilities and services. The distinctive feature of the first class hotels in India is their high standard and quality accommodation that caters to the needs of all kinds of tourists. Equipped with all the modern facilities, the luxury hotels in India promise to offer world-class hospitality and personalized services to tourists visiting India.

Hotels in India offer visitors for online hotels booking. It helps visitors to choose the best hotels according to the services, facilities, place and other things. Booking hotels online is the best service provided by the internet to the people. Online hotel booking provides some seasonal offers and the main thing is price comparison.

Hotels in India are categorized in different classes like seven star hotels, five star hotels, three star hotels, budget hotels, etc. Hotels are providing their guests an ultimate leisure and fitness experience and include an indoor swimming pool, comprehensive gym facilities, a beauty salon, sauna, massage and steam rooms and snooker and table tennis facilities, Bar, Restaurant, 24-hours room facilities, car parking, travel information, transportation and other luxury facilities.

Besides the five star and luxury hotels, the India offers some other hotels providing world-class accommodation at affordable prices.

Get information about Hotels in India which is provided by the major Indian hotels Directory, it provides hotels booking in all over in India, Hotels in Delhi and also provides the tour package in India.

Hotels in India

'Hotels in India' have supply of 110,000 rooms. According to the tourism ministry, 4.4 million tourists visited India last year and at current trend, demand will soar to 10 million in 2010 - to accommodate 350 million domestic travelers. 'Hotels in India' has a shortage of 150,000 rooms fueling hotel room rates across India. With tremendous pull of opportunity, India is a destination for hotel chains looking for growth. The World Travel and Tourism Council, India, data says, India ranks 18th in business travel and will be among the top 5 in this decade. Sources estimate, demand is going to exceed supply by at least 100 per cent over the next 2 years. Five-star hotels in metro cities allot same room, more than once a day to different guests, receiving almost 24-hour rates from both guests against 6-8 hours usage. With demand-supply disparity, 'Hotel India' room rates are most likely to rise 25% annually and occupancy to rise by 80 per cent, over the next two years. 'Hotel Industry in India' is eroding its competitiveness as a cost effective destination. However, the rating on the 'Indian Hotels' is bullish. 'India Hotel Industry 'is adding about 60,000 quality rooms, currently in different stages of planning and development and should be ready by 2012. MNC Hotel Industry giants are flocking India and forging Joint Ventures to earn their share of pie in the race. Government has approved 300 hotel projects, nearly half of which are in the luxury range. Sources said, the manpower requirements of the hotel industry will increase from 7 million in 2002 to 15 million by 2010.

With the USD 23 billion software services sector pushing the Indian economy skywards, more and more IT professionals are flocking to Indian metro cities. 'Hotel Industry in India' is set to grow at 15 per cent a year. This figure will sky rocket in 2010, when Delhi hosts the Commonwealth

Games. Already, more than 50 international budget hotel chains are moving into India to stake their turf.

Hotel Industry in India

The hotel industry in India is going through an interesting phase. One of the major reasons for the increase in demand for hotel rooms in the country is the boom in the overall Economy and high growth in sectors like information technology, telecom, retail and real estate. Rising stock market and new business opportunities are also attracting hordes of foreign investors and international corporate travellers to look for business opportunities in the country . Hotel industry is also inextricably linked to the tourism industry and its growth has added fillip to the hotel industry. And with Conde Nast Traveller ranking India as the fourth most preferred travel destination and Lonely Planet selecting the country among the top five destinations from 167 countries, India has finally made its mark on the world travel map. The arrival of low cost airlines and the associated price wars have given domestic tourists a host of options. The opening up of the aviation industry in India has led the way for exciting opportunities for the hotel industry as it relies on airlines to transport 80% of international arrivals.

Moreover, the government's decision to substantially upgrade 28 regional airports in smaller towns and privatisation and expansion of Delhi and Mumbai airport will improve the business prospects of hotel industry in India. Substantial investment in tourism infrastructure is essential for Indian hotel industry to achieve its potential. The upgrading of national highway connecting various parts of India has opened new av enues for the development of budget hotels here. The Government of India's Incredible India destination campaign and the Atithi Devo Bhavah campaign have also helped the growth of domestic and international tourism and consequently the hotel industry. In recent years the government has taken sev eral steps to boost travel and tourism, which have benefited the hotel industry in the country.

Five Star Hotels in India

The booming tourism industry of India, a top world tourist destination, has also led to the growth of the Indian hospitality industry. The huge number of tourists, both international and domestic, are catered to and taken care of by the Five star hotels in India, who offer warmth. comfort and contemporary facilities to the guests.

The hotels in India maintain very high standards of service quality and this is evident from the hospitality offered by the Five star hotels of the country. Accredited across the world for their sophistication, style, grandeur and superior services, the five star category hotels are the ideal place to lodge for a truly rewarding vacation.

The Five Star hotels in India offer a host of services and facilities to corporate as well as leisure travelers. Luxurious and spacious rooms, sumptuous delicacies, ample recreation options and fabulous meeting and conference facilities are the characteristics of these hotels. Besides these, many of these hotels also come up with lucrative holiday packages for the convenience of the tourist and travelers.

Many of the Five star hotels belong to the reputed hotel groups of India, like the Taj Group, the Oberoi Group, the ITC Group, the Welcome Group and many others. All of them feature among the luxury hotels in India.

Five star hotels are found in many cities of the country like New Delhi, Kolkata, Mumbai, Bangalore, Agra, Hyderabad, Chennai, Jaipur, Chandigarh, Pune, Khajuraho, Jodhpur, Panaji, Srinagar and others.

So, expect good value for your money and enjoy a relaxed and luxurious holiday by lodging in any of the Five star hotels in India. The warm hospitality offered amidst royal comfort will surely leave you mesmerized.

Star Rating System Hotel Requirements for Four, Five Star etc.

We take an objective approach in rating hotels. For any particular hotel, we consider a wide array of factors, including ratings from independent ratings systems, media recognition, and post-trip surveys of our customers. All these points of data (at least three and as many as 12 for each hotel) are plugged into a weighted formula, which calculates our star rating. These calculated ratings are then reviewed to help ensure they reflect any current developments or changes occurring since the compilation of the rating.

In cases where the available data is insufficient to meet our standards, we make an effort to perform additional research, including further review of media and additional visits to the property. We may also consult members of our editorial team for factual information regarding a hotel.

Because we take great pride in the objective nature of our ratings system, we neither take business considerations into account when computing any given rating, nor do we use ratings as a negotiating strategy with suppliers.

Hotel Class

A hotel's star rating is an indicator of the general quality of a particular hotel, and is wholly dependent on the data available to us. The descriptions below indicate what you should be able to expect from a hotel in each of the star classes. These descriptions provide general data, based on the many sources of information that go into our star rating. Circumstances such as ongoing renovations, overbooking, and specific guest needs can affect the quality of your stay. (Be sure to let the hotel know any special requests or requirements you have at check-in.) Star ratings do not necessarily reflect all the amenities or services that might be available at a hotel, and some amenities and features may not be available in every room or at every property with a particular star rating. The features and amenities described here are often not available at holiday rentals, apartments, inns, bed-and-breakfasts, and other speciality hotels.

Economy

A one-star establishment is expected to offer clean, no-frills accommodation with minimal on-site facilities for the budget traveller for whom cost is the primary concern. Guestrooms generally are small, functionally decorated, and may not have a private bathroom, in-room telephone, or amenities. Onsite dining is usually not available. Public access and guest reception may not be available at all hours.

Value

These limited-service establishments are expected to offer clean, basic accommodation. These properties may offer some business services but generally lack meeting rooms, baggage assistance, and full fitness and recreation facilities. On-site dining is usually limited to coffee or Continental breakfast service. Guestrooms generally offer private bathroom, telephone, TV, and limited amenities.

Quality

Three-star establishments place a greater emphasis on style, comfort, and personalised service. They generally feature on-site dining room service, a pool and/or fitness centre, a gift shop, and may provide baggage assistance. Conference rooms for meetings and extended services for business travellers are usually offered. Guestrooms offer more extensive amenities and more careful attention to decor and comfort.

Superior

These upscale establishments usually offer a fine-dining restaurant, lounge, and room service with extended hours. Service features usually include baggage assistance, concierge service, and valet parking. A conference centre with up-to-date technology and full business services are usually offered. Public spaces and guestrooms are thoughtfully designed and constructed with high-quality materials. Guestrooms generally offer stylish furnishings, high-quality bedding and bath products, and a wide array of amenities.

Exceptional

The finest hotels in the world. A five-star hotel is characterised by luxury appointments, superlative service, and the highest standards of comfort. Five-star hotels offer originality in architecture and interior design, high-grade materials in construction and décor, and such special touches as fresh flowers and plants in abundance. These properties also maintain a high staff-to-guest ratio, gourmet dining, and 24-hour room service. Guestrooms offer ample space, the finest furnishings and decor, premium bedding, and luxury bath products. Room amenities generally include highspeed Internet access and CD and/or DVD players. Five-star resorts may offer additional recreation facilities such as tennis courts and golf-course access. On-site spa services, a top-notch fitness centre, and a pool are generally available, as well.

Not Rated

Half-star ratings these hotels have not yet been rated. We have adopted the half-star as a unit of measurement in our five-star scale. The great variety of property types, the wide array of amenities, and the range of property-class characteristics around the world require a classification system of greater precision, which the half-star provides.

Characteristics of Star Hotels

5 star : Extrior should be posh eligant beautiful Good clean environment car park. Minimum 25 rooms attached toilets for rent. Hot cold water in bathroom, window curtains, good lighting furniture - interior designing by well known interior decoratoratedAC rooms with good quality carpets. Building more than 2 storeyed, swimming pool, separate changing rooms (Male/Female) facilities in Five star.

(1) Reception (2) Cash counter (3) Enquiry counter near entrance - person employed highly educated experience and skilled, conference

room, bookstore, beauty parlor, authorised travel agency, bank, cosmetic shop, medicine shop, compulsory each room telephone - visiters lobbt. Entertainment - song dance music separate dinning hall, music systems, channel piped music, modern uptodate elegant furniture, bar,coffee shop, restaurant in the vicinity of the hotel.

Facilities - Food should be national and international type. Excellent quality skilled cook, helps and helpers. Modern coursty to the customers, clean uniform - knowledge of foreign language, good command on English, Hindi, 24 hours open telephone reception service - enquiry, clean good laundry service - good quality linen.

4 Star Hotel - Exterior should be posh and elegant, good surrounding environment, parking facilities, atleast 25 rooms for rent, attached clean toilet, shower bath, 24 hors hot and cold water, carpets, furniture, curtain, upholstry of top class quality. Internal decoration expert, Building more than 2 storeyed, lift facility, clock room, separate M/F. modern facilities - Receiption,enquiry, telephone, book shop, travel agency telephone d each room. restaurant, Authorised Bar and permit room, kitchen should be clean - Modern gadgets, hence productivity of water increases food - both national and international and wine also. Trained skilled workers, clean uniform, modesty, coursty being polite to customer, top quality blankets, pillows, towels good quality furniture also.

3 Star: Good attractive sturdy construction, good clean surrounding, car parking, atleast 20 rooms + toilet attached for rent. Bathrooms tub, compularoy shower - hot and cold water 24 hrs. 5 per cent rooms should have AC furniture, carpets, curtains of the good quality. If more than 2 storeyed lift is compulasory, separate Male/Female cloak room, experienced qualified people employed, bar, bank, travel agency. each room telephone, clean and uptodate if permission granted bar etc Clean kitchen, Indian & Western food clean uniform, English speaking clean laundry facility, clean warm blanket and towels, good music - entertainment facility.

2 star: Clean environment study building minimum 10 rooms + toilet attached rent. 75 per cent rooms must have attached toilet. Toilet & Bath - remaining 4 rooms share one bathroom hot cold water, 25 per cent rooms with AC, special clean well ventilated lighted rooms. Receiption desk, telephone call bwll or phone in each room, good food - dining facility, clean kitchen, skilled workers, English speaking modest coursty - good linen - blanket etc.

One Star Hotel - Atleast 10 rooms with toilet, 25% rooms with attached toilet bath. 4 rooms - one toilet share, hot cold water, well lighted, well ventilated rooms, cosy comfortable furniture, reception gdesk, telephone facility, clean special dining hall, testy clean food, skilled workors - clean uniform, modest polite to customers, good quality hotel keeping.

Hotel - Five star deluxe hotels

Single rooms	*Area standard for bedroom and bathroom*
Single	180 sq.ft.
Double	200 sq.ft.
Bathrooms	45 sq.ft.

4-Star & 3 star hotels

Single A/C. & Single non A/C	120 Sq.ft.
Double A/C & Double non A/C.	140 Sq.ft.
Bathroom	36 Sq.ft.

2 Star & 1 Star hotels

Single A/C & Single non A/C	100 Sq. ft.
Double A/C & Double non A/C	120 Sq. ft.

(All rooms should have proper ventilation and ceiling fans)
Bathrooms30 Sq.ft.
or subject to local byelaws.

Failure to satisfy the above conditions will disqualify hotel from consideration for star category. Source - Govt. of India, Department of Tourism - rules

Classification fee - for star hotels:

1 star	=	Rs.	2,000/-
2 star	=	Rs.	3,000/-
3 star	=	RS.	4,000/-
4 star	=	RS.	6,000/-
5 star	=	RS.	8,000/-

With effect from 27.7.1998.

Pune Municipal Corporation rules for granting hotel licences permits / grade - gradition of hotel etc.

Prerequisites for obtaining a licences (Hotel)

(1) A printed or typed application addressed to the Chief Health Officer P.M.C.

(2) A map/plan 3 copies of the blue print plan - location size dimension along with site plan.

(3) If this land is owned by XYZ his letter of consent is essential ale
(4) If the person own's the land they he should furnish a proof that he owned the land e.g. a receipt of property tax paid by him.
(5) If he owns the place/or is himself a tenant he should possess and therefore furnish a receipt of the rent paid.
(6) If he is a partner he should show legal documents regarding partnership deed etc.
(7) Article and memorandum of association.
(8) Electricity meter and water. Municipal tap connection -record and receipt.
(9) A green signal No Objection Certificate from the Fire Brigade Dept.
(10) No Objection certificate from the Construction Department (Dept. of PWD).

These conditions apply only for hotels and restaurants.

Pre-requisite for stalls/handcard etc. :

1. If the location or area is within a hutment/stums then a No Objection Certificate from the slums Amelioration Rehabilitation Dept. as well as a certificate recognition identification card.
2. Written permission regarding stall/shed/handcard. from the concerned department.
3. If machinery is needed or is to be installed a permit number certified by the concerned department is essential.
4. In case of a wine shop/toddy shop - liquor along with a legal permit on excise permit from the dept. of excise a xeroxed attested copy is essential.

For Grading Hotel 100 points will be allotted

If 100 points 75 points will be allotted to 'C' category.

The remaining 25 points are divided, 20 points for all types of amenities e.g. Health/sanitation/Hygiene 'C' facility.

5 specific types of facilities (a) Natural light (b) AC/ clean air pollution free environment etc.

If the necessary conditions are not fulfilled by the owner or proprietor then a licensee is not issued or it is not reissued, it is immediately cancelled by the P.M.C. Department. If the owner has according to A,B,C category followed the rules then alone he will be allotted points but if the owners has failed to fulfil essential conditions then such a person will be given - negative points (negative marking) because all these conditions are very important healthwise and to bear strict adherance to these laws is legally binding upon the customer. If a given hotel/restaurant is not fit or is in competant in terms of obtaining a license then a legal action against such a violater/owner will have to be taken or his license will have to be cancelled or his hotel will always be branded/labelled as a 'C' category hotel.

'A' CATEGORY

Hotels and eatering places Inns how to maintain Hygiene/ cleanliness a chart of the points allotted to each.

(1) To wash kitchen utensils crockery hot water/soap should always be used and such pots should also be disinfected and a facility for drying the dishes should be there -points 3

(2) The workers, helpers/cooks should have a bath room to wash hands felt etc. (disinfectant - antiseptic) - points 3

(3) For servants hired at the hotel compulsory bath every day, nails cut haircut, clean washed clothes to be worn by them - points 3

(4) A resting room for cooks/servants with lock and key also provide locker to keep their cloths - points 3

(5) Where the cooked food is kept or stored (Kitchen store room pantry take precautionary measures to keep flies/ insects/ cockroaches, antic, away. - point 3

(6) Upto 6 feet from the land/floor disinfectants like DDT etc. has to be sprayed and minimum abd wall should be washed everyday - point 1.

(7) For serving food an indepenant arrangement should be made the tables, trolleys, serving trays should be kept absolutely clean and also a very clean place to store them - point 1.

(8) From the hotel the garbage/dirt should be removed atleast 3 times a day - dust bin - point 1.

(9) For clients/customers a clean soap and a clean towel to wash/wipe their hands mouth/clean wash basin - point 1.

(10) For serving food trays/trollys should be clean/with antiseptic solution to safeguard the health of the people
as well as a storage place to store them - point 1.

GRADE 'B'

Natural light and clean air fresh air a chart prepared for points allotted to them -

(A) Semi cool temperature to be maintained or artificial semi cooled temperature maintained by AC/cooler, free circulation of air - points 2.

(B) The hotels should have oil painted walls only - point 1.

(C) Where there is a stove or coal uses there should be a chimney or exhaust fan used (where such coal *is* not used such hotels/Inns were in category a & b gets one extra point each - points 2.

GRADE 'C'

(1) The location/site hotel should be easily visible and the license should be hung outside on a board visible to the naked eye - point 1.

(2) The place where food, drinks are prepared should be totally independent - point 3.

(3) In proportion to the hotel a bathroom with municipal tap should be fitted alongwith the meter/to minitor reading. The drain dirty water should be connected to the municipal drains properly.- points 2.

(4) Tiles for flooring care should be taken to see that there is no water sepage/water proofing should be done for such floor, should atleast be washed once in a day - poins - 10.

(5) The workers/servants em clothes should be washed clean of he/she is suffering from infections/contagious desese he should not be employed e.g. Scabies, leprosy, skin diseases it. He should be given a midd anticeptic soap, clean towel to wash his clothes. If his hands are not clean he should not be allowed to touch food items-points 10.

(6) Utensils, glasses, cups/dishes, sausers should be washed very clean before they are put to use - points - 10.

(7) The dustbin trash can lid should have a coaltar covered (inside & outside tin container). The garbage should be emptied only in Municipal bins atleast 2-3 times in a day, clean the bin thoroughly every time. points - 2.

(8) The walls should be plastered with lime - chuna atleast twice during the year. April and October first week. If the walls are painted with oil paint, or varnish they should be wiped with mild soap/foam-points 10

(9) Prevent flies/cockroach/duest from settling on food items. Food should be stored in glass bpxes prepare food enly in kitchen and not outside - points - 10.

(10) The drinking water should be absolutely pure and very clean glasses should be used to store them. They should be stored cn 15 inch stand with tight lids/ cover and if it has a spout to pour out water-points 10.

(11) Where the licence board is fixed placed toilets etc. open drains should be kept away from them. The persons should never utilise these places for sleeping - points 5.

(12) Maintain Hygiene and proper sanitation all over the place. points 2.

Restaurants and hotels the fees for each are Rs. 190/- temporary licence. Star hotel Rs. 500/- per year and Rs. 600/- per year. There are about 2500 hotels in Pune, therefore Rs. 190/- is the fee for temporary license, hence P.M.C. gets Rs. 4,75,000/- per year from them. There are 175/- star hotels in 'A' Grade.

PUNE: PAST PRESENT AND FUTURE

Pune has always been recognized as the "cultural and educational capital of Maharashtra" or popularly known as "Oxford of the East". Pune is one home to around 5,00,000 students out of which 2 lakhs from outside of Pune region. About 14,000 of such students are foreigners who come from nineteen countries across the world. However, Pune evolved as an industrial township only after the setting up of the Explosives (Ammunition) Factory at Kirkee during the Second World War. The next milestone was the entry of the Kirloskar Oil Engines 1945 which was the first collaboration between Kirloskar group and Associated British Oil Engines Export Ltd., U.K. It thus paved the way for Pune to develop its strength as an engineering hub. A little later Finolex (Chabria group) and JN Marshall group set up their manufacturing units along the Mumbai-Pune belt. Thus, Pune's development into a business hub is literally like its metamorphosis from a traditional agro-based economy to a knowledge led system and from a 'conventional traditional society to a modern cosmopolitan one'. Today, Pune is often referred to as 'Detroit of the East (Industrial township)'. The subsequent mushrooming of industrial growth along the Pune-Mumbai highway i.e., the development of the Pimpri-Chinchwad area to accommodate refugees from Sindh and Punjab (1947-Partition). The year 1956 wittnessed the setting up of Hadapsar Industrial Estate by Pune Municipal Corporation. Its policy of octroi exemption on the raw material and machinery resulted in the setting up of industries in and around Hadapsar. Later in 1960, MIDC (Maharashtra Industrial Development Corporation) set up a huge industrial estate on 4000 acres of land at Bhosari in the Pimpri-Chinchwad Industrial Complex, which resulted in a phenomenal growth of auto and auto-component companies such as the Swiss company-Alfa, Laval, Sadwik Asia, SKF

Atlas Compo. These companies made Pune the hometown for production. Later, bigger companies such as Buekau, Wolf, KSB Pumps, TELCO, Bajaj Auto and Hindustan Antibiotics established their base in Pune. Thus, the period between 1960-1990 culminated in transformation of Pune into an 'auto-hub' with the production of wide range of vehicles from two-three-four wheelers to trucks, buses, luxury cars. Along with the production of automobiles, a large number of ancilliary units- components assemblies and sub-assemblies needed for automobiles were also set up at Pimpri-Chichwad; examples include cutting, metal coating, fabrications, chasis building. However, the period between '1990s-2000' marked the period of consolidations and rationalization of the industry. The parallel economic reforms, the scrapping of Monopolies Trade Restrictive Act, End of License Raj-redtapism and the forces of liberalization-'opening up of our economy along with the strong currents of globalization started transforming the industrial sector into optimizing on man-power costs, putting in quality systems adopting new strategies to adapt to the changing times. The period between 2000-2005 was the growth phase. A survey conducted by MCCIA (Mahratta Chamber of Commerce, Industries and Agriculture) in 2005 threw light upon the large number (65%) of proposals from medium and large industries to set up manufacturing operations in Pune after 2002. Such manufacturers were interested not only in setting up auto-component units but also polymer, rubber parts, machine tool units. Today we find that there are thousands of such units which cater to bulk orders both from domestic as well as foreign clients thus, in turn generating employment for lakhs of people in India. Another crucial factor responsible for Pune's development has been the phenomenal growth in agro-business, the setting up of grapes wineries, horticulture, floriculture product. Today there are 12 wineries in Pune, along with the rapid growth of agro business has been the phenomenal growth of food processing industry, its giant leap from mere 78 units in Pune upto 500 units-operating in key areas such as spices, dairy fruit and vegetable processing, cereal processing, confectionaries, ready-to-eat food. At present, nearly 70 units export a variety of products to world-wide destinations and accent for Rs.150 crores of exports i.e., 2% of national processed food exports. The demand for convenience food has been trigged by socio-economic, cultural, as well as demographic factors such as migration of IT workers from other states, a change in the eating habits of local people and the tendency to buy out different types of food. Thus, the food-processing industry has a Rs. 2000 crore segment, contributing to nearly 1% of total national food-processing turnover.

There are 30000 people directly employed by the sector. The crucial factor of migration of IT workers has resulted in the demand for different types of cuisines thereby leading to the subsequent proliferation of multi cuisine hotels and restaurants across Pune. Today, Pune is also known as a Cyber-Software city; infact, it is Information Technology and Bio-Technology which have emerged the new drivers of the Pune Economy. The IT and BT (Bio Technology) sector has growth from Rs. 250 crores to Rs. 6500 crores since 2002. IT sector generated employment to the tune of nearly 200000 people with an addition of 4000 people in 2006-07. Today, Pune has 600 IT companies and software exports are $3.49 billion contributing to 10% of national software exports. The rapid developments of IT park at Hinjewadi first of its kind in India has resulted in attracting giant key companies such as Wipro Infotech, Tata Technologies, Mahindra British Telecom Ltd. At present there are 10 SEZs in Pune out of which 8 are in the IT-ITES segment alone Pune as mentioned earlier is also known as the Oxford of the East which now boasts of 6 universities with 600 college and PG (Post Graduation) depts. Today, Pune is home to nearly 500000 students out of which 8000 are foreign students from 62 countries. Out of the 5 lakh students, 2 lakh are from outside the state. Due to Pune's new status as an IT city as well as Detroit of the East. It has attracted lot of manpower from all over the country looking for better job opportunity. At present the four business segments that dominate Pune are auto and auto-components, agro and food processing, IT-BT and education. IT Export over 2008-2009 and Billion in Pune boasts with many more to follow. There are around 1000+IT companies and several IT training institutions in Pune. Pune has the highest Internet Penetration in the country one in every 5 uses Internet. Around 2,20,000 people are working in the IT sector. Supercomputers were developed by C-DAC at Pune Refer (MICCIA IT Directory 2009). Thus, today Pune which was earlier described as a pensioners' paradise has blossomed into a major IT and automotive hub not to speak of its educational institutions, service industries and hospitality. Today, it is branded as Detroit and Oxford of the East and has emerged as the new international business hub. Pune's engineering strength- well educated technically sound population.Pune's proximity to Mumbai port and its booming export-oriented business has it buzzing with activity. It not only boasts of top notch engineering colleges and management institutes that it attracts lots of students at an early age. This has become advantageous for all the companies who are in search of skilled workers.

Howeever there are certain key factors associated for transforming Pune into an industrial hub:

(1) Its proximity to Mumbai JNPT

(2) It is a centre of prosperous urban markets along with Mumbai, Nasik, Aurangabad.

(3) Well- developed engineering supply base.

(4) Availability of man-power at reasonable competitive wages.

(5) Competitive property rates.

(6) Good Communication infrastructure.

(7) Availability of a ready market and a strong and consistent customer base.

(8) Entry of MNCs and foreign collaboration ensuring a steady demand for a plethora of products.

Today, Pune boasts of being an Cyber Software (Info Tech hub) IT city. At present Pune is also home to well known giants of the Indian software industry like Wipro, Infosys, Satyam, Tata technologies, TCS, Kanbay, Veritos, Cognizant PCS and Mahendra British Telecom. A further feather in the cap is the 'Indian Institute of Software Engineering' coming up in association with Carnegie Mellon University USA.

In 2009 there were 92 software IT companies located in and around Pune. (Major software companies in Pune, http://www.nauki2000.com/careers/s pune.php3 dated21-8-2009.)

A Brief Update About the New Hotels in Pune

Today, Pune has emerged as a 'Detroit of the East' as were as a 'IT BT Cyber City- vibrant city', always on the move. Thus, Pune remains one of the most frequented cities visited by business tourists as well as leisure travellers. As mentioned earlier the entry of Pune city on the international business map, the entry of MNC's, foreign collaborations establishment of many excellent hotels in Pune ranging from cheap to Budget to Three-Four-Five star-business (corporate) hotels.

The need for a 'Budget Hotel' arises especially when a person has a limited expense account, at the same time wants value for every rupee spent. There are quite a few budget hotels here such as Amir Hotel (located near Pune Railway station) 'Hotel Shalimar, Hotel Rainbow Retreat, Hotel Sapna Executive, Hotel Royalty, Celebrations Inn, The Elite Suites, Shanti Hotel, Hotel Alankar. At present, there are 43+Budget hotels Refer (http://www.indianhotels.com/hotels in india/hotels in Pune/budget-hotels 21-12-2010). The need of a 'budget hotel' arose as nowadays we find an influx of 'budget travellers' who want to explore the city. Budget hotels provide accommodation for backpackers, tourists travelling on a shoe-string budget. The accommodation provided is extremely comfortable and cozy and along with many contemporary facilities at an affordable reasonable price. The tariffs at these nominally priced budget hotels include all meals. Most of these budget hotels are located in close proximity to major business areas and tourist attractions of Pune. The best known Budget hotels provide well equipped Conference Halls or Board Rooms and associates equipment necessary to hold business meeting and corporate events. Other facilities available at these hotels include travel desk, in-house laundry, medical assistance, car parking, money changing (foreign exchange) counters, credit card, secretarial services etc. For all those who are looking for comfortable yet reasonably priced stay in Pune 'the Budget hotels are the best option'.

The List of Budget Hotels in Pune

1. Baron Lakeside Resort
2. Farmers Inn
3. Hotel Alankar
4. Hotel Royalty
5. Celebrations Inn
6. Shantai Hotel
7. Hotel Amir
8. Hotel Ashwini
9. Hotel Ashiyana
10. Hotel Ashoka
11. Hotel Choice
12. Hotel Emerald Park
13. Hotel Ketan
14. Hotel Deccan Park
15. Hotel Deluxe
16. Hotel Dreamland
17. Hotel Gauri
18. Hotel Homeland

19. Hotel Kalasagar
20. Hotel Kapila
21. Hotel Lokesh
22. Hotel Madhav
23. Hotel Mayur
24. Hotel Meru
25. Hotel Nandnvan
26. Hotel Natraj
27. Hotel Pleasant
28. Hotel Rajdhani
29. Hotel Ranjeet
30. Hotel Shalimar
31. Hotel South Court
32. Hotel Span Executive
33. Hotel Sriman
34. Hotel Swaroop
35. Hotel Tourist International
36. Maurya Residency
37. The Pichola
38. The Residencies
39. The Samarat Executive
40. Hotel Sapna
41. Hotel Parichay
42. Seasons Service Apartment
43. Hotel Excellency

Three Star Hotels in Pune

The Three star hotels are moderately priced and provide warm hospitality, quality service and are equipped with modern facilities. A luxurious stay at a pocket friendly price and the feeling of being card for 'A home away from home' are some the benefits. The rooms and suites at the three star hotels are tastefully furnished. The dinning facilities include a choice of menu such as Chinese, continental, Indian delicacies. The state of art conference rooms, banquet hotels, open lawns as venues for corporate meetings and latest audio-visual equipments secretarial services. Thus, the three star hotels are statements to offering hospitable and efficient services at affordable price.

At present there are 17 B Star Hotels in Pune.

1. Amer Al Asian
2. Ashish Plaza

3. Central Park Studio
4. Hotel Studio Eshque
5. Centurion Spring Hills
6. Hotel Madhav International
7. Hotel Shree Panchratna
8. Hotel Ashirwad
9. Hotel Raviraj
10. Hotel Regency
11. Hotel Woodland
12. Kendal Palace
13. Panchashil Hotel
14. Season Hotel
15. Shree Panchratna
16. Taj Ginger Hotel
17. The Senator

Four Star Hotels in Pune

To cater to the needs of IT entrepreneurs, businessman, the Four Star hotels offer luxurious accommodation with modern facilities. The rooms are A/C fully furnished, ISD facility, 24 hours room service, tea-coffee makers. The Restaurants cater to various types of national as well as international cuisines accompanied by a well stocked bar. The elegant banquet halls, meeting rooms, conference halls, latest audio visual equipments-video, tele-conferencing and other state of the art technologies etc. At present there are 13 Four Star hotels.

1. Goodon House
2. Hotel Aurora Towers
3. Hotel Central Park
4. Hotel Kohinoor Executive
5. Hotel Deccan Rendezvous
6. Hotel Sagar Plaza
7. Quality In Centurion
8. The Oakwood (Business Hotel) Suresh Talera Group.
9. The President Hotel
10. Royal Orchid
11. Lemon Tree

12. Hotel Sadanand Residency
13. Quality Inn, Centurion Park.

Five Star Hotels in Pune

These hotels offer accommodation to business magnates, entrepreneurs who frequent the city on work and can afford to and are willing to spend that extra buck for cutthroat luxury. It offers sweeping luxury coupled with state of art facilities, technology video conferencing, A.C Room, tea/coffee makers, DVD, refrigerators, JSD, 24 hours room service. A gastronomical delegent and sojurn into various types of national and international cuisines for the real connoisseurs of food and wine. A completely well stocked up bar (stocking ehociest spints liquour, wine etc.).

At present there are Six 5 Star hotels with many more to follow such as Leela Kampinski.

1. Best Westen 'The Pride Hotel'
2. Hotel Sun N Sand (formerly known as Holiday Inn)
3. Le Meridian
4. Taj Blue Diamond
5. Marriot-Convention Centre
6. The Corinthan Boutique Hotel and Spa.

The Ministry of Tourism, Govt of India has released statistics regarding number of hotels and number of rooms in different cities of Maharashtra in the year 31-12-2005.

In the city of Pune there were 3 Five Star Deluxe Hotels with a capacity of 428, whereas Five Star hotels were 2 and hotelrooms were 330. There were 2 four star hotels with 125 rooms. There were 5 Three Star hotels with 268 rooms and 6 Two Star hotels with 72 rooms. At the same time 2 hotels with 73 rooms to be built were put on the awaited list. The total no. of hotels were 22 with 1478 rooms available. However, quite a few more hotels are coming up in and around Pune such as 5 star Business Hotel at Hinjewadi (IT setor is located here) Another one is coming up in Balewadi (sports complex-Junior Commonwealth Games Oct 2008 were held there.

Another Four Star hotel is coming up at Kalyani Nagar near Pune Airport. Quite a few new Five Star Hotels are being developed. The Inter-continental Hotels are promoting a 5 Star hotel with a capacity of 250 rooms (Hyatt Regency) (Airport) Vimanagar near another major 5 Star hotel is being built at Hinjavadi IT city by Kollte Patil Developers Ltd.

The famous Lemon Tree Hotel group is building another three hotels.The IHHR Hospitality is also building a 5 Star hotel in Pune district. Krizm Hotel group is also building a Star hotel near Pune Raliway station. It will be a 7 storeyed and with 220 room Sariver Hotels and Resorts is also planning to build a hotel with 120 rooms called as 'Hotel Pune' at Nagar Road. Another prominent group that is Goel Ganga group is constructing Hotel at Vimanagar near the airport called as 'Hotel Orchid'. Panoramic Universal Ltd. is building a 5 Star Hotel near Baner village – 360 rooms (proximity to Balewadi Sports complex as well as Aundh where major IT sector companies offices are located. These latest additions to the hotel list were obtained through MCCIA on their website project today.com/ Project Print.aspx. dated 17/12/2010. Projects today are India's largest data base on new projects.

Concept of Serviced Apartment

Serviced Apartments have become the need of the hour as it is relatively cheaper compared to hotels and is just like 'a home away from home'. A serviced apartment is a type of furnished apartment available for short term or long-term stay, which provides amenities for daily use. 'The term serviced apartment is used when referring to an alternative for hotel accommodation for short and long stay leisure and business travelers. The very concept of service apartment originated in USA, even today 86 per cent of the world's stock of serviced apartments is still located there.

Serviced apartments are gradually emerging as the trendiest place to stay for both corporate and leisure travelers today. It is a rental facility, like a hotel where you can stay for a few days or a few weeks/months depending on the nature and purpose of your visit. Today, many guests prefer to stay at service apartments when they relocate to stay at service apartments when they relocate to a new city and have to look for a permanent place to stay. The reason as to why serviced apartments are the preferred choice for those who seek transit accommodation either for a short term or extended stay is because living at a serviced apartment feels much like living at home.

Serviced apartments operate much like hotels – you reserve rooms by calling or writing to the property, no extra charge are paid for services such as house-keeping, maintenance, and utility. They are usually 30 per cent to 35 per cent less expensive than to hotels. The pricing at service apartment is predicated on longer duration stays, thus resulting in significantly higher occupancy ratios. They are much more spacious as compared to hotel-rooms, also if a person wishes to cook he/she can cook in the kitchen. Another redeeming feature is about 24 x 7 security, along with TV and direct-dial telephones, internet connectivity. The kitchen utensils, refrigerator, gas, micro-wave oven, food Processors are provided by S.A. along with free laundry service.

Service Apartments (SA) are a relatively new concept. Very often SA can have only one single-room or studio apartment with a kitchen etc.

Single Room Occupancy (SRO) is often a multiple tenant building that houses one or two persons in individual rooms, because toilets or kitchens are shared between those SRO's are primarily rented as a permanent residence.

A Studio Apartment is also known as a studio flat or efficiency apartment or bachelor/bachelor etc. style apartment it is self-contained small apartment which combines living room, bedroom and kitchenette into a single with barring a bathroom. Housewives, bachelor/efficiency apartments are much smaller than studio apartment. They have a much lower rate as compared to regular service apartment.

An Apartment Hotel is a serviced apartment complex that uses a hotel-style booking system. It is often similar like renting an apartment, however with no fixed contracts and occupants can checkout whenever they wish.

An Apartment hotel is thus a flexible type of accommodative instead of the rigid format of a hotel room or an apartment. The length of the stay in these apartment hotels vary anywhere from a few days to months to years.

These apartment hotels provide a 'holiday home' but are serviced. Essentially an apartment hotel combines the flexibility of apartment-living with the service of a hotel.

The concept of an Extended Stay Hotel originated in the USA. It intends to provide more home lime amenities. Such hotels are popular with business travelers on extended assignments, families in the midst of a relocation and anyone else in need of temporary housing. They are also used by travelers who appreciate the larger space a typical suite provides.

In a vibrant city like Pune, which is the hub for multinationals and IT, ITES sector, Serviced Apartment is a fast emerging choice of long stay executives, NRIs, and frequent travelers. Serviced Apartments, offer the convenience of hotel with the privacy and warmth of a home. Business travelers and holiday makers prefer living in a serviced apartment as it is cheaper, has more space and privacy as compared to a hotel.

There is a big Service Apartment complex at Kharadi as well as Magarpatta City where the IT offices are located. The SA project 'Living Waters' offers budget accommodation at cheaper rates as compared to the hotels. SA stands for the luxury facilities of hotels at affordable rates without compromising on service, quality. Today, SA is, in fact, fast emerging as an smart and convenient alternative to hotel suites.

It serves as a stop gap arrangement for business family holidays for a few days/weeks. Serviced Apartments (SA) is indeed a home away from home. The Serviced Apartments (SAs) are well equipped with AC kitchen, round the clock attendants, daily housekeeping, Free WI-fi - Internet service, free laundry service, cook, 24 x 7 security. Hence the feeling of staying at comfortable and most importantly affordable is well. Such Serviced Apartments (SAs) by 'Living Water' are also located at Viman Nagar, Kore gaon Park. Today for the discerning travelers, businessman, entrepreneur MNC executive, corporate tourist a cost effective alternative to hotel stay are SAs. 'Cosmos' service Apartments have literally changed/transformed the face of hospitality industry by providing luxurious 1 – 3 bed rooms with spacious living room, fully equipped kitchen, pet friendly unlike hotels, with complete A/C climate control, TV, Internet – Yet easily affordable at Kore Gaon Park.

Today, we find survival such locations where SAs are located for e.g. 'Bella Vista' is one of them – It provides us with the best quality service with all the necessary amenities and to make our stay pleasure and the maid servant option is also provided.

According to 'Bella Vista' Serviced Apartments (SA) Manager, they have been providing quality service to corporate clients for the past 5 years or so. In recent years, there is an increased preference for furnished service/serviced apartment's concept in transit accommodation amongst corporate clients especially for those who travel very often, and those who need to stay for long periods in transit for projects. 'Bella Vista' also offers Corporate Apartments - Luxury Serviced Apartment (fully furnished) with a home-like ambience. Hence for our corporate executive who has to come to Pune for work for a couple of weeks, it is the best option for e.g., if a person is required to stay for a few weeks the best option is a SA or Serviced Corporate Apartment.

Concept of Serviced Apartments (SA) is fast catching up in Pune as stated by Ms. Veronique Siracett, General Manager of Pune Oakwood Chain "There is no proper accommodation for expatriats or for people staying for a long period, say three to six months." SAs are the perfect mix of space and service which is much better than having a private maid in an individual rented apartment. The deposit is limited as compared to the rent of an individual apartment. All facilities and services (housekeeping, restaurant, business centre, fitness centre, and swimming pool) are provided as in a hotel but in a smaller scale, which makes the place more intimate, personalized and friendly.

According to industry sources, 'The cost of an apartment hotel is approximately 20 percent less than the cost of staying in an ordinary double room in a hotel of equivalent standard. On an average, a guest staying at a Five Star hotel pays Rs. 400/- for his laundary and spends anywhere about Rs. 2,000/- on his daily break-fast, lunch, dinner combination, thus apartment hotels are very economical from a long-term perspective.

The Benefits of Serviced Apartments (SAs) are

1. Corporate and Business Individuals save at least 30 per cent leasing quality SA in Pune.
2. As compared to hotels SA charge per room and not per person.
3. The price of SA is inclusive of VAT and Service Charges unlike hotels that have hidden cost too.
4. SA makes often feel at home.
5. All benefits of hotels such as maid service, cots, baby sitters etc. are also provided in SA.

Serviced Apartment (SA) makes one feel that one is in the private space of a home and get indulging in hotel service. Serviced Apartment (SA) is the preferred choice of people from a new culture and selling and expats they never have to compromise on their life-style.

The cost of a Serviced Apartment (SA) can vary from Rs. 7,000/- to 11,00,000/- per month for a well equipped 3 bed room amenities including swimming pool, garden, gymkhana. The tariff charge for Serviced Apartment depends upon the length of the stay. It is economical for prolonged stay.

Today many hoteliers, prominent builders see huge potential in the market due to increasing demand for a short-term housing for MNCs, business travelers. Many real estate developers are building Serviced Apartments and then leasing them out. SA have better occupancy rate as compared to hotels. The occupancy rates in SA categorizing were 74 per cent in 2005.

Serviced Apartments are also seen as a lucrative investment option for the high level of efficiency and high profit margin. The growth in key sectors like IT, BPO, Manufacturing and Tourism has propelled like bullish temper of the trend of SA in Pune.

Many corporate who travel from other countries or nowadays, NRIs, Indian Immigrants use Serviced Apartments as a stop gap arrangement while searching for a permanent house. At present there are quite a few SAs located at Kalepruray Oakwood International Chain, 'Seasons' Naik Navare Group Manisha, Living Water, Cosmos, Bela Vista, Beverelly Hills and thus are many more to come.

In short SA is the in thing today! Serviced Apartment has more space and more privacy, more freedom, cost effective, because not only a saving can be made on the cost of the apartment, also, because SA come with fully equipped kitchen facilities, there is no need to eat out all the time. They are convenient, especially when travelling with a family because the whole family can stay in one apartment. Serviced Apartment offers a home away from home, with all the modern convenience you would expect.

Hotels and Restaurants in Pune

(1) Concept of a Hotel

Hotel, which is the communication code for the letter 'H' is aloso a simple of hospitality of a home away from home a hppy stay in a healthy place. Hotel or Inn is defined by British Laws as a place where a bonafide traveler can receve food and shelter, provided he is a position to pay for it and is in a fit condition to be received. Hence hotels has to provide food an loding to the travelers on payment and has in trun the right to refuse is travller is drink, disorderly or is not in a position to pa or the services.

Whereas restaurent derived from the French word Restrau-means to go to a place and eat food and come home – this menas that a restaurant does not have lodging facilities – to stay there unlike a hotel.

Dictionary-webster Eglish dictionary defines hotel as "a building or institution providing lodging, meals and service to people". From the point of view of users a hotel is a institution of commercial hospitality. It offers its facilities and services for sale individually or in various combinations. As a product for sale, a hotel consists of the following elements, Together they determine its saleability and price.

(a) Location – Which implies accessibility and convenience to the clients.

(b) Facilities – Refer to quality of bedrooms, function rooms, restautrants, bars, transport, and axi facilities.

(c) Services – Comprises speed, efficiency degree of personal attention.

(d) Image – Is the way in which a hotel pertrays itself and emerged from the above factors. It however, depends on atmosphere, appearance, its goodwill, the name of the hotel and its association with the type of people who patronize it.

(e) Price-Is determined by all the elements mentioned above. It is the value given by the hotel throu its service reputation and the general satisfaction of its patrons. Therefore hotel can include a restaurant but not the vice verse.

Brief History of hotel – its origins in the world – with specific reference to its development in India – particularly in Pune.....

The Hotel industry is perhaps one of the oldest commercial endevours in the world. The first inns go back to the 6th century. Bc and were product of the urge of travel began by the invention of the wheel. The earliest inns were ventures by husband and wife teams who provided large halls for travelers to make their own beds and sleep on the floor. They also provided modest whole some food and thirst quencerss like wine. Entertainment and recrestion was provided by the hosts wife or lady member. The entities cooking services and recraction was provided by husband and wife team and family. These conditions prevailed for hundred years. The industrial revolution in English brought ideas and progress in the business of inn keeping. The Development of railways and steamings is made traveling more prominent. The industrial revolution also changed travel from social or government travel to business travel. There was a need for quite and clean service. The lead in hotel keeping was taken by the emerging nations of Europe expecially Switzerland. It was in Europe that the birth of an organized industry took place. The small hotels came into existence and they provided a variety of services. In early Englang public houses were normally called inns or taverns. Normally the name inn was reserved for finner establishment. Catering to noble persons and minsters of Christian Church. The houses visited by commoners was known as a taverns. In Fracne a similar dstinction was made with finer establishment known as "hoteliers and the small houses called as cabrets. The word hotel was used in England in about 1760 and after a passage of over 80 years. In Americas loding houses were called inns or coffee houses.

The real growth of modern hotel industry took place in USA beginning with opening facility Hotel in New York in 1794. Therer was the first building erectd for hotel purposes. This led toe a great compititon between different citites and resulted in big hotel building. Some of the finest hotels of USA were build in the area WALDORF AUTORIA, but the real boom in hotel building came in the early 20th century. The depression of 1930s had a disastrous effect on the hotel industry. It was felt that hotels will never recover but the out break of IInd World War gave a tremendous lift. This prosperity continued through war years into the 1950s when 2 new concepts emerged viz.

(1) Hotels and (2) International chain operations. Today hotels cater to all ness, wishes of guests and the future holds promises for a further progress of modern hotels. When man started traveling by horse or walked he wanted to stay where he and horse got good hence the nedds to saty a palace to stay and eat hence in ancient India the concept of a Dharamshala-Sarhi – in India a guest – Atithi was treated as a God "Atithi devo Bhava". In ancient Indiaplace of pilgrimage – Dharmashalas were build as the need for accommodation plus eating kept on increasing. Hence now this was considered to and occupation. Earning money by serving people food and shelter. After the industrial revolution neeed for producer to appoint distributors there need to stay away from home hence hotels erer started. Later industrialists, enthusiastic tourists, politicians, needed a place to stay. After industrial revolution of new occupation were started one of hen being hoteling. In Refreshment houses- Upahar Graha – food drinks were served. The need for novelty of items was felt by merchants. In London city alone there were 3,000 coffee houses. Ancient Indian tradition of Atithi as ealier explained have been narrated in the accounts of books written by Marcopolo (1271) (626, 645) Hunyatsen. Beginning of the 19th Century there were many eateries- (Khanavalis) for e.g. Portuguese-George, Parseas-George Victory Hotel, Luxurious Hope Hall. They built Dharmashalas (constructed roads laned trees, dug water bells, lakes. In North India Mohamed Tuglak built and Phirosshaha Tuglak, Shershahs Suri and Moghul rulers like Akber Jehangir, Shahajahan Built (Jahaara Begam – Azad Park)

As soon as Transport and Communication increased in big cities no. of khanavalis (eateries) and Dharamshala increased.

2 types – (1) Rich (2) Middle class – Dharamshala

After decline of Mugul rule British rule started these eateries got converted into western type of hotels. Big cities like – Bombay, Calcutta, Delhi, such hotels were started. Even though Dharmashalas remained popular many foreigners came to India often stayed in Western British style Hotels as well as for Indian, Indian type hotels the British built hotels manly for themselves and foreign tourists 60-70 years back Bombays Tajmahal like hotels were started by British and Swiss ownership with all facilities/amenities. E.g. Billiards table, Lunch, Dinner breakfast, tea, coffee were given. Travellers tourists travel by sea route – Boating facilities provided. In 1840 – in Bombay – of Parsis gentlement Mr. Panalji Pestronji built a British type hotel – he was the first man to build such a hotel very well managed – beer Bar well equipped later started hotel near Fort area (Bombay) 1871 John walsk started Elsplanade hotel he himself designed building for hotel for management, he had hired British people – Hotel had 130 rooms. In 1886 with capital of Rs 0 lacs capital started 'Great Eastern Hotel'. In India before Iind world war very few hotels, 1940 no. of hotels/restaurants in big cities increased because foreign tourists came here but even them their number was limited. After independence no. of hotels and tourists increased. In 1962-63. in India total no. of hotels with licenses and government approval-186 total no. of rules 7,085. 1962-63 star hotels classification started, 1982 onwards government approved hotels – 405 rooms 29, 332 along with that non authorized hotels no. also increased.

Taj hotels started by JRD Tata on 1st April 1902 in Bombay – Capital invested Rs. 30 lakhs. JRD visited many European countries and tried to build such type of hotels. Taj 1904 hotel built 5,000,00 pound cast 'Taj' is rated as 10th Best hotel in the world. Fully equipped 5 star hotel. Later on old palaces converted to Taj Hotels e.g. Late Palce – Udaipur. Lot of foreign tourists come here. Hence these hotels have contributed a lot of foreign exchange to India.

Hotels in Pune – In earlier in Pune only Maharashtrian men owned hotels – family enterprises. But as soon as industries increase, educational changes, change in occupation – people had to travel as well as stay hence Khanavals (eateries) were converted into hotels. After industrialization in Pune many people fromm other regions started coming here. Iranis – Cafes, Udipi hotels. Today Pune many Udipi-settled here 35-40 yrs.

Eg. Mr. Gundhuraj Shetty – owner of Modern café is settled in Pune for 40 years. After Udipis Chinese, Punjabi, Gujarati, continental, fast food is gaining lot of importance.

	1972	1978	1985	1990
No. of Hotels in Pune	24	35	48	147

Pune City star hotels have increase a lot

1987	*Blue Diamond*	*Hotel Amis*	*Gulmohar*	*Sanman*
Rooms	92	52	32	22
1990	92	52	32	

1987 4 star hotels was not.there. Whereas in 1990 star and 4 star where there. In 1987 Pune 6 star hotels and no. of rooms, 127 whereas in 1990 sixteen hotels, rooms 593. Star hotels have increased to great extent in 1990.

Characteristics of Hotel Industry

M-Edward Deming has discussed distinguishing economic characteristics of hotels and catering industry. According to him the true measure of quality service is the ability to meet the customers needs. Unlike a product, hotel industry services are intangible, perishable, complex, immediate and shapeless. Given below are 10 characteristic of the Hotel industry.

1. Service Intangible – all services of hotels are intangible and they must come up to the satisfaction and expectation of customers. There are many intangibles like lighting, decoration, atmosphere, location and activities of the staff.
2. Service immobile – The services of hotel industry cannot be transported over long distances. They must be made available to the people wherever they are. As pointed out by economist Jagdish Bhagwati, there is immediate consumption of services / mobility of agents.
3. Wide dispersal of services – Due to immobile services, there is wide dispersal of hotel / catering establishments. Small and large hotels / restaurant are spread all over India.
4. Services are perishable – Food, flower products, and services of hotel and catering industry are perishable. This is because they cannot be stored like a manufactured product. A room not sold is a loss. The unutilized capacity because of seasonal fluctuation in demand poses a great difficulty in the way of hotel industry.
5. Labour intensive – Being a service industry, hotel or catering industry is labour intensive. Personalized service is the key note to ultimate success. Quality of staff determines quality of products/ services. A large number of staff equipped with operating as well as social skills is required in the industry.
6. Huge investments – The investment in land, building, furniture, equipments is necessarily high. Even the expenditure for wages and salaries, power, lighting etc., to a high degree is fixed cost for hotel and catering industry.
7. Narrow safety margin – In hotel / catering industry break even volume is very high and the gap between break over and total

capacity level known as safety margin is very narrow. Even a small drop in volume results in huge losses.

8. Round the clock operations – Hotel / catering industry is a round the clock operation, particularly in the lodging section. Working hours are more than those of the commercial establishments.
9. Comparatively stable and perennial demand – Hotel / catering industry is in a more advantageous position as it has a perpetual demand. These services do not become outdated and their demand is not much affected by cyclical fluctuations.
10. Low working capital – Most of the hotel and catering business is in cash and whatever credit business is there, it is for a short period. Again the inventories are stocked in small quantities and for a short period as most of them are perishable. Similarly, there is no question of some processing and finished product inventory.

In several ways, a hotel is a many splendoured thing. It provides large revenues to the Government, offers vast employment opportunities and makes a customer feel sovereign, accounts for the bulk purchases of a variety of items, hosts specialized fairs and exhibitions, earns sizeable foreign exchange for the country, and also sponsors social and cultural programmes.

Hotel Industry as Employment Multiplier

Under section 'Employment Multiplier' in the chapter 'Theoretical Perspectives', I have discussed the role of industries, especially the sophisticated ones, as Employment Multiplier. It also has a reference to how the hotel industry generates myriad of jobs. The following paragraphs discuss the cascading of this multiplier effect which is mainly through different types of sub contracting.

Hotel industry has brought many new and varied groups into the employment market, thereby enhancing income and purchasing power of the groups concerned i.e. ultimately of those employed in such venture. This certainly provides for occupational mobility for enhancing purchasing power, in short a redistribution of income. Some hotels are run by women entrepreneurs adding a new dimension to the earlier system and thereby providing fresh opportunities to women. Running of hotels, restaurants and other eating places also provide considerable employment primarily to the local people, though in some cases hotel industry also imports certain kind of specialized workforce from other parts of the country.

Furthermore, hotels are a useful source of revenue for the Government. Bulk of foreign exchange is from overseas tourists. In 1985-

86 in Maharashtra alone, the industry gave about Rs. 45 crores by way of sales tax, and Rs. 6 Crores as luxury tax. Additionally there is also revenue for the Government through property tax, municipal licenses, electricity bills, duty, customs and excise duty. Hotels generate speedy cash flow of money and rolling support for credit card business. Hotel Industry thus offers lucrative careers to young boys and girls, and helps the Government also. Development of hotel industry also helps hosting collaborators both from within India and outside. That is why there are various types of Star Hotels and restaurants such as Turf Club, Boat Club, Residency Club, Poona Club, etc. Similarly the influx of industries from outside Maharashtra or outside India makes demands on the supply of multi-cuisine and services. Hotel Industry as such requires the services of various agencies right from market for food grain, poultry, milk, meat etc., to the specialized (expert) services of engineers, architects, accountants, PROs, Pest Control, Interior Decorators, Landscape gardening, Luxury buses and limousines, etc. Thus, the quality and smooth operations of hotel industry depends on continuous inputs and support from many agencies listed above. The hotel industry in its turn gives rise to a multiplier effect, enhancing growth. Apart from economic growth, the broadening and expansion of various segments of population from different regions of the country also lend a distinct composition and universalistic flavour to the city. Today many girls (graduates in Hotel Management / Catering etc.) are seen in Five Star Hotels starting from reception to occupying even executive positions in the hotels. Earlier working in hotels was considered to be a taboo – girls were looked down upon – thought to be cheap. Today, however, the scenario has changed. We find many smart young girls working side by side with boys. Previously only Christians, Anglo-Indians, Parsee girls worked but now girls of all castes and religions work, e.g. in Hotel Taj in Mumbai as well as Hotel Blue Diamond a lot of Maharashtrian Brahmins are working in areas like interior decoration, management, etc. The advertisement shown on T.V. about Taj Hotel depicts the hostess as a young dynamic girl managing enumerable tasks with a lot of poise, grace, confidence and courtesy which is a functional imperative (Parsonian term) for the survival of the hospitality industry in India. A trained class of hotel employees ranging from CEO's, Front Desk Management to Receptionist is required in hotels. A fleet of servants are hired by hoteliers right from scavengers, gardeners, washer men, janitors, to bell boy, cooks, helpers etc. All types of skilled and semi skilled workers are hired here. Hence there is always a rising demand for them and subsequent training. Service industry and its sophistication and its ever

increasing demand for training in catering and hotel management augurs well for the economy. CAs, ICWAs, CS, are needed along with maintenance engineers, architects, interior decorators, civil, structural engineers as well as Medical doctors in times of emergencies. They also need the services of AC maintenance, lift maintenance, supply of cars, tourist taxis, books, magazines, newspapers, video-audio cassettes, office stationery ,etc. This too is sub contracting. Thus, Employment Multiplier is not subject to employment within but also from outside.

BIBLIOGRAPHY

1. MCCIA (Mahratta Chamber of Commerce and Industries, 2009) IT Directory Pune, 2009, Published in Association with CREDAI, (Promoters and Builders Association of Poona and MCCIA, Trade Tower, Senapati Bapat Road, Pune – 411 016.
2. MCCIA (Mahratta Chamber of Commerce and Industries, 2008.), Industrial Directory of Pune, 2008, Published by MCCIA, 'A' Wing, Trade Towers, Senapati Bapat Road, Pune – 411 016.
3. MCCIA (Mahratta Chamber of Commerce and Industries, Feb 2008), Pune Profile: An Analysis ofManufacturing – An Intelligence Report on the Growth of Pune Industries, Published by MCCIA, 'A' Wing, Trade Towers, Senapati Bapat Road, Pune – 411 016.
4. 'Projects Today' 17-12-2010 <projetstoday.com>/…/project print.aspx (compiled from MCCIA Website – process.
5. 'Place-wise Number of Approved Hotels and rooms in Maharashtra as on 31.12.2005) compiled from the Statistics released by Ministry of Tourism, Government of India (compiled from MCCIA – Process)
6. http://www.indianholidays.com/hotels in india/hotels in pune/five-star hotels/
7. http://www.indianholidays.com/hotels in india/hotels in pune/five-star hotels/budget hotels
8. http://www.indianholidays.com/hotels in india/hotels in pune/five-star hotels/three star hotels
9. http://www.indianholidays.com/hotels in india/hotels in pune/five-star hotels/four star hotels
10. Hotels in Pune - http://www.indianholidays.com/hotels in india/ hotels in pune-in-pune.html dated 21.12.2010
11. http://en.org/wiki/serviced_apartment
12. http://en.org/wiki/studio apartment
13. http://en.org/wiki/apartment hotels
14. http://en.org/wiki/extended stay hotel
15. http://www.punehotels.org

6

Social Dimensions of Industries

Culture of Eating Out

Various sections in this book have reiterated that it is not always the demand that generates supply, but very often the supply that leads to demand. This can be best illustrated by not only the phenomenal growth of hotel industry in late 1960s – 70s and continuing further; but also by the proliferation of eateries and restaurants in Pune during the same period.

It is noteworthy that the eateries in Pune are not confined to local cuisine. They cater to regional, state-wise and countrywide preferences in cuisine. Various restaurants specializing in international food such as Chinese, Thai, Mexican, and Continental have come up. Another vital aspect has been the impact of globalization – the concept of franchising, for example Barista coffee, McDonalds, Pizza Huts and Dominos Pizza. All this reflects the ever increasing gastronomical delights. The taste buds are often stimulated by an array of visual, appetite cum curiosity stimulating display of foods as well as attractive exotic café names - a vital component of saleability of food products.

Hence in strictly economic terms, it is not always the demand that generates supply, but also the supply which generates demand.

If Five Star hotels cater to the satisfaction of discerning clientele who have more resources at their disposal, the street food vendors cater to lower income groups. Others cater to floating student population as well as middle class employees or casual visitors to the city. It is also because of such varied supply to suit all pockets that the culture of eating out thrives. The new consumer class, particularly of software specialists and experts, provides a significant clientele for the food industry in general. The emergence of this class or group also signifies considerable interaction and interchange between different regions and nations. This in turn also helps the culture of eating out. A variety of cuisine is offered to those who desire to entertain business partners to good food in a good ambience. The requirement of newer and newer expertise in the field of catering also increases.

In addition to all these, nowadays many star-status hotels organize food festivals specific to different regions such as Gujarat, Karanataka and even continental countries such as Italy. Some examples of these events are *paratha* festival, *kabab* festival, or Khyber (north-west frontier) food festival. The availability of such food certainly provides for a better exchange of various tastes and fancies, thereby sustaining the culture of eating out. The investment in such concerns runs into crores. Similarly the membership fees of clubs also reflect a very wide range to suit different sizes of the pockets of the clientele. In hotels, the bulk of occupancy comes from corporate world. As mentioned earlier, Mr. S.L. Kirloskar had foreseen such necessity when he started the first star hotel Blue Diamond in Pune. Now there are many; for example, Suresh Talera's Oakwood Business Hotel located on Deccan Gymkhana. In this way the demand of the new socio-economic group becomes an important consideration in the supply of eateries and services. People are not compelled to eat and enjoy only what is offered to them. The demand side has acquired equal importance as the supply side. The multiplier effect unleashed by these services thus allows for a special growth of hotel industry. However, as already mentioned, one must not forget that this would not be possible without the support of the changing cultural milieu sustained by changing structural arrangements like family, caste, region, nation, etc. Side by side with the economic prosperity goes socio-cultural change or transition and as such both the processes have to work in unison. Economy, society and culture are the three points of a triangle.

Variety itself denotes the basis of stratification which in its highly advanced stage means elite and exclusive posh eating places such as 5-7 star hotels and clubs which constitute a device of exclusion. The emergence of a variety of eating places signifies a similar trend; for example Barista Coffee, Pizza Hut, McDonald's – just to name a few. They are

'Avante garde' of modern India. In addition to several other factors mentioned above the double income families have helped consolidate this habit of eating out. DINK stands for Double Income No Kids. This means enough money for trying out new dishes which have been made possible by the various types of restaurants, Punjabi, Chinese, and Continental. Thus, rising levels of education, income, better jobs and careers have also contributed to different eating places in Pune both in the city, as well as the cantonment area. Hence, there has been a very remarkable transition if not transformation from need based eating out to eating out for variety, socializing and status. The concept of eating out has been on the rise especially after 1970s-80s. This is further enhanced by the proliferation of different types of hotels, restaurants, cafes, etc. To reiterate, it is the supply of different types of food that generates demand. To recapitulate, eating out today has become a very common thing due to variety of reasons which are listed as follows:

1. Out of Necessity

Many a times one comes across many students frequenting small restaurants e.g Hotel Vaishali. Many of them are from outside Pune or live faraway. They have long hours at college. At times working girls/ boys who live in hostels or as paying guests, are often regular customers. Office goers who have long hours of work, often eat small snack or lunch to supplement their home tiffins. During my interview I have come across quite a few who eat out daily – Many are often single / bachelor boys – hence it is more out of necessity that they start eating out which gradually becomes a routine. Most of them are from outside Pune, stay alone here with no family.

Moreover nowadays quite a few school going children often get pocket money to buy fruits. They eat *wadas*; *bhaji*as as mid-day snack, very often working mothers give them more pocket money. In Mumbai, tiffins are available on railway stations. In suburbs like Dombivali and Mulund, the working women often buy such tiffins in the evening. In the afternoon they eat at mess / office canteen.

A new phenomenon in Pune is on the rise in the case of old – senior citizens – especially single ones. Many times we come across senior citizens buying tiffins for lunch / dinner. They are too old or too weak to cook at home. Instead of hiring domestic help they prefer home made, home delivery; often on monthly basis door to door service is available and is supposed to be fairly reliable.

2. Working Couples

Today's working couples often invite guests outside in hotels due to paucity of space, lack of privacy and more because it is very convenient. As earlier mentioned, today's birthday celebration, marriages, thread ceremonies are all held in big hotels, therefore necessity is the mother of invention – people are always on the look out for new untapped avenues of food.

3. Socializing

Socializing is a very important sociological process which starts from birth. Socialization especially with peers / old friends / buddies is often done in hotels. For example, some old school batches have their yearly get together in a particular restaurant. Fergussonians meet on Sundays at 10 o'clock in the morning at Vaishali. Socialization is both formal as well as informal. Informal one is like chatting with old school / college friends over a cup of tea and snacks, or after hectic day shopping. Socialization not only strengthens solidarity but keeps us in touch with happenings, events and points of view. At times it can lead to serious discussions. Friends meeting one bright day decide to become partners in a joint venture. Semi-formal kitty parties are also held in restaurants. Very often formal socializing becomes an integral part of the life of a business executive, software manager, etc., e.g. cocktail, drink party with boss and other colleagues. Very often at cocktail parties business deals are struck. Social drinking has become a norm of conduct in the upper middle rich and neo rich class. The etiquettes, sophistication, glamour and the ambience of a hotel can often lend a magical touch – soft music and dim lighting create an atmosphere. In my interviews I came across many software / business executives regularly frequenting hotels with family members, friends, associates and partners. Many times business deals/ contracts are struck at business luncheons. Rotarians often meet at a certain hotel weekly.

Today the entry of women entrepreneurs into different fields such as software has also further accentuated socializing. Eating out, drinking, dancing or attending banquets have become a status symbol. Very often in newspapers and magazines there are pictures of prominent industrialists cracking open a champagne bottle at restaurants like Le Meridian. This often contributes not only to publicity but to gain patronage. Very often, especially on Thursdays or Sundays (Industrial Holidays) one comes across hotels being flooded with customers (car owners, upper income bracket families) for buffet luncheon at star hotels like Blue Diamond, Holiday Inn, etc. This is transaction from purely ascriptive status to newly achieved status.

I have already quoted Daniel Bell "As income rises propensity to spend on items of leisure, recreation and other personal services rises". This holds true in case of eating out. Upper middle rich class or elites of society are seen frequenting big hotels also for a display of wealth. This is what Alwin Toffler terms as Leisure Industry. "Ambience, Affluence, Cozy quiet atmosphere are the key words in today's hospitality industry". Very often this new found social status is manifested in hosting or attending dinners. Often business is mixed with pleasure e.g. Software executive entertaining foreign partners in ethnic and posh joints. Sociologically speaking, with the status, goes role. If one occupies a certain status (privileged position), he or she also has the responsibility and duty as a social citizen e.g. the Rotarian Governor has to often organize charity balls and music concerts. Very often top industrialists frequent certain hotels. Mr. Rahul Bajaj likes to go to Blue Diamond, which is in a way patronizing it. This is Particularistic Vs Universalistic. Therefore, such hotels offer regular clients discount. Hospitality combined with business is the key word. Social status, occupation and income play a very pivotal role in the status / position the person occupies. One of the repercussions of the changing occupational structure is that now we find a steady increase in the number of skilled workers instead of just labourers. This in turn necessitates more technical institutes to train the workers. Today's foreman supervisors are often men armed with engineering or polytechnic diplomas. A glance at job advertisements in newspapers can tell us how professional training is stressed. To cater to such needs, a wide variety of education is also available. Different professional courses can be done. There are different management schools and computer institutes in Pune. Young professionals are subsequently absorbed into lucrative jobs. Many of the interviewed in this study were at least science graduates – some post graduate – engineers. Many of then were armed with degrees / diplomas in Management, thus being a cut above the rest. There is a change from traditional form of occupation to modern technical type; therefore it is a transition from ascriptive to achieved status and also at times departing from traditional family norms. Most of them are working couples except three single highly trained professionals. Most of them like to go out with wives, family and friends.

Today's economy is fast changing. The twin processes of globalization and liberalization of economy, entry of more foreign companies, increase in credit and banking facilities (latest being telebanking, e-commerce). The fast pace of industrialization along with urbanization has changed the texture of Pune itself in the past 30 to 35 years.

To sum up, the rising prosperity and sophistication of the clientele lead to increasing demand, and therefore becomes a dynamic factor in economic development. Software companies in Pune have further accentuated the process as they patronize various expansive clubs. This in turn has helped many to discard traditional taboos about the food and alcoholic drink. For example, nowadays several Marwari businessmen are members of the Residency Club. There is a shift from restriction to relaxation, from puritanical to liberal attitudes (Reference group behaviour). The motto seems to be Epicurean pleasure– Eat, enjoy and be happy. In this way economy, society and culture are three strands of a single entity. They complete the triangle.

Industrialization as Social Multiplier

We have already seen how the functioning of multiplier effect of industrial advancement is reflected in the multifarious and sophisticated allied services of which hotel industry forms a very integral part. In this part we may focus on the socio-cultural dimension of industrialization. It is not easy to describe the social changes which the business organizations bring in the social fabric of a city. But one can see the new social patterns in the restaurants, in conference halls, in business organizations and associations.

When professional services find the growth of industries lucrative enough to come and operate in Pune, when new firms of auditors, legal advisors, architects, interior decorators, management consultants, advertisers, and specialists in a variety of fields converge upon a city in search of prosperity, the Multiplier Effect crosses the threshold of economic connotation. It results into reducing social distance. For example, women working in hotels were looked down upon earlier, but today it is not so. They work side by side with men right from front desk to CEO. As Prof. Hagan has pointed out, new occupations are much less caste oriented than the traditional ones. One may say there is a kind of democratization of the job market.

The rapid social transformation of Pune is due to several factors, but one of the most vital one is the industrial leadership. Most of the growth of Pune is from within and much under its own steam. The Kirloskars, the Parkhis, the Garwares were all local people. Even now one finds a whole new generation of technicians struggling hard to achieve success in industry. Many of them are young graduates in Physics, engineering, chemical engineering, electronics and they are starting new small scale industries in increasing number in the city and the regions surrounding it. The industrialization of Pune has brought about a change in their value judgment. The industry has acquired respectability and the ambitious young men of Pune are today aspiring to have an independent enterprise of their own.

The upsurge of the ambition in men wanting to go ahead is the motive force that has brought Pune to prominence as an industrial city. It is increasing and intensifying. Young men are making various things, be it electronic instruments or furniture. They run shops, manage industries, or audit accounts. This multiplication of productive activities may look diverse and often disjointed, but the unity of purpose and single mindedness of men to achieve success is the same.

Women Entrepreneurs

The traditional face of Pune Industry is also changing fast. Many women have entered in so far male dominated field of business. They are not only managing service oriented business but a number of women are in manufacturing line as well. About ten years ago, there were about 300 women entrepreneurs in industry and service sector in Pune. MAWIM (Maharashtra Association of Women Industrial Movement) indicates the figure to be manifold by now.

New Industrial Society

In post eighties instead of aristocratic intellectuals or social activists, prominent position in the social hierarchy has been taken over in Pune by the leaders in industries. This is because they contribute to the city's income and provide employment to a large section of society. They also provide an opportunity to ambitious young men to do creative work. Their efforts have also brought a place for Pune on the industrial map of the country. Thus, the Kirloskars, Bajajs, Firodias, Kalyanis, Pitties, Garwares, Sathes, Malhotras, Shirkes, Lunkads, Agas, Sangtanis, Wadias, Chabrias, who are Pune based industrial families, occupy esteemed position in the social stratum of the city. Top industrial houses of India like Tatas and Birlas have also their base in Pune. A number of multinational companies like Philips, Sandvik, SKF, ICIM, Backau Wolf, Atlas Çopco, Mahindra have set up their sophisticated manufacturing establishments in Pune. The combined result of the efforts of all these companies and local entrepreneurs is the fast industrial progress of Pune and it has earned recognition for Pune as the home of sophisticated quality products. Therefore, it is no wonder that the five among the present blue chip shares of the stock markets of India belong to Pune.

Leadership in Performance

Pune city boasts of not only the largest number of industries next to Mumbai- Thane belt but also the performance of some of the industries tops the ranks in the national economy. Every year the *Economic Times* publishes reviews and performance of the industries on various parameters. Reviews of 1986-87 and 1987-88 highlight some of the features of the Pune industries when SKF Bearings figured at number 3 for the gross profit as percent of total capital employed (25.17%). Bajaj Auto ranked first in the category of earnings per share for Rs. 10 paid up (64.6%) where in percent dividend also it topped the list with 80% figure.

Among the private sector giant companies' profitability ratios and earnings, many prominent companies like Bajaj Auto, Pieco Electronics, Kirloskar Cummins, Bharat Forge, Century Enka, Garware Nylons, Bajaj Tempo Ltd. figured in the list. As per the ranking of *Economic Times* based on the profitability and earnings of the companies, there have been at least three Pune companies figuring the list of top ten ever since 1983-84. Other details of this survey follow. Pune industrial area is proud of the achievement of some of its industries.

Table 1 : Companies in Pune Figuring in Top Ten (1983-88)

Year	*Name of the Company*	*Rank*
1983-84	Kirloskar Cummins Ltd.	No.3
	Bajaj Auto Ltd.	No.4
	Bajaj Tempo Ltd.	No.5
	Chloride India Ltd.	No.9
1984-85	Bajaj Auto Ltd.	No.3
	Bajaj Tempo Ltd.	No.4
	Maharashtra Scooters Ltd.	No.6
1985-86	Century Enka Ltd.	No.2
	Bajaj Tempo Ltd.	No.7
	Bajaj Auto Ltd.	No.8

(Contd.)

(Table 1 Contd.)

Year	*Name of the Company*	*Rank*
1986-87	Bajaj Auto Ltd.	No. 1
	Maharashtra Scooters Ltd.	No. 5
	SKF Bearings (India) Ltd.	No. 10
1987-88	Maharashtra Scooters Ltd	No. 1
	Bajaj Auto Ltd.	No. 2
	SKF Bearings (India) Ltd.	No. 6

From the above table it can be seen that Bajaj Auto Ltd. has figured in the top 10 in each of the 5 years, while Bajaj Tempo Ltd. has figured in two years, and Maharashtra Scooters Ltd., and SKG Bearings (India) Ltd. have figured twice during the last five years.

Features of Changing Diaspora

Another vital aspect of the city's colourful mosaic has been the changing diaspora which can be looked at from three angles:

(i) The influx of immigrants, both from different language groups as well as regions. They comprise Marwaris, Gujaratis, Tamils, Punjabis etc. They have not only set up businesses and factories, but have also contributed to Pune's cultural ethos.

(ii) The influx of students from all parts of India as well as from abroad for obtaining technical, and professional training, mainly in management and computer courses.

(iii) Last and equally important has been the influx of highly trained people from all over India and abroad. They include personnel from executive cadres, CEO's. The growing foreign collaboration also brings high profile business persons from abroad. Hence, Pune has become a cosmopolitan city, always on the move.

Ever expanding service sector has also contributed to the changing ethos of the city. This service sector now encompasses health facilities – ultra modern hospitals, growing demand for gyms, health spas, etc., recreation facilities, increasing number of theatres, auditoriums, multiplexes, museums, holiday resorts, hotels, restaurants, communication and mass media, creation of international consortiums and convention centres, conference halls and the growing craze for event management.

The central problem in this study is that of consumption and its positive aspects. The growth / proliferation of number and types of hotels, restaurants, clubs of various star categories catering to regional, ethnic, international types of cuisines vindicate my stand that supply also creates demand. The proliferation of eateries, hotels, pubs and clubs has resulted into not only direct employment but also concept of indirect one – franchising and supplying of food, houses, laundry, security etc. The language of thrift / and abstinence is discarded. The notion of ambience, taste, luxury, cozy atmosphere in the privacy of a hotel dominates the scene. There is also change in the concept of eating out. Today a slight modification in the Keynesian notion of 'production – income- saving' is necessary. There is a *prima facie* skipping of saving by entertaining business partners and clients in posh hotels, thereby indulging in consumption to clinch business deals / contracts. Hence today consumption is spending as an investment for the future. There are changes in standard of living and ideas of living, style of life, thereby negating Veblen's concept of conspicuous consumption as wastage.

In this way Pune has both facilitated, and enjoyed a level of consumption as a result of the favourable and positive function of variables like employment, earning capacity arising out of productive activity, quality of its education, social and cultural space for innovation and expanding of not only economy but also of the mental horizons.

7

Role of Immigrants in Pune's Socio-Economic Development

In the previous chapter we have discussed how the culture of eating out has made inroads into the once orthodox Pune Communities. Along with several factors mentioned therein, the migrants in Pune, especially after 1947-50s have also led to a change in the texture of the social as well as the cultural fabric of Pune. In this section we will elaborate this further.

Immigrants and Food Industry

Pune was once known to be a conservative traditional, but educational city. Earlier Deccan Gymkhana area was more modern and Pune cantonment obviously more cosmopolitan. After the advent of Rajneesh Osho Commune, Koregaon Park became 'international' with hordes of foreigners coming into the city.

Gradually popular culture penetrated the once traditional orthodox, puritanical, ethnocentric and at times almost xenophobic culture. Influx of immigrants has lately made the city quite heterogeneous, replacing the homogenous society of the bygone era. Today it is jokingly said that it is almost impossible to find truly authentic Maharashtra food in Pune. A variety of eating places testify to the changes in taste and for different kinds of food right from the traditional menu to various regional ones like the Punjabi, the South Indian, the Rajasthani, the Gujarati, the Western, the Thai, and the Chinese reflecting the changing composition of diaspora. A whole range of ethnic food is now available because of immigrants. Along with this there is a continuous inflow of entrepreneurs, kitchen staff and other experts.

It was during 1930s that Irani Muslims came to Pune from Persia due to acute famine and drought there. The first generation of Iranis migrated to Pune to seek out a living and started selling tea, bread, meat rolls Muska pav, bun bread, tea, khari etc. They found both the climate and the clientele good. Business started doing well. Hence these temporary migrants decided to settle here. Today the 3rd – 4th generations run the business of Irani cafes. Chinese immigrants came during the British period. Chinese joints in the city are at least 80 – 100 years old (e.g. Kamling on main street camp is 102 years old). They tried to popularize their food, of course with a little Indian adaptation. Parsees (real Persians) fled Iran to protect their faith, made India their homeland and have immensely contributed to the Indian industry. E.g. JRD Tata and Godrej. They have also contributed to Indian food culture. E.g. Dorabjees' Eatery in camp is the oldest, set up in 1850s. today the 5th – 6th generation runs it. Sindhis and Punjabis came in 1947, after partition of the country. They were very self-respecting and enterprising people, who never begged for food or money. They entered into Hotel, Textile business e.g. Mr. Kapoor of Hotel Amir (near Pune Railway station) – a 4 star hotel, was from Lahore with only Rs. 50/- in his pocket. Sindhis too have entered into hotel business e.g. Ramlaxman Hotel Pvt. Ltd. is owned by Mr. Bhojwani family. Holiday Inn franchises and sub contracting is also with Bhojwani family. Gujarati businessmen have entered into Hotel business for many years e.g. Hotel Ritz, opposite GPO was owned by Thakkar family for 125 years, trying to popularize Gujarati food in a semi alien environment like Pune. South Indian (Shettys – Udipi) migrated from South Canara. Earlier their small restaurants and cafes were confined to their pockets in Rasta Peth and Mangalwar Peth. But today we find even in Deccan Gymkhana area, Mr. Jagannath Shetty, the owner of 'Vaishali' and 'Roopali' who migrated from Udipi way back in 1950s, has occupied a very strategic location here.

Today there has been a decline in the number of Irani cafes, and increase in Udipi cafes. Many of the Irani café owners have died, or mortgaged their cafes or their sons do some other business. E.g. Café Sunrise is now owned by Shri Gunduraj Shetty. Lucky is also now owned by a non-Irani Shetty. The evergreen film star, producer-director Dev Anand reminisced about his walks to Lucky restaurant during his days in Pune – drinking tea and eating khari, bun bread and *salais* – slice of bread; slice was pronounced as 'Salais' by the waiters at Lucky. He used to walk down from a lodge at Prabhat Road. He was a struggling actor working at Prabhat Film Company way back in early 1940s.

Expansion of educational institutions and the increasing influx of students belonging to different groups from Kashmir to Kanyakumari, have made Pune a melting pot of different ethnic groups(students). Hence today different types of food are available even on the streets (Street Food Vending, SFV – hawkers). Since mid 1990s, there is advent of Pav Bhaji (Punjabi), Kacchi Dabeli (1990s Gujarati), and Chana Bhatura, while in 1970s it was *bhelpuri, panipuri, samosas, idli, dosas*. Today even pizzas are sold on street cafes. Wada Pav has become the National Food of India.

Because of Symbiosis Institute and the influx of foreigners, especially Africans, Thais, and Iranis, a mini street food chowpatty has emerged near GPO. Similarly one is found near University circle which springs surprises, right from Chinese to all Indian dishes on demand. A lot of Irani, African students hang out there till late night eating chicken, bread, etc. Hostel mess is shut on Sundays, in the evenings, so the hostelites also need to go out for food. This generates demand, and hence supply of a variety of food coupled with reasonable pricing and ready availability. This is another factor associated especially with street food.

Another aspect has been that after the establishment of industries in and around Pune it has resulted in the recruitment of executive cadres from different parts of India e.g. a lot of South Indians especially from Kerala occupy top executive positions in industries in Pune. Hence a triangular relationship is evolved which necessarily generates demand, and thereby supply; just as supply generates demand.

The proverbial chicken and egg dilemma presents itself even in this respect as to whether socio-cultural development precedes economic development or whether they (socio-cultural changes) both demand and encourage economic development.

Especially in the late 1978-80 there has been a great deal of change about not only type of food but the norm of eating along with family, friends as well as entertaining guests (official/business partners). Eating out now is not considered to be a taboo in most of the homes except for a few hang-ups about non-veg. / food or alcohol or during four months of Chaturmas – Shravan when onion and garlic are strictly prohibited. Many middle aged men and women executives are welcoming a new change and today they give pocket money to their school and college going children to eat outside. Today family structure has changed from big joint family to relatively small family- nuclear family. The status of women too has undergone change. They are highly educated, working outside. Hence very often they buy food from outside or take their guests outside which is indeed convenient. Such necessity creates demand and thereby supply. Very often one notices businessmen or partners discussing with clients in big star hotels. Hence very often business is mixed with pleasure. Often foreign collaborators and partners are taken out to ethnic joints e.g. Banjara Hills, Sanskruti etc; hence, the proliferation of different types of food ranging from street food to Five Star hotels. If one were to study from economic point of view one would say demand generates supply but here it is vice-versa. When Punjabi, Gujarati dishes were new, they were in demand.

On the restaurant and hotel front today we not only get Indian food, but also Mexican, Greek, Thai, Lebanese, Swiss, Chinese, Italian, Continental food along with Punjabi, Gujarati, South India, Oriya, Bengali (latest addition) and of course Maharashtrian food is available. The concept of fast food is fast catching up. Franchisees like Pizza Hut, Dominos Pizza and the latest Mc Donalds have sprung up. International 5-7 Star grade hotels like Le-Meridian, Holiday Inn, have emerged.

Therefore, we find that socio-cultural change in society acts both as a facilitator of economic development as well as a beneficiary of such development i.e. on one hand it generates employment – revenue taxes to the Corporation, Government, as well as due to presence of certain infrastructural facilities – transport, communication, industrial development, it is beneficial to the citizens. Business executives contribute to the exchequer – revenue for e.g. a lot of tourists come here as requisite infrastructural facilities are provided by the State and Central Government. They contribute to income generation and usher in the much needed economic development, especially for a third world developing country like India. In Pune, during the racing season (July – November) hotels and clubs are booked full. So in a nutshell, apart from changing habits and tastes of people, it is the socio-cultural change in the society (mainly influx of immigrants : Chinese, Irani, Udipi, Gujarati, Parsees, Muslims and of course different Europeans (Osho Rajneesh disciples) which makes new type of food available right from the street food to Five Star Hotels.

That is why the study not only cites the examples of Star hotels but also different types of hotels and restaurants like Maharashtrian, Gujarati, Punjabi, South Indian, Continental, Mughalai, Parsee, Irani Cafes, Chinese, and so on. This typology has been further extensively used in the interview schedules (especially interviews of business, software executives as well as those of hoteliers).

In this case development of service industry – tertiary sector – activities of leisure or what Alwin Toffler terms as 'Leisure Industry' in his famous book "*Future Shock*" is applicable to the study of hotels and restaurants. As people's horizons expand, new tastes develop so people spend on leisure activities. Hence today when one uses the term service sector, it has a positive two way relation to development. Service sector not only generates employment (income generation) but also contributes a great deal to the development not only in terms of infrastructural facilities or other aspects of development, but also influences socio cultural aspects of society. Often when one uses the term development it implies economic development, but in this study it has a greater social cultural dimension as well. Sociologically it affects all basic institutions like caste, marriage, family. It also affects occupation, education, cultural habits, input through media, generation of new ideas in society – folkways, mores, fashion and several other changes in society. Though service sector is used to understand the development of post industrial society (Daniel Bell), it can also be applied to the third world developing country like India.

Immigrant Population of Pune

1. Irani Muslim

Irani Muslims migrated from Persia in 1930s – due to heavy drought in the country. They came to Pune in search of employment and started Irani cafes – selling tea / coffee, biscuits, *khima pav* and other non.veg. dishes at a very cheap rate. At first they were temporary migrants to Pune city, but after doing brisk business, they decided to settle down here permanently. At present their 2nd or 3rd generations are running the family business. In the study a lot of reference has already been made to Irani café e.g. Marathi literary masterpiece – 'Puneri'- Joshi's detailed description of Lucky Restaurant. The present generations of Iranis are not much interested in running the family business – they do other types of business also. The rise of Udipi hotels in Pune (prime location – Gymkhana) has to a certain extent affected their business. Even the patronisers to these cafes are constant. Ninety per cent people visiting them are men.

2. Punjabis

This is a community always on the move. After the partition of 1947 many Punjabi migrants came to Pune. Today we find that the Punjabi Community has carved out a niche for themselves by their sheer hard work. They are extremely industrious and enterprising and self respecting people. Not a single Punjabi ever begged for food or money. Many illustrations can be given. Mr. Harbans Lal Aurora came from Lahore with just Rs. 50/- in his pocket. Today he is a proud owner of Hotel Amir – 4 Star Hotel since 1967. Omprakash Aurora too was forced to migrate from West Punjab (now a part of Pakistan). He too is a successful Hotelier – uncle of the owner of Hotel Aurora Tower – the tallest building in the Cantonment area, as well as a luxurious 4-5 Star Hotel.

Today we find that many of these immigrants are educated and since 1955 they have a Punjabi Cultural Association – Now they allow even non-Punjabis to become members. Among some other Punjabis are the Malhotras of Weikfield Company (Jelly Crystal). Today they also dominate internet business.

Mr. Ashwin Vakil, owner of Chandan Stores was also a refugee. The cycle business in Pune is dominated by Punjabis viz. Sikhs e.g. Singh Cycle Mart – as well as Automobile Service Centres. Cloth – Fabric business is one more area where they tend to dominate. (Gurunanak Textiles).

The Punjabis therefore have not only contributed to industry, but industrialists like Mr. Khosla (Khosla Plastics) have donated generously to Pune University's Chemistry Department, thereby strengthening the nexus between industry and educational institutions. They have also contributed immensely to hotel industry, for example dishes like chola bhatura, samosas, tandoori chicken have become the 'in thing' today. They have assimilated themselves into an alien community at the same time maintaining their cultural ethos. Mr. Preetam Singh Anand – owner of Anand Food Bakery and Shoppe was a refugee from Lahore in 1947. Many of them speak excellent Marathi and take active interest in the happenings of the city. Shere Punjab on Bombay Pune Road is a witness to their spirit – Dhaba culture. The popular Bhangra Folk Dance – its modern version, Bhangra Pop is a hit amongst the young generation. The Punjabis also undertake a lot of charitable activities.

3. Sindhis

After partition of 1947, they too were forced to migrate. They too are a very self respecting, hard working, industrious and enterprising community. They never begged for food or money. They used to sell embroidered handkerchiefs, laces, embroidery blouse pieces, papads, and pickles, at time even combs or brushes on trains. Recalling the post partition days, it was a common sight to see these poor refugees earning an honest living be selling their wares on Bombay Pune Railway Train and Stations.

Sindhis are the most adaptable community. In Mumbai itself, Ulhasnagar, a small suburb of Mumbai, is today a sprawling suburb because of Sindhis. In Pune the pioneering efforts of Shri Sadhu Vaswani (1948) of Sadhu Vaswani Mission carried forward many activities, especially in areas of education for girls. They started St. Mira's college for girls, other schools, hospitals for the needy, destitute and orphans. They have also tried to carve out a niche for themselves. Sindh Society at Aundh houses most of the prominent Sindhis e.g. Mr. Nari Hira, owner of popular *Citadel Magazine* and *Stardust* has his office and residence there. Sindhis have dominated textile business, fashion sarees and dresses. Construction business too is dominated by them e.g. Late Atur Sangtani; and now his son Lalit Sangatani, Gera Builders. Mrs. Nalini Gera, daughter of Atur Sangtani is Editor and owner of *Maharashtra Herald* (newspaper). Mr. Lalit Sangtani is also associated with Symbiosis Institute, he is the President of it. Many are involved in trade, share business and insurance. The owners of Finolex Pipes / Cables – Chhabrias are Sindhis too. They have left a landmark in the hotel industry as well, E.g. Mr. Bhojwani (owner of Holiday Inn, who also owns Ramlaxman hotels private limited – is a franchiser for Holiday Inn). They have fully tried to assimilate themselves with the Marathi community though at times with resistance or opposition from the local community. Yet they try to maintain their distinct identity e.g. they observe own rituals like Chetichand New Year, birth celebrations of their saint Jhulelal or birth days of Shri Sadhu Vaswani – (November 25). It is a meatless day. They are also involved in Mithai business as well e.g. Karachi Sweets.

4. Marwaris

They have migrated from Marwar province in Rajasthan for centuries together, and are mainly traders, merchants, dealers e.g. grocery, grain stores, diamond, gold merchants, money lenders. Today Pune's pride – Pravin Food Masale- is owned by a Marwari – Chordia Group. Textile business too is dominated by them – sarees shops like Princess, Shangun on Laxmi Road, Pannalal Lunkad Textiles. They are also involved in building construction business. The famous jewelers – Ranka Jewellers. Mr. Fathechand Ranka is the President of Pune Gold Business Association. Jain community is engaged in a lot of charity activity. Share market or business too is dominated by them. E.g. Transport business in Pune – (Bafna Auotomobiles or Navlakha Transport). Jain Irrigation Systems Pvt. Ltd is a major industry. Their exquisite cuisine e.g. Sanskruti ethnic joint – Hotel garden type located near Loni Kalbhor Opp. Philips Factory is a rich, cultural and gastronomical delight. Their dance, music and arts are delightful. Chittod, a luxorious hotel located on J.M. Road serves lavish food. Among street vending – Marwadi Kulfi is very famous.

5. Gujaratis

They have lent a distinct flavour to Pune's culture through the stomach as well as entertaining. Ritz hotel – owned for 125 years by Thakkar family has popularized Gujarati meals (Dhoklas, Undhyu). They are mainly engaged in trade, commerce, business, money lending, share business, jewelers – Mehta (Camp). Construction business too is dominated by them. They have their own educational institutions – Pune Gujarathi Kelwani Samaj – School and Colleges. There is often a stiff competition between Gujaratis and Marwaris in business. Gujarati – Street food vending – *kachhi dabeli* has a distinct Gujarati Kacchi flavour. Gujarati dance – Ras Garba – its modern variation – disco dandiya is very popular amongst the younger generation.

6. South Indians

They have migrated to Pune for centuries, right from the rule of Peshwas when artisans from Andhra Pradesh, Karnataka, Kerala, Tamil Nadu were invited. Later on many of them settled down here for generations together, especially in areas like Rasta Peth or near KEM hospital. They have literally created a mini Chennai or Kerala there (like ghetto). All the food varieties along with delicacies are readily available here. Many of their families have adapted to Marathi language. Surnames like Polkamvar, Dhagamvar are originally Tamilians, but they speak fluent Marathi. The famous saree shop "Kundan" has weavers from Andhra Pradesh.

The entry of Udipis (Idli, Dosa joints) though originally OBC's from South Kanara, today have become prosperous (new found achieved status). Today many South Indians occupy top positions not only in Government services even in Maharashtra Government, but also executive positions in industries in and around Pune.

Late Dr. B.V. Rao – founder of Venkateshwara Hatcheries (Venky's) now selling ready to eat chicken nuggets, kababs, and *keema* burgers hails from Andhra Pradesh. So they have not only contributed through food but also through textiles. Mr. Suresh Kalmadi, M.P., originally from Karnataka State; owns Sai Service and Poona Coffee House (A Multicuisine restaurant) opposite Deccan Gymkhana Bus Terminus.

7. Chinese

Chinese migrated from China more than 100 years ago. They are mainly involved in restaurant business e.g. Kamling, Chinese restaurant in cantonment area is 110 years old. Girls and women are involved in beautician business – hairdressers e.g., Hong Kong Hair dressers in cantonment area. Men are involved in leather shoe business. They have select outlets in camp area.

8. Parsees

For many centuries they have migrated from Persia (now Iran) – original Persians. They are simply involved in industry and business. Thermax – Mr.Rohington Aga turned Thermax into a multi crore business. Tata's Telco is located at Pimpri-Chinchwad area. They also dominate hotel and restaurant industry e.g. Dorabjee's is hundred and twenty years old. It is the oldest eatery in Pune. It is literally like an institution – catering business is flourishing – latest Dorabjee's bakery is located on Ganeshkhind Road. They run several charitable trusts. The famous Marzorin and Pasteur bakery are located in camp area.

9. Muslims

Ever since the Mughal rule – many conversions took place. Bohras (sec of Muslims) dominate business e.g. hardware. Many of them are involved in leather business. Mr Norman Latiff (owner of Latiff – Mughlai food since 1960s is very well known. The Khoja (Muslim Sect) community led by his Royal Highness Prince Agakhan is involved in many charitable organizations. Agakhan palace where Gandhiji was kept under house arrest during British days is today a National monument. Many of the Muslims are involved in antique business. Mr. Hamid Dalvi was a social reformer amongst Muslims. They have outlets for chicken /mutton shops (butchers) as well as sell biryani / kabbabs and especially in Pune cantonment area during Bakri-Id – set up stalls at Shivaji market.

10. Christians

For many centuries Christians have lived here. They are involved mainly in educational institutions – Missionary schools and colleges. Many of them own shop for books and other articles. Very few are involved in hotel business – mainly bakery business, cake orders.

8

Street Food Vending in Pune – A Sociological Perspective

As already mentioned earlier, in the traditional Pune Society 'eating out' was looked down upon, if not entirely 'tabooed' due to the notion of purity, pollution, not to say hygiene and notions of status and prestige of the family. In such a society street food vending (SFV) was like a thin end of the wedge. It was mainly confined to items of food which were dry and not really cooked like roasted peanuts, puffed rice, etc. Later certain items like *pakodas, batatawadas* made their way in to the repertoire. Yet partaking of such food was confined to poor sections, menial labourers and craftsman. However, today, there has been a sea change in the consumption pattern and the items available as well as the class of consumers which cuts across caste, education, income, occupation and age.

In addition, there has been an entry of vendors belonging to different regions such as North India, South, Gujarat, Rajasthan, and even Chinese food so as to cater to the taste and fancy of the ever-growing different wage earners' strata and groups. No wonder that the clientele has also changed considerably right from daily wage earners, menial workers, and students from various regions of India, not to say foreigners. All have considerably added to the items made available. Cost wise eating off SFV is both cost saving and yet caters to the changing taste and fancies regarding food.

Objectives of the Study

(1) To find out as to who are the real consumers of SFV

(2) To find out as to whether there is any correlation between Age, Caste, Class, Income, Occupation, Education and Consumption of SFV.

(3) To find out as to who are the SF Vendors, whether they are local or migrants.

Methods

I have essentially used purposive sampling (Non-probability) in the area adjacent to Kamala Nehru Park where there is a proliferation of SF vendors. The method of data collection is observation. I had earlier tried to interview the vendors but they were quite reluctant to answer my questions, they mistook me to be a spy of Pune Municipal Corporation and were probably scared about the temporary nature of their licenses.

I intermittently used complete (non-participant) observer role where I was completely an unnoticed observer without revealing my identity. At certain times I was a partial participant (observer participant) observer. I ate certain food items or often asked them to pack them for me sometimes I tried a small talk with the proprietors, so that I could observe them and their customers in their operating skills like cutting, serving food, hygiene etc. (presentation of food items) I would often take a walk in the park in the mornings, afternoon, late evenings or walk over to the opposite side of road, get into the shops on the pretext of buying groceries, medicines, etc.

Findings

(1) Most of the Street Food Vendors are settled in Pune for more that 10-15 years, and are literate.

(2) Women hardly participate, except for chopping vegetables and fruits.

(3) Children in the age group of 5-12 years are often hired to wash dishes or act as 'Mobile waiters.'

(4) Very often *haftas* (bribes) are paid by *paanwalas* to police hawaldars or they often are served free food, *paan*, tea etc.

(5) SFV cuts across all sections of society ranging from daily wage menial earners, students, youngsters, couples, and old people to four wheelers owners, children. Age Group is 3-80 years.

(6) Students often eat here due to necessity. Many of them are paying guests, hence they eat outside and chat with friends (socializing).

Many of them work outside. Often on Sunday's college mess/ canteens are shut; hence necessity generates demand, thereby supply of variety of quick tasty and reasonably priced food has been increasing.

(7) Old people enjoy it. They have the leisure; eating street food is a recreation for them, and a novelty too as they had not eaten many items earlier. Either, they were not available or were forbidden. They are very often lonely, uncared for at home and hence indulge in eating out. Many of them are BP, diabetic patients. They violate food restrictions – low salt, oil/fat free, sugar free. Films such as *Baaghban, Shaukeen, Joggers Park* are exemplified here by the 'senior citizens of Pune Kamala Nehru Park Road.

(8) There are seven crucial variables such as age, class (economic), education, occupation, income, old age, ethnicity and reasonably priced tasty food.

In short SFV is enjoyed and relished by groups right from daily wage earners, college students, young children, couples, working people (e.g. bank employees) as well as by retired pensioners – old people (earlier holding prestigious positions – as Income tax commissioners, lawyers, Central / State Government employees, etc). The place of street food vending has become a melting pot where the differences of age and status are obliterated. Consumption of SFV and the like has broken all the barriers of age, gender, strata (income), education, and occupation. Thus, SFV can be considered to be a development offshoot of the changing notions about consumption.

Street Food Vending (SFV henceforth) is essentially a third world country urban phenomenon which falls under the category of informal sector. The chapter discusses SFV's conceptual definitions and is supplemented with a few case studies, using observation method near Kamala Nehru Park (Pune) area, where there has been a proliferation of Street Food Vendors selling food ranging from simple *bhelpuri* to *pavbhaji* and pizzas to cater to a wide spectra of society cutting across age, caste, religion, ethnicity, class, income, region, linguistic states, education, professions (occupations) children, students, young couples, professionals, families and old senior citizens (geriatric aspect).

In a city like Pune, conventionally known as 'Oxford of the East' and today also an 'industrial cyber-software city', with the growth in population and rising incomes, the eating habits of the citizens of Pune (Punekars) have changed. These changes are reflected in more outdoor eating, changes in tastes and preferences and larger availability of a variety (plethora) of food items ranging from snacks – *bhelpuri, samosa* to *idli, dosas, pav bhaji*, pizzas, sandwiches, veg. burgers and *puri bhaji, chola bhaturas*, non-veg. tandoor, Chinese and of course *Vadapav*. In the case of SFV, the sociological process of adaptation is put into action, whereby culinary skills of regions, at times even other countries such as China, Italy are available here. Pizzas (Italy) Haka Noodles, Manchurian, Non Veg. food (China) cater to the taste buds of wide spectra of Punekars. SFV refers to reasonably priced tasty tangy food, *'Swasta ani Masta'*.

Innovation of new food items such as '*wada pav*' a synthesis of potato wada (Patti) and bunbread, two slices inside which it is sandwiched is an Indian (Mumbaite) adaptation of a vegetable burger which is in fact a mini meal having clientele ranging from daily wage earners, college students, young children, couples, working people to families, thereby obliterating caste, class, income, education and occupational differences. In short, necessity is the mother of invention. The cheap price and near completeness of *wada pav* in terms of satisfying hunger has in fact transformed it into India's fast food as well.

The increase in outdoor eating has been not only due to rise in incomes, but also due to dispersal of work places, a rise in outstation students, working people and paucity of time to cook at home. The changes in tastes have been brought about additionally by the migration of people from other states, which introduced their native dishes in Pune for e.g. *idli, dosa*, Gujaratis – *Kacchi Dabeli*. Thus, to put it sociologically, it is social processes of assimilation, adaptation and innovation. Yogendra Singh (2000): "Within India, the trend to consume and patronize food items of other regions and its culinary practices by members not belonging to that region is now fast growing due to increased inter-regional migration". The non-veg dishes have become popular among the Punekars especially the Brahmins, who a decade ago completely shunned it. A socio-cultural change has occurred; simultaneously it is the impact of westernization and modernization, exposure to a new set of values and reference group behaviour. Hence today we find many earlier non-meat eating castes and communities emulating the western or meat eating communities, a via media to attain social acceptability, thereby social ascendancy – a near complete debunking of the socially prescribed norms of purity and pollution and other dietary taboos associated with it. Therefore the concept of purity and pollution associated with food, especially liberal use of onion garlic, tomato associated with non veg foods has been obliterated.

There is also a simultaneous growth in open air eating with food served from stalls, carts and on pavements – e.g. Pav Bhaji, Misaal have become very popular and especially in the evenings (Sundays) we find throngs of youngsters, four-wheeler owners binging on it. Jains have their version of Pav Bhaji i.e. without potatoes, onions, but they still enjoy eating out. Here the clientele is also varied from low income daily wage earners (Wadapav, Misaal) to middle class to the rich (owners of costly imported cars (neo-neuvo rich).

Along with such a sociological analysis of SFV, a conceptual definitional perspective is also essential, so as to understand the special characteristic features, dimensions of SFV. SFV is essentially a third world county urban phenomenon, predominantly found in South East Asian countries – India, Thailand, Malaysia, Singapore, etc. and African Latin American countries. Sociologically speaking it is a functional imperative, (Parsons, 1934) and methodologically speaking it is its ontological / and epistemological aspect which require a very close examination.

Conceptual definitions of SFV, and Informal Sector SFV is a small size (micro size) enterprise which usually avoids regulations and taxes. SFV employ less than 10 or at times less than 20 people. Very often household / domestic servants are also included under informal sector. It is a very small-scale operation and very often sub-contracting is done. For example Asian and African countries constitute the bulk of the urban survival especially entry of women, who constitute the poorest and lastly there is a traditional pattern of apprenticeship.

Characteristics of SFV

1. **ILO Kenya Convention (1972):-** has listed six peculiar characteristics of SFV (informal sector). Ease of entry, no highly specialized training is needed here. (i) Reliance upon the use of indigenous resources (ii) Family ownership (iii) Small scale of operation (iv) Labour intensive and adaptive technology (v) Skills are acquired outside formal school system.
2. **Jacques Charmes (1970):-** He has defined informal sector as marginal productive activity covering street hawking garbage and rag pickers and casual labourers. Indian statisticians have often used 'non-registration under Shops and Establishment Act as one of the key criterion for defining informal sector activity. It can be under a tree, in a basement or on the pavement. These are temporary structures, often operated illegally. Often no electricity is used. kerosene lamps are used.

3. **Hans Singer (1990):-** He describes informal sector enterprise like a riddle which is hard to describe. You know it only when you see it. It works in somebody's backyard, under a tree, in front of a dwelling or by a road side. Such street enterprise is made up of non-permanent materials e.g. thatched roof top, plastic polythene vinyl covering. It resembles a shack (*tapari*), often a dilapidated structure, or often an open air hut.

4. **Victor Tokman (1990):-** He has enumerated special features of informality. Accordingly trading is one of the points for entry for migrants into a city, as well as traditional life time activity for many working poor. In any cities of Asia and Africa, street trading acts as both a residual occupation with marginal and sub marginal incomes and an economic ladder that offers some type of upward mobility. SFV will continue to draw entrants as long as there is urban unemployment, lag behind population and labour force increase. Government is faced with tensions arising from necessity to combine and control accommodation.

Tokman has given the features of this sell out area (SFV) (1) Small scale of operation (2) Informal Structures (3) Use of traditional technology (4) Unprotected labour markets (5) Ease of entry for low skilled (6) Low economic returns (7) Tendency for activities to operate on pavements at railway stations, or other public spaces e.g. parks, gardens, outside city theatres, auditoriums, schools, colleges, and at picnic spots.

Positive aspects of the role of informal sector are its capacity to absorb labour and its role in provisions of goods and services at lower cost.

Negative aspects are: It has a deleterious effect on public sector revenue and it encroaches on public places for e.g. Railway station platforms, footpaths, parks, gardens.

The informal sector contributed to nearly two-third of employment in Mumbai in 1991, and more or less the same in Pune. Features of informal sector are (1) generally lack of adequate resources (2) This results in small scale of operations and lack of access to basic inputs such as space, finance etc. The distinctive features of this sector which form the basis of informal – formal sector dichotomy are given by Papola (1994).

Papola (1994) on SFV Features

(1) Small scale of operations generally based on size of employment which has less than 10 workers. It is self generated employment (self employment).

(2) Informal structure and family ownership. Extensive use is made of family labour and there is a limited division of labour. There is no formally structured organization.

(3) Use of traditional technology, labour intensive, low productivity techniques etc.

(4) Unprotected labour market. The supply of labour comprises mostly of new entrants in the labour market. Generally they are immigrants of young persons unable to get access to the formal sector. The informal sector bears the brunt of excess labour supply which is reflected in low wages and insecurity.

(5) Ease of entry in contrast to the difficulty of entry-unto formal sector. The skills have been generally acquired outside the formal education system.

(6) Earnings in the informal sector are low as compared to earnings in the formal sector. Generally 50 per cent or lower. However, earnings are much higher than what migrants from rural areas would have earned at the place of origin.

(7) Many of the informal sector activities operate on pavements – public places. This gives rise to harassment by authorities. There is thus a sense of insecurity.

The landmark of the popularity of the concept of informal sector, since its inception is mentioned by Keith and Hart (1973) in the introduction of their study of Ghana (Africa) a third world country. The activities in the informal sector are unlicensed, untaxed, unprotected, and without any involvement in legal contracts.

UNDP (1996) has stated that 'Informal Sector can be a major source of employment in developing countries as job creation takes place with it, as it provides opportunities of self-employment. It also provides goods at lower cost. This is especially significant in Third World countries, where a sizeable proportion of the population lives below poverty line. Adams and Paul (1987) and Lever (1996) have pointed out that it is able to foster and provide opportunities for entrepreneurship skills which may transfer into formal sector over a period of time. For example, a person selling roadside batata (potato) wadas, after a period of 3 – 10 years can join a mess or canteen or even start a small restaurant some day. Thirty-five years ago, Mr. Ramakant of Lonavala was a roadside potato *wada* vendor located on Mumbai Pune Highway NH4. Today he has transformed his business into a big restaurant named 'Ramakant International (a flourishing business). Another example is that of Diwadkar's Batata wadas near Karjat (suburb of Mumbai). Thus, SFV is one such occupation which does not require formal education or training and employs less than 10 people, provides tasty reasonably priced food- a wide variety as well as affordability cutting across wide strata of society – caste, class, income, age, education, and occupation and acts as a facilitator for rural migrants to work, though lowly paid. However as a coin has two sides, the negative aspects of SFV are it is unprotected, at times illegal activity and often encroach upon public places, thereby obstructing pedestrian, vehicular traffic. It also generates a lot of garbage – leftover papers and food adding to environmental hazards – pollution, entry of rodents – rats/cats, stray dogs hovering after food leftovers littered on the streets. A major hidden aspect is that of child labour and hygiene (in preparing, serving food-health hazard). Nevertheless an increasing number of people in a growing metropolis eat street-food. The working people often supplement home lunch boxes with Street Food. When working overtime they eat snack and tea outside so SFV is an accepted form of necessity / entertainment / leisure and recreation among middle class families.

SFV in Pune

SF vendors locate themselves where a large number of customers come near schools, colleges, parks, railway stations – platforms, offices, banks, theatres, auditoriums, hospitals etc.

Major Findings of Meera Bapat's Survey (1992) on Street Food Vending in Pune

(1) Almost 40-50 per cent of SF Vendors are proprietors of their enterprises for nearly 5 – 10 years. Some of them have lived in Pune for 2 – 3 generations and nearly 70 per cent have lived in Pune for nearly 10 – 15 years. Most of them are at least literate, have attended secondary school.

(2) Barely 10 per cent of these have regular licenses from Pune Municipal Corporation, or at least profess to have temporary licenses i.e. six months only.

(3) Nearly 22 per cent of SFV have to do it to supplement their incomes and about 10 per cent of them have previous experience of apprenticeship (Small scale of operation).

(4) SFV has expanded in industrial urban sector like Pune. It is often a popular form of entertainment / leisure / recreation, especially for middle class families, on holidays, Sundays and especially among the poor as a source of affordable food, due to economic compulsions.

(5) Most of them do not use modern technologies, except mixers, fruit juicers or at times a hand operated aluminum centrifugal churner / mixer for extracting juice from pineapple, watermelons, sweet limes etc., but they use fresh stock of materials as they have no facility for storing food – no refrigerators. Very little skill is needed.

(6) SFV gives them reasonable income; some of them make a lucrative business out of it e.g., Paanwalas, earn more than Rs. 1000 – 2000/ per day. Moreover they pay no income tax. Those food items which cater to economically better off clientele yields higher income to SF vendors.

(7) Very few women are involved in SFV, except for helping in washing, chopping or selling traditional items like missal, potato wada, thalipeeth, pohas and use of domestic skills.

This study finds SFV located near schools, parks, colleges, banks, auditoriums often selling guava, watermelon (seasonal) berries (chanya-manya- bright cherry red small wide berries), cucumber, roasted maize corn (bhutta) peanuts, chanas, ice lolly, cheap cold drinks, pepsicola (a cheap variation of western popsicle i.e. semi liquid fruit flavoured ice candy sold in a plastic bag which one can sip from.

The proliferation and abundant variety food ranging from simple *bhelpuri* to *dosas, puri-bhajis, idlis* to non-veg, pizzas, *pav bhaji*, Chinese, *missal, khichdi* (pearl sago), chicken, tandoor tikka dishes and *wada pav*. Yet these items are reasonably priced ready to eat (fast food) and tasty and tangy to tickle taste buds. The clientele for SFV comprises of a wide strata of society including the poor and daily wage earners, manual workers, etc. Today SFV has become a 'buzzword' of urban life style which is triggered by necessity for example outstation students and working people need such food. It is also a form of leisure for family outings, picnics, and for old people it is like eating the forbidden fruit which was earlier not allowed due to notions of purity and pollution.

Case Studies of SFV Near Kamala Nehru Park (done 10 years ago)

It has been more than a decade ago that the names and prices mentioned in the following pages were elicited. Now the prices of the street food mentioned here have gone up three fold at least. The same vendors are no more. Nevertheless, the popularity of SFV continues, and so does the validity of its sociological significance.

(a) BHELWALAS

(1) Bhola Bhel – The owner is a middle aged person around 50 – 60 years and has been a constant feature fixture for more than 35-40 years.

He has hired an assistant boy to help him in cleaning, cutting, serving bhel. He sells wet as well as dry bhel (mixture of namkeen, sev, boiled potatoes, onions, tomatoes, chillies, coriander, puffed rice (churmuras) and flat hard crispy purees). He charges Rs. 5-6 per plate. He serves dry bhel in newspapers, wet bhel in glass dishes and uses cardboard flaps (for spoons). He stores wet tamarind and mint, green chutney in big porcelain jars (used for wet Bhel) and during summer adds raw mango pieces to enhance the tangy taste. His stall is open from 9 – 9.30 a.m. in mornings till 1.30 in afternoon and from 4.00 – 8.45 p.m. i.e. till the park closes. He stores dry stuff-namkeen in glass showcase type box with compartments. It is mounted on his hand cart. His clientele ranges from the age group of 3 – 80 years cutting across caste, class, income, education, occupation. People also visit the place on holidays.

(2) Rajesh Bhelpuriwala – The owner is a young man of around 35 – 45 years and has been here for the past 15 – 20 years and he too serves in a similar way as that of Bhola Bhelwala and clientele is also the same. He owns another stall known as 'Jay Bajarang Bhel'.

(B) PANI PURI (Golgappa)

(1) Sangita Panipuri – The owner is around 25-35 years. He charges Rs. 6- 8/- per dish. He serves in deep saucers (meant for soups). He too stores *puris* in glass showcase type box compartments and the tamarind chutney in China clay glass jars. He uses Municipal Corporation water for the *pani*. His clientele includes more youngsters and couples. The panipuri is extremely tasty, spicy and tangy

(C) SANDWICHWALA

(1) A1 – The owner is around 30 – 35 years and has been selling here since 1997 -98. He sells sandwiches for Rs. 10 – 20. He sells jam, veg, cheese, chutney and even club sandwiches. The cost of sandwich is directly related to the ingredients used. He uses genuine Amul Butter and Cheese and Sandwich bread, good sauce/ketchup and often buys from Aaswad Bakery on the opposite side of the road. He serves in plastic plates and provides paper napkins. His clientele includes mostly outstation students from nearby colleges or young working people. Mostly in the evenings the place is thronged by youngsters. Necessity generates demand, hence supply.

(D) CHAIWALA (Tea Stall) – The owner is around 30 – 35 years and has been a constant fixture for the past 10 – 15 years. He sells tea for Rs. 2.50, Masala Chai for Rs. 4/-, Malai Chai for Rs. 5/-. He also sells half glass tea (called as cutting chai). His stall is open from morning 8.00 till evening 7.30. His clientele ranges from daily wage earners, office goers, students, and elderly people. The tea is very tasty, refreshing and addicting at times.

(E) PEANUT SELLER –The owner is a middle aged man 50 – 55 year who has been here for the past 25 – 30 years. He serves roasted peanuts and chanas in newspaper cones and sells each one for Rs. 2.50/-. About 30 years ago it used to cost only 25- 30 paise. Due to sharp rise in the price of groundnuts the cost has shot up. His timings are from 9.30 a.m. – 8.30 p.m. at night. His clientele includes small children, young couples, students, picnic goers etc. Peanut is considered to be a poor man's snack. One is often reminded of Hindi/Marathi film in which the Hero and Heroine (Lovers) would share a cone sitting in the park or at seashore, completely love-lost which symbolized the epitome of romance. Noted legendary film director Late Shri Hrishikesh Mukherjee in his classic films such as '*Choti Si Baat*' and 'Rajanigandha' has shown such scenes. Marathi novels especially by noted novelist N.S.Phadke describes the young couple (love birds) huddling together eating peanuts. Earlier buying peanut cone and a small garland (gajra) for the lady love was the 'in thing' for dating. Today, though not much has changed, it has become a class indicator. Sociologically speaking the social processes of cooperation, adaptation and accommodation are involved in such a simple act of buying a humble peanut cone and sharing it. This was especially so in earlier days of paucity of money, concept of sharing, togetherness, saving and frugality in Pierre Bourdieus term 'taste of necessity' or ideas of simplicity in life meant.

(F) SANTOSH KACCHI DABELIWALA AND RAGDA PATTICE OWNER – He is around 35 – 40 years and has been around for 10 – 11 years. He sells it for Rs. 3.50 – 4 comprising of 2 bread buns filled with boiled potatoes, sev, groundnut, onions, pomegranate seeds and the special Gujarati masala filled inside. His clientele includes young college students, couples, and families. On Sunday evenings the place is very crowded. Ragda pattice are potato cutlets served in chana (white chick pea) gravy/ sauce with tamarind chutney which is a talk of the town for youngsters. Very often children (child labour) aged from 6 - 12 years act as mobile waiters and clean dishes.

(G) MULTICUISINE MINI MEAL AND SNACKS

(1) Shinde Snacks – The proprietor is a young person around 30 – 35 years. He owns two stalls. He sells potato wadas, misaal, poha, upma and of course wada pav. He keeps his stalls open from morning 8 till 9.00 at night.

He also undertakes outdoor catering orders for *wadas*. He does brisk business and by 10.30 a.m. in the morning most of the snacks are over. He has hired two helper boys. The stall has been there since 5 – 10 years. His clientele includes daily wage earners (early morning), around 8.30 – 9.30 a.m. its park senior citizens (pensioners), a little later it is Bank of Maharashtra employees, KNP park supervisors and students.

Very often Senior citizens order pohas, wadas and sit and eat in the park and often tell the owner/assistants to serve dishes by bending the fencing of the park.

(2) Swami Samartha Snacks Centre – The proprietor is around 40-45 years and has been here for the past 7 – 9 years. He serves Dosas, Upama, Wada Pav, Sheera (Sweet Suji Halwa) Misaal and now Chola Bhatura and Puri Bhaji.

His clientele includes young college students, working people of age group 18-30 years. Mostly outstation students throng the place, sitting on their parked two-wheelers, gobbling and chatting with friends. Most of them stay in hostels or as paying guests here. The stall opens at 8.30 a.m. in the morning. By late evening i.e. around 8.30 – 9.00 p.m. the stalls shut down.

(H) PAANWALAS

(1) Rakshita – The owner is around 35 – 40 years. He opens the stall at around 10 a.m and shuts it at 11.30 at midnight. He sells Banarasi, Poona masala, Calcutta, Maghai, Kimam, Meetha paan (tutty-fruity), Tobacco – as the number increases so does the cost and strong flavour – Brand names such as 500 – 600 'Paanchso cheso' depict the purity of tobacco added. An ordinary paan costs Rs. 3 – 5 and depending upon the freshness, virginity of the Indian piper plant leaf (paan) as well as ingredients added such as gold foil, silver foil, the piece can shoot upto Rs. 100 – 500/- per paan. He also sells paan masala, gutka, Goa, paas paas, Paan Parag, cigarettes etc. though legally banned by the Government of Maharashtra.

(2) There is another stall once owned by an elderly man whose two sons manage it now. The clientele includes office goers, especially in the afternoon (post lunch). Youngsters eat minimum 5 -6 paans per day. They characterize the place perched on their expensive motor bikes using expensive outfits, goggles, aftershaves (Ray ban goggles, imported jeans). Today eating paan is a status symbol often engrossed in chatting, whiling away time or eating paan on credit. The elderly man used to often label

them as 'Bade Baap ki Aaolad'. Today even girls are trying to emulate them. A few years back noted Marathi film stars – Ramesh Bhatkar (detective serials) and many others used to throng the place. It is a matter of prestige.

(I) FRUITWALA – The owner is around 30-35 years. His wife around 25 – 30 years helps him in cutting fruits. She uses rubber gloves and serves in steel or plastic plates with forks and paper napkins. He sells cut bananas, apples, chickoos, grapes (seasonal papaya, pineapple, water melon, oranges, sweet lime). He sells at Rs. 20 – 25 per plate (a dry fruit salad). The clientele includes young outstation students, children, couples from middle / upper class families. On holidays it is jam packed.

SEASONAL STALLS

(1) Dilbahar Bombay Kulfi (only summer) – The owner is around 35 – 45 years old. He sells Mevadi Kulfi, chocolate, pista, mango, Kesar (seasonal) badam, ice cream. Kulfi is an Indian version of a thick creamy ice cream bar often made out of condensed milk (*rabadi* style – a popular North Indian sweet dish). This stall has been here for the past 15 – 17 years. The clientele includes middle and upper class and four wheeler owners, especially in the evenings. It costs around Rs. 20 and above.

(2) Snacks Point – Owner is around 35 – 40 years. He also owns a stationery shop 'Shirish Traders' nearby. He sells pot ice cream in Kesar, Mango, Pista, Chocolate, Strawberry flavours. His clientele includes children, couples, families, and upper middle class.

(3) Maize Bhutta Seller – The owner is a woman around 30 – 35 years of age and has 2 young sons aged 6 – 13 years. She sells Bhutta for Rs. 5 – 8. She roasts corn, applies salt, masala, lemon juice, and chillie powder. Her clientele includes children, youngsters, students, couples. She serves mostly in the evenings.

(4) Narial (Coconut Water Wala) – The owner is around 30 – 35 years. He sells *narial paani* for Rs. 8 – 10. The price of the coconut depends upon the virginity of the coconut its creamy side (Malai) and sweet taste of the water i.e. old one would have turbid water with a salty taste. The clientele includes young couples, fitness conscious (joggers) health diet freaks, old people, children, and Joshi Hospital patients. This is a hospital situated nearby, hence caters to the demands of the patients especially post surgery (stomach, heart, kidney, liver) patients. As is observed in case of peanuts cones many times young love birds /couples similarly are seen sharing one coconut, using two straws.

(5) Nimbu paani / Aam Panna Seller – The owner is around 40 – 50 years of age. He uses corporation water and stores it in two steel drums and sells 'nimbu sharbat' (lemon squash) for Rs. 2.50 and Aam kaccha panna for Rs. 5. The clientele include children, students, and old people. It is necessarily a thirst quencher, refreshing cooling drink. He does brisk business in the two summer months, April and May.

Thus, the SFV around KNP cater to a wide variety of food which is reasonably prices, tasty and which cuts across a wide spectrum of society i.e. caste, class, income, age, education and occupation.

Major Findings

1. SFV vendors use corporation water.
2. Haftas may be paid to policemen. I have especially noticed it in case of paanwalas once or twice. Some times police throng these places. But so far no hawker's stall has been confiscated. Women hardly participate except for the fruitwala whose wife helps in chopping fruits.

The customers here are of ages between 3 years to 80 years or so. While observing street food vendors most importantly their customers, there have come across seven important variables:

1. Age group 2. Class 3. Occupation 4. Income 5. Education 6. Old Age 7. Eating – out, reasonable rate :

1. Young Age: Students, especially outstation ones are frequent visitors / customers here. They are between the age group 17-18 to 27-28 years. Most of them are college students, studying in nearby college's e.g. BMCC, Symbiosis, Fergusson, etc. They come from far off places like Mizoram, Manipur, occasionally African students also come here. Many of them stay is hostels or as paying guests. Often on Sundays College mess and canteens are closed, hence the demand comes out of necessity.

2. Very often middle class / upper class students who are two wheeler owners flock this place out of necessity – very often they stay far away. Very often they hang around here till late at night. At times they come from extra tuitions. Sometimes they are apprentice at company office like Dr. Beck or recently at Soft Bridge Solutions, a software venture.

3. On holidays they often eat out here, for time pass and get together with friends. Mostly working boys / girls come here for a cup of tea or snacks after a busy day at work to catch up with friends, chatting etc.

4. Today eating out has become more of a norm / fashion, trying out new varieties every day and socializing. It is often necessity that generates demand; hence supply (triangular relationship). The youngsters often laugh gregariously, talk loudly. There is not a single dull moment, verbal teasing or, at times passing rude, lewd comments at girls is also involved.

5. Very often though double parking is not allowed here they do it. In Parsonian terms 'norm of deviance' i.e. repeatedly violating the rule knowingly? Today's pop or mass culture has emerged; very often these youngsters curse old citizens as to why they come out late in the evening. Many of them belong to upper middle class, have expensive two wheeler, imported jeans, goggles, after shave (expensive) eat most of the time especially pan, chain smokers. They belong to rich / neo-rich class (hidden money, black money). In modern terms Pune in a way has been "Bunty-Bablized".

6. Especially every morning a bunch / group of pensioners come to the park for walk, chatting with friends. Most of them are highly educated e.g. Ex-Municipal Commissioner, Income tax Commissioners, lawyers, Central / State Government employees now retired. They receive regular income by pension but often like to come here – relax, enjoy and be happy. A few of them stay with their sons – daughters-in- laws who are often working women and have no time, and take no interest in them. They have careless / indifferent attitude towards the in-laws. Son too is indifferent. There are conflicts at home. Many of these senior citizens men have lost their spouses-wives, hence are alone. Due to paucity of space and lack of privacy / single men / widowers come here. They find similar company in the park. Often in the morning at 8-8.30 a.m. they buy snacks – *pohas, batatawada* from Shinde Snacks and enjoy. They often discuss present politics, bygone days, cricket corruption with their friends, in general they socialize here. Films such as Shaukeen, Joggers Park, Baghban, and a couple of Marathi films such as Unn (Sun), Pauss (Rain), Goud Gupeet (sweet secret), "Tu Tithe Mee" (after me), mirror this reality. Many of these pensioners are economically self sufficient but are often not cared for at home. Many are heart patients, BP – blood pressure, Diabetes, Arthritis, etc. but eat in spite of restrictions at home e.g. sugar free / salt / oil free – low cholesterol. They enjoy themselves by eating indulging in a little deviance – eating forbidden things – picnics, outings and exercise, and most importantly peace of mind. This has also been exemplified by the study 'Adjustment to the changing status and role of old age' a study of old aged persons in Pune city by Anupama Keskar (1990). As has been stated – many of the old pensioners manage their free time, leisure time, especially mornings. This free time is a compensation for a life-time of hard work. Most of them sail in the same boat, suffering a sense of role loss, loss of status. The park and the plenty of SFV outside provide them an anti-dote to cope with life. Very often these pensioners are lonely at home due to either death of the

spouse, or sons and daughter living separately in Pune, or living in another city or at times abroad. It is an empty nest for them.

Conclusion

SFV is enjoyed and relished by group's right from daily wage earners, college students, young children, couples, working people e.g. bank employees as well as by retired pensioners – old people. Earlier holding prestigious positions like to have a fling (food binge) on items of food (considered to be a taboo) helped in merging or rather obliterating the age and status difference. Thus, consumption of SFV has been considered to be a development, offshoot of the changing notions about consumption.

Appendices

Appendix – 1

Historical Background through Marathi Literature
[Content Analysis of Marathi literary sources portraying the attitudes towards eating out]

It has been a backbone of this book that side by side with the economic prosperity goes socio-cultural change, or transition. Since literature is a mirror to society, a brief survey of relevant contemporary literature can corroborate this entire process of transition in a very interesting way. For example, earlier in this book, we have mentioned Gandhian ideology and the traditional philosophy of total denial of materialistic pleasure. Both these concepts are optimized in the language of thrift written large in some of the legendary icon novels such as 'Shyamchi Aai' (Shyam's mother) by Sane Guruji.

Challenge to traditional authorities is reflected in some films of the transition period. A famous Marathi film '*Kunku*' by the legendary director and producer Shantaram starts with a young orphan girl forcefully married to a old widower who has a grown-up son, almost her own age. The rest of the film is about her rebellion, not allowing her husband his marital rights and her struggle for survival in the adverse circumstances. However, the end is happy, the husband realizing his mistake and he himself gets her ready to marry her off to a suitable partner.

We have also noted how the typical pundits gradually caught up with the epicurean pleasure of eating out, and trying different cuisines at home also. The noted Marathi humorist writer late Shri P.L. Deshpande has written satires on the culture of recipe books and the women experimenting their culinary skills on their poor husbands and children. In one of such satires, he describes a woman, Mrs. Kavyakalabai Korke, demonstrating a recipe from a book in women's club. The name of the dish is 'almond skin sweet upama (sheera)'. Mrs Korke shows to her spectators how only the almonds' skins / peals must be used and almonds thrown away. In another classic case of 'Sabudana Khichadi' (pearl sago preparation), a newly married inexperienced girl takes her refuge in a cookery book. But unfortunately the relevant page slips and she bifurcates the word as 'Sabu' (detergent soap) and dana. Thus, instead of pearl sago, the soap makes an entry into the pan and the poor husband starts eating it as though it was snow flurry or bubblegum. Literary stalwart, Late P.K. Atre's autobiographical book '*Karheche Pani*' comprises reminiscences of his early childhood and young college days in Pune i.e. in the early decades of twentieth century. The book is a good indicator of the times.

Atre migrated to Pune from a nearby village Saswad, when he was still a young child. Gradually he got fascinated by Pune which was relatively a very modern place compared to his native village. At that time there were no restaurants (uphargrihas) in Pune as the concept of eating out was not at all popular. Atre's book takes us on an interesting journey of how the eateries were gradually set up in the orthodox Pune.

We have already discussed how the concept of eating out, or drinking tea and coffee was popularized partly because of necessity. Even though the British started bakeries, the Parsees and the Christians here were among the fastest to grab the business opportunity. The city also saw the advent of Muslim Irani cafes at about the same time. As a result, eating non-veg. (at least an egg omelette) ceased to be a taboo, but only after some struggle. Till then it was relished secretly. This stage has been captured in different interesting ways in several books including novels, written a little later.

There was one place called 'Matekar's Hotel' during 1915 or so. The conservatives gradually started frequenting this place. Matekar's *missal* was famous. Up till now the fastidious, choosy, fussy people of Pune had not tasted the Missal dish. It was a mixture of Moongdal or Matki legumes along with onion and 'puri' in a tasty spicy gravy. This hotel was located near Kotwal Chavdi behind Paranjape wada (House).i.e. in Central Pune. Every evening the Punekars started eating at this place. Matekar's Upahargriha was the starting point for more *upahargrihas* which came up one by one. But the other eatables available here were very few. Often biscuits would dissolve if dipped in a cup of tea and form a soup like solution. Near Tulshibaug there was a shop called Mama Basundiwale where the Punekars relished hot basundi (thick milk kheer type dish). Near Pune's Nagar Wachan Mandir (library), two Brahmins sold snacks, the 'jalebi' was famous here. Adjacent to Kotwal Chawadi, two Muslims sold tea. No Hindu had ever dared to step inside here, even though the tea was very tasty. (Religion played a key role as well as the concept of purity/pollution) But one Hindu Sanskrit school teacher named Mr. Govind Hari Thorat, once dared to go and drink tea there. He often used to praise the tea made by the Muslims (considered to be a sort of dare-devil rebels). Another modern Upahargriha known as "Darvas Shantisadana" was opened near "Kirloskar Theatre". There were small rooms for customers and the waiter boys had metal badges and *khaki* uniforms. Tea was served in cups and saucers. Tea cups, tea pot (kettle), milk jug, sugar jar, and spoons used to be neatly arranged in a tray. It was labeled as revolutionary type of upahargriha. A lot of people started thronging the place and very soon it became overcrowded. Very often the waiter boys were bribed 2 annas for reducing the bills. Soon it had to be shut down due to heavy losses incurred by the owner.

Lemon and Soda cold drinks were started in Pune during 1916 – 18. Ice-cream was not available in shops. Later *bhaiyas* sold ice cream on the road, cutting and serving it on banana leaves (nature's own plate, disposable and eco friendly). On Fridays, Balaji Kabli, Bengal gram dal (phutanas) Pandharpuri dale, pink sweet lozenges and *chiwda* were sold on the roadside. Near Rameshwar Mandir a cold drink called *ghota* (mixed with *bhang* like *thandai*) was sold. Atre and his school friends once experimented drinking 'ghota' ground on a mortar and pestle, a tumbler full served in a brass vessel, and almost got intoxicated. On Sundays and Wednesdays a bazaar of second hand things (a flea market) was held in Pune. A lot of people came here to buy things. The streets used to be crowded here. By night at 8.30 p.m. everything, every where was silent (a sleeping town). At that time not many people roamed around here. No road Romeos or street walker hustlers were seen at that time. At that time there was very little traffic. Prostitutes were seen only near temples. Even orthodox people were attracted to prostitutes. Hence, after 8.30 p.m. such men used to walk around streets, visit prostitutes and come back as family was very important for them. Many prostitutes wandered near Tulshibaug and Jogeshwari Temple, near Balaji Temple in Budhwar Peth area, near Belbaug. So called decent prostitutes used to stay near Globe Cinema Theatre.

This description of Pune dates back to the early twentieth century. At that time the Punekars hardly saw silent films which were screened by Industrial film pioneers Jimnagar and Preli. Mr. Atre had seen a film by paying only 2 paise. During Atre's childhood there were only two bridges that connected Pune (1) – Lakdi Pool (Narayan Peth), and (2) – Dagdi (stone) pool (Mangalwar Peth).

Mr. S.J. Joshi, a well known Marathi literary writer and an author of several good books has written *'Puneri'* (a Puneite). In his inimitable style he describes how going to an Iranian café in camp or Deccan Gymkhana area was a great romantic adventure. The author, along with his friend, had visited Lucky Restaurant on Deccan at a very young age – school going – 13 to 14 years. He felt extremely ashamed about his shabby clothes. During those early days smartly dressed boys and men were seen walking or roaming around Deccan Gymkhana. While strolling around Deccan Gymkhana, he happened to notice Lucky Restaurant by chance, and his mind was confused as to whether Lucky came first or was it Deccan Gymkhana. It was considered to be an ultra modern restaurant and it is still considered to be a pivotal landmark in the process of modernization of Pune. He strolled along with his friend Balkya Saranjame. Eating an egg was considered to be strict taboo amongst Brahmin families. Hence, he was scared at first. So on that day they had tea and Khari biscuit only. Both belonged to typical Sadashiv Peth – Brahminical environment. Hence Balkya was relieved that Joshi was not inclined to eating it (egg) on that day. Yet he felt that he had become a rebel by eating cake which contained an egg. During his college days, however, he became a little bold and carried 4 – 8 annas in his pocket and became a frequent customer at Lucky Restaurant. Soon he got habituated to the idea of spending several hours there and observing people. He used to read Marathi novels (romantic ones) and soon realized how every thing about them was so unrealistic. But at a tender / young adolescent age, lasting impressions are almost etched / engraved upon one's mind. Whenever he visited Lucky, and saw the special rooms, he felt that couples inside showed affection to each other. He used to fantasize it in his mind and tried to imagine himself in their role. He too aspired and longed for a girl to meet him. But he felt crestfallen due to his own disheveled appearance. For many days together he and his friend Balkya just sat at Lucky and had tea, but one fine day after mustering a lot of guts / courage (After climbing the steps of rebellion – tea, *maska pav*, biscuits the highest peak was of eating an omelette and toast); he tried to teach his friend Balkya (short form of Balkrishna – Baby Krishna – from rural background

– Bhor) how to use fork and knife for eating an omelette and also told him not to mash it like Puranpoli (Marathi delicacy). Later on the thrill of adventure of eating an omelette too was lost but even then they both continued to visit or literally worshipped Lucky Restaurant as though it was a temple. He kept on imagining at times, even day dreaming of sitting in a special room at Lucky along with his beloved and romancing with her. But he could not find a girl friend there. The baker had a daughter Lucy whom both of them loved (but unexpressed love). After marriage, however, for old time's sake his friend Balkya, along with his wife, managed to go to a special room in Lucky. One day Joshi also took his wife to Lucky. Balkya and wife ordered an omelette and he taught her how to use a fork and knife for the first time. She was trembling scared stiff. He later on told her that he had specially brought her to a special room – for some romantic moment and he kissed her for the first time. Such was the spell of Lucky that converted a Sadashiv Peth boy into a modern man – a romantic hero teaching him how to eat an omelette. Even today he makes it a point to go to Deccan Gymkhana and stare at Lucky – nostalgic memories of his bygone young days flooding his mind. Today, however, the picture has changed. It is no longer a point of attraction for the youngsters and he wonders as to whether any couple ever goes into those special rooms. Today, he finds youngsters going out there out of necessity of eating food and romance that blossomed in his young days is hardly seen today. It is the end of that golden romantic era. He is saddened by the dwindling number of Irani Cafes in Pune and compares Cafes to social institutions. But now they are lack luster, dilapidated crude structures in pitiable condition. He feels that the Udipis have defeated the Irani Cafes.

According to Joshi, before 1978, Pune's Western part was largely dominated by Brahmins – predominantly Chitpavan Brahmins, on the other hand near the erstwhile Kirloskar Theatre near Nanawada, the New English School was not only for Brahmins, but also other castes. His school Nutan Marathi was only for Brahmins, and he could not develop friendship with any other caste person at all in seven years. The children from Deccan Gymkhana belonged to upper middle class – children of lawyers, Doctors, Engineers etc., and were rich well to do, better off as compared to children from Sadashiv and Narayan Peth. Nutan Marathi School was for simple poor families having fake sense of pride in their tradition – middle class white collared people. The author Joshi belonged to a junior middle class stenographer's family, his father worked as a steno in the British office near Huzurpaga School. The girls at these schools were very beautiful and could be recognized even from a distance. Joshi worked as a clerk for 32 years in Government office. He was somehow fascinated by Deccan Gymkhana area. He had 2 – 3 friends living in that area. Once he visited one of his friends and had almost a cultural shock of seeing aunty (friend's mother) in a saree which was normally worn during weddings. He saw his friend's father's sister riding a cycle from college. He was astounded by the modern clan. He felt the life on Gymkhana was like Utopia (fantasy – a land of happiness). He felt ashamed of his appearance viz. (backblock variety Sadashiv Peth up-bringing). He remembers the Gymkhana of his childhood where he enjoyed walking down that road, especially during his college days. But now after living on Deccan for the past 25 years, he feels the entire area has changed today. He considered himself to be a commoner, at times even a misfit, in Gymkhana. Bygone days Gymkhana was more of an idyllic fairy land. Previously retired ICS Government Officers built bungalows here, their children either did medical /engineering or went to F.C. College. Girls were very versatile and talented, played badminton or tennis. Women were busy with their club activities. But today, alas. he laments the scene of Gymkhana changing. Today's bungalows are full of tenants. crowded. The glamour and prestige of being a Rao Bahadur has disappeared today, there is only a landlord. The old fashion bungalow owners have gone, new ones have even changed the names like 'Usha Swapna' to 'Matru Smruti'. He is deeply saddened by the present condition of Gymkhana. Till 1930 – 35 Gymkhana was a fairy land which is deeply imprinted on the mind of Joshi. He was the sole B.A. graduate in his entire family, but at the same time he continued to write. He tells us how Dehu Road, Wanori, Kirkee Ordinance Factory, Depots started. He joined as a clerk in Wanowari Military Accounts, worked there for 32 years, prior to that he worked on meagre wages as a temporary clerk but continued to write in newspapers – first writer of the family. During his childhood Pune was very much like a small town. Gymkhana had barely 50 – 75 bungalows. Jangli Maharaj Road, Tilak Road, Laxmi Road, did not exist at that time. Bhikardas Maruti existed outside the city (considered outskirts of city).

The growth of Cantonment was responsible for counter acting factor in the second quarter of the 19th century, with creation of plural societies very different from the city. New elements, new communities along with the British settled here leading to a gradual transformation. Immigrant artisans also settled, but they, however, were hardly integrated in the social set up of the city.

Mr. Shyam Bhurke in his book '*Pune Ek Sathvan*' has given a very extensive account of Pune seen by him from 1968 onwards when he joined Bank of Maharashtra as an officer. He was from Satara. After retirement he decided to settle down in Pune. He thought of Pune being a pensioner's paradise. He liked Pune's hills, greenery, rivers and the clean fresh air in the evenings. He has humorously described the fitness regime of Punekars climbing hills - Fergusson hill, Law college hill etc. He is also proud of being associated with Pune which is better known for its pioneering educational institutions. The Punekars are very happy, contented and enjoy life. Even though Pune has spread laterally, and vertically, with new tall buildings and multistoried towers (e.g. Aurora Towers in cantonment, or Parvati towers), some old houses still exist in the by lanes – quiet places still.

Main roads are becoming noisy now, whereas if one were to live in a colony like Sahakarnagar, Parvati, one could still catch a glimpse of nature. Bhurke is saddened by the increase in vehicular traffic on the road today as compared to 1968, when Pune was famous for the cyclists. Today it is being over powered by scooters, motorcycles, cars, etc. The roads are littered with rickshaws so much that often one would require to book a rickshaw to even cross the road. Previously Pune was very sparsely populated as a result of which if one were to stand on the footpath and just point out at a hotel, the owner would serve him tea. Today it is impossible. Even though Punekars are criticized for their miserliness, rudeness – curtness, people from outside Pune, after coming to Pune, often like to settle down here.

Pune's Lakdi pool reminds one of the sad battle of Panshet – especially the defeat. At that time it was a jungle. Lakadi Pool meant a bridge made with wooden planks and what we call today as Deccan Gymkhana was a total jungle during the period of Peshwas. The river today is a major link to the city (Laxmi Road) from Deccan Gymkhana or other parts of Pune. Today Bhurke states that the girls (college students) are freely roaming around on the streets often caught teasing boys. He remembers the first electric lamp being fitted on Lakdi Pool and the crowd that had gathered to see it. Previously there used to be kerosene lamps. Another phenomenon is the availability of readymade sweets, sweetmeats, snacks, namkeen as well as milk sold in polythene bags. One of the pioneering names is that of Chitale. Their Shrikhand is very famous and often exaggerated that the Chitales have made Pune a tasty, famous, readymade food place. The serpentine queues for their Bakarwadi are famous. Even outsiders relish them, especially Mumbaikars. Chitales are famous for standard product and uniform pricing and reliability, the efficient management of milk business from Bhilawadi (Sangli), mechanization – pasteurization – storage. Chitales started making sweetmeats in the 1950s in Pune. Today the third generation is efficiently managing business.

Mr. Abasaheb Garware of Garware enterprises believed that there is no short cut to success. Garware Nylons manufactured fishing nets, nylon and wall ropes. They gave donation to college and schools, e.g. MES College is known as Abasaheb College or Bhave School now is known as Mrs Vimlabai Garware School.

Today's Deccan Gymkhana and Hong Kong lane are simply inseparable. Even if one is not able to go to real Hong Kong, one walk into this magical lane is simply worth it. At the beginning of the lane there is a florist who sells fresh beautiful flowers. College girls throng this place for a lot of artificial jewellery, shoes, cosmetics. English / Marathi Book shop, imported goods, perfumes, greeting cards, presentation articles, hair pins etc. are sold here. Today in Deccan as well as Shivajinagar area among every five houses there is at least one NRI person.

Deccan is famous for cricketers, e.g. Prof. D.B. Deodhar lived here. Bhurke mentiones that during the times, novels of Shri. N.S. Phadke influenced young boys and girls, and how couple used to visit Café Good Luck or Lucky on Deccan. One example is Phadke's novel *'12 number chi bas'* (Bus No. 12). But today it is 'Vaishali,' the hub of College students. Vaishali is like a second home to most of the students who often bunk college. (F.C., B.M.C.C.). Dating and chatting are common sights here in the evenings.

Mr. Bhurke has described the atmosphere at Fergusson college in 1920, given by Mr. A.R. Deshpande, a writer from Vidharba. "The hostelites were slightly senior – chatted, gossiped, often wore dhoti kurta, black coat and hat. The boys, girls from city had to walk to the college as there was no mode of transport available at that time. The college professors wore *pagadi* or a stole round their necks and came by tongas. Some of the students, especially boys, were impish, very often they chewed a pan or beetle nut in the classroom. The boys from Nagpur often wore dhotis in a peculiar fashion which resembled sarees, because it was not bifurcated behind.

The great stalwarts like Agarkar, a social reformer, was once the Principal of Fergusson College. The annual fees for Deccan College was Rs. 10 during Agarkar's time in 1880. He, along with Lokmanya Tilak, started New English School. Bhurke goes back and forth while narrating Pune i.e. prior to 1947 as well as later, hence the book oscillates between past and present and looks into future – as Schlesinger had stated: "The long arm of the past is not behind us but within us, hence it affects the present as well as has its seeds for future". Hence when we look into the historical background of Pune one cannot afford to forget the present as well as think in terms of the future.

Poonam Hotel was formerly owned by Mr. Nilubhau Limaye – first hotel to be owned on co-operative basis. Even the waiters, cooks and helpers had a share in the ownership of the hotel. Today it is owned by Kripe Udyog or AV Bhat Udyog Samuh (group). From 1968 Bhurke was resident of Pune. At first he stayed with his friend Patwardhan on Apte Road in a house called Vaidika Ashram, a small type of residence - 2 rooms, and a verandha and a common toilet. He was a tenant. He often walked down Jangali Maharaj Road. Now he cannot accept that Balgandharva, the Sangeet Maestro is no more. Balgandharva Rangamandir was built by PMC. The golden era of Balgandharva and his famous plays and Natyasangeet seems to be still heard in the hall. The people of Pune literally worshipped Balgandharva – the first actor to enact women's roles when women were not allowed to act on public stage. He did it to such perfection that many of the women in the audience did not know that it was a man playing a woman's role. Near Balgandharva Theatre even today Jasmine strings and 'batata wada' are sold; even at Tilak Smarak and Bharatnatya Mandir - two other auditoriums. The Atre – vs N.S. Phadke controversy is famous in Pune. Sambhaji Park today is famous for its street food vending – Bhelpuri as well as electrically operated merry-go-round. It is called lover's park.

AIR is still famous for its singers and programmes. While passing through Gansehkind one is reminded of the Chaphekar Brothers – murdering Mr. Rand, the British officer who was in-charge of controlling the plague epidemic that rocked Pune in 1896, the atrocities committed by the officer still haunt on the minds of many Punekars. Pune is known as the seat of learning and University of Pune, established in 1949 bears testimony to the fact. It is famous for its advanced academic pursuits as well as greenery.

Savai Gandharva Festival in memory of Mr. Rambhau Ganesh Kundgolkar (after his death in 1952) is one more feather in the culture crown of Pune. All the famous musicians, singers from all over India come to Pune and sing or play musical instrument in memory of the great legendary maestro. Singers like Shri. Pandit Jasraj, Tabala Maestro Zakir Hussain have performed here. Pune's Shaniwar Wada reminds us of the golden era of Peshwa rule in Pune. Music stores selling tape records and tapes of famous singers e.g. Alurkar Music House on Karve Road are always crowded with people. Karve road links us to Kothrud Hingane and Paud Road. Millions of two wheelers are seen here now. The legendary writers like P.L. Deshpande lived here. Different drama associations such as Progressive Theatres Association thrived here. The city has seen careers of well known theatre and film personalities such as Dr. Jabbar Patel and Dr.Mohan Agashe blossom here, with revolutionary productions like 'Ghashiram Kotwal'. If one were to walk on Prabhat Road, one would hardly find people walking here, because two / four wheelers have captured the roads. Today Prabhat Road is full of buildings and flats. Old bungalows are being pulled down giving rise to new apartments. Many NRI parents live here alone phenomenonof 'empty nest'. In short, old order has changed giving place to new.

Appendix – 2

Articles from Newspapers and Magazines : A Gleaning

The British started eateries – bakeries, restaurants and finally hotels for their own tastes and comforts. However, the Parsees were not too far behind to imitate them. In fact, many hotels in the cantonment area were managed by Parsees from early 20th Century till about 1960s or even later; while Iranis were also quick in starting Café Restaurants (1920 – 30). The Maharashtrians did not have much of the concept except running 'Khanavalis' (Community Mess) for either immigrants from villages, students, bachelors or labourers in factories. Later on with the advent of college education; they felt the need for teashops and small eateries catering to the lower middle class. They were called 'Upahargrihas' (Refreshment houses). Eating out was looked down upon if not all together a taboo. With the advent of Irani Cafes and college education as well as white collared jobs, eating out of necessity as well as visiting Irani joints became possible. Eating non-veg food was still a taboo and as such relished, though secretly. Whatever hotels existed were essentially for the benefit of the lower middle class (e.g. Poona Guest House). However, this picture changed gradually giving rise to the emergence of eating places. The pace of industrialization and its changing character (sophistication) created a demand for relatively sophisticated and quality food which would satisfy the palate of middle and upper middle classes. Of course the echelons of bureaucracy such as ICS could avail themselves of the fare available in the cantonment areas, like Murat ore, and clubs like Poona or even Royal Connaught Boat Club. The qualitative and quantitative change in the nature of industrialization created the demand for a sophisticated Five Star hotel which would cater to the new rising class.

Interviews of the owners of hotels and restaurants, along with a few other sources have helped in this study to trace how this phenomenon of sophisticated restaurants and hotels started and developed in Pune. The earlier part of this book has already discussed it at length. Now is the stage to reinforce this through gleanings from contemporary newspapers and periodicals. This may be called 'Purposive Deliberate Sampling' as against the usual survey method.

1. Indian Express 12th August 1999 – Pune Panorama – Article, Amit Dasgupta.

Emerging lifestyles are not only in pubs, but also in the men appointed in the interiors of stores. Pune's lifestyle has changed and there is improvement in standard of living. Pune's smaller families with growing incomes like most of the urban Indian have greater buying power. It is especially true of the bludgeoning middle class. Whether it is automobiles, restaurants, pubs and even snack serving pool.

The average Puneite today considers an evening out at a favourite pub or snooker parlour or eating out with family very common. The star variety of restaurants, hotels and pubs that have sprung up in the city over the last couple of years testifies the fact. So much so that it no longer raises eyebrows when Puneites prefer to organize a wedding in a hotel rather than a conventional Mangal Karyalaya.

2. The 'chat pat' cantonment (khau galli) Indian Express 2.8.1999

The SFV caters to all varieties of Indian Fast food such as Kacchi Dabeli, Chatpatti Chaat, Khatta Meetha Dhokla. Old favourite customers have been visiting this place ever since food has been sold on a hand cart. (Main reason being its reasonable pricing and variety).

Pune's changing lifestyle: People love Chinese (especially weight watchers), continental, Thai food. But contrary to the popular notion it is not so much the influx of multinational brands or satellite channels that have influenced the lifestyles. It is search for convenience coupled with the new found affordability.

3. Citadel January 1999

Le-Meridian – A class apart, opulence and luxury are their signature tunes, the latest from the hospitality industry to grace variety. Mr. Julian

Grasim, G.M. of Le Meridian, a 7 – 8 star hotel termed it as the 'most happening place' in the city.

4. Citadel October 1998

All for Pizzas. Pizza Hut on Jangali Maharaj Road – the world's largest pizza chain with over 1,25,000 restaurants all over the world makes Puneite's mouth water.

5. September 1998 Citadel

Jazz Garson, the Thai Menu is changed every 4 months thus change, novelty and variety constitute essence of hospitality, breaking the monopoly.

6. Citadel 1996 November

Extends hospitality industry, has exquisite cuisine and flawless catering, entertainment. Most of the industries have their corporate offices in Metros. This also leads to an exodus of highly qualified professionals in hotel industry towards Pune. Hence it means business for Pune.

7. Citadel May 1996

Magazine *La Dolce Vita* : There are eateries and then there are eateries and in the season of sun, summer vacations, you are probably with guests and what better way to entertain in style than to take them on a gastronomic trip and give them a taste of Pune's culinary culture. Today Italian restaurant, the Café Tarium has taken the Puneites by storm.

Sarja (a restaurant owned by Lata Mangeshkar) at Aundh, Sanewadi, Baner Road – the Malwani food is the latest food. Sarja means the 'sun'. The Swiss cheese garden owned by ABC Farms (Koregaon Park Road). Open air restaurant, Zaika, Mughalai Delights, Riverview Garden Restaurants – at the junction of river Mula – Mutha owned by Mr. Sharad Pingle (tranquility of 'Egyptian Pyramids') serves Chinese, Continental and Persian food).

8. Citadel September 1993

If number of luxury hotels in a city is any barometer, it looks like good living is in. In three years there will be no less than seven glitzy new hotels in Pune and even the big chains are clamoring for piece of action.

9. Citadel December 1996

Throwing money, socializing – pub culture is fast catching up in places like Black Cadillac, 10 Downing Street.

10. Citadel August 1999.

Whither Pune's Iranian Cafes?

The Iranian café has become the very symbol of what an eatery can mean to an average man on the city streets: everything for now is well. But will it last? Some think its future is uncertain. There are only 15 cafes left in the city, about 1/3rd the number that operated a generation ago, says owner of Café Naaz – Mr. Abdul Jaffer. Many Irani peasants, farmers, due to famine in 1920 – 30's, had migrated to Pune. The new generation of Iranis prefers to gò abroad or do other types of business rather than manage Irani Cafes.

11. Pune Times 17th March 2000

Chaat Toppers – Hardayal Maurya, Proprietor of Manmeet at FC Road states that Pune has some of the qualities of Lucknow – a kind of easy going attitude, fond of eating out. Everyone likes to try different types of food other than Gujarati, Maharashtrian, Punjabi, and South Indian – Hence introduction of Lucknowi Chaat.

12. Times of India 7th April 2000

'Aai Ga': Marathi food Snack Centre and Bhelpuri Centre on Paud Road.

Times of India 3rd March 2000

Malwani food – Take away food 'Soul Curry'

The Mavin Kurve couple who sells Mutton vadas etc; coastal cuisine as well.

A quick round up of different hotels as well as to what experts have to say about food – nutrition – aesthetics etc., at the same time food for thought – entry of microbiologist by training venturing into cheese making followed by a frank interview with Mr. B.M. Shetty (Vice-President, Pune Khadya Peya Vikreta Sangh) as well as the growth of pubs, bars culture in Pune a quick glance at Pune's well known Bakeries (a reminiscent of British days – especially Cantonment area in Pune) synthesis of tradition and modernity. Also an article on the entry of Maharashtrians into Hotel management courses. The study growth of 7 – 8 Star Hotel – Le Meridian, Holiday Inn. Pune's fast food culture growing – Pizza Hut. A brief interview of the top hoteliers – their opinions about Pune being a hot spot for hotels. A brief encounter with top notch hoteliers in Delhi, their frank opinions about the future of our hospitality industry. The appendix section ends on a note on changing lifestyles of Pune – at the millennium.

13. December, 20th 1990, Citizen Magazine (Indian Express, Pune)

Irani cafes – cozy corners: Irani cafes need no introduction. Lucky Irani Café and Good Luck ; both the restaurants are very popular and many political discussions have taken place in Café Good Luck over a cup of tea. Deccan Gymkhana was different in those days and the concept of going to a restaurant was not exactly common. Now, however, Good Luck is a landmark for any one giving any kind of direction. Naturally it is impossible to miss it. In the early days, Good Luck Chowk was considered the end of the town. It was a point where old Bombay Pune Road began. Beyond the restaurant there was nothing, recalls the owner. Now of course it is the centre of activities. A couple of years later in 1932, at yet another street corner, this time near the old city, Regal opened its doors to its customers. The Café was the second venture of Mr. Padsha who had earlier started Café Canada at Gadital Chowk. Its situation at the corner of the road and facing Lakdi Bridge made it a favourite with people taking strolls down the road. The situation is no longer the same, says the present owner Mr. Mohamed Aga Padsha. "Our ancestors thought that by choosing the corner business was guaranteed. However, they could not foresee the problems caused by increasing traffic." Padsha should very well know, at the junction of roads parking is the biggest problem faced by patrons.

Everyone would prefer to go to a place where they can park their scooters and cycles nearby. If they park outside, they have to park correctly or else they go to other place. In Camp area, one of the places is Naaz started by Jaffrey Bros. During those times, Quadir Jaffrey recalls, it was the undisputed and famous café. Almost anyone who visited Pune station will be familiar with the Café famous for its Nankatais and cakes. 1961 was a bad year for Puneites (Panshet floods) and the Irani restaurant owners suffered heavy losses when flood waters hit the city. Lucky, Café Good Luck, Sunrise, Regal were all washed away, recalls the owner of Good Luck. Our relatives came to help us out. All Cafes had to start from scratch again. Has the infiltration of Udipi Café and its steaming Idlis and coffee, crisp dosa, divided the clientele? While no clear cut answers are available, this does appear to be the case to a certain extent. Take Sunrise for instance. Started in 1956, Mohammed Sadiz Niroo was one of the partners. Now 75 years he has handed over reins to his son Mehdi Niroomohamed. Initially called Kazemi after original owner, the name was changed to Sunrise. Amongst other places into which Nirro once had a share are Café Olympia and Cafe Try luck in the cantonment area. Meddi Nirromand remarks that the typical Irani Restaurant culture which the Iranis are well known for was actually a legacy of the British. When the British were here they had their typical tea houses and after they left, the Iranis took over. There was a severe drought in Iran and many of the Iranis came to India after hearing that it was a rich place where they could make good money. They stayed on and now the younger generations have been born and brought up here. Café Sunrise has had more than its share of ups and downs. The entire place was washed away in 1961, but once again tragedy struck in 1982 when miscreants burned the place down. "My father just had the place redecorated, wooden paneling, false ceiling etc." – recalls Mehdi who wanted to turn it into a 'A' Grade Hotel / Restaurant. But after the fire, they decided to keep it simple. Sunrise began serving South Indian dishes to attract more clientele, comments Mehdi. This view is reiterated by Mr. Mohammed Padsha of Regal. "Customers who wanted to drink a lot were common when non-veg food was served. And drunken person meant trouble. So we opted out". However, he hastens to add, "It's not that we are a copy of Udipi restaurants, and even Udipi restaurants are fast diversifying into bigger restaurants serving non-veg food, and now we even have permit rooms and serve liquor. We do not sell alcohol because of our religious beliefs. Since non-veg food is preferred after drinks. We felt it was better to be totally veg", he says. Naaz turned veg. a few years ago. "The caterer always caters to the majority" states Abdul Quadir and therefore the non-veg. Samosas were struck off the menu. People are fed up of non-veg. and we cater to people's changing tastes. As a result he too stopped serving non veg. food. Eggs are of course the exception and in all places one can still get tasty omellets. D.P.Pillay (waiter of Regal since 1949) says, "Udipis made no difference. However, rising costs are bound to affect our business. Most cinegoers from Alka talkies, however still cross the road for a cup of tea in the evening." "We depend on Alka crowds" says Aga frankly. Says Mehdi Nirooma, "Udipi people are much better organized. They brought all their staff from their native villages and so we had to change". Everyone stresses that the customers' choice is very important and therefore changes in the menu had to be made. "We cater to a different class of clientele and therefore Udipis have not in that sense really affected us," feels Abdul Quadir. He adds that the present Irani Cafes are continuing the tradition started by their ancestors of serving food at cheap rates. "We are still the most economical," he maintained. While most of the cafes are in snacks business, there are still a few famous one who sell Biryani – well known among these are Diamond Queen / Blue Nile. Comparatively low prices, good quality, quantity and quick service are some of the reasons for their popularity. While Blue Nile is still relatively young, the Diamond Queen has been around since the British days. Although changes have been made in the interiors, they still retain their old world charm. One of the other old time places is George which also existed during British days. These days however not only the menu, but the décor is changed. The aptly named 'Welcome' chairs are fast being replaced by easy wooden chairs imported from England, Poland, Belgium and even Singapore. Contrary to the belief that they require more care, the chairs have in fact lasted for several years without any kind of repairs. "The older generation always went in for old time furniture and fixtures", comments Abdul Quadir.

Old timers also remember the Juke boxes which were one of the attractive features of those places. One of the last existing Juke Boxes was at Café Sunrise. However, this too was burnt down in the fire which destroyed the restaurant. It is not an easy business and this is borne out by Jaffrey, who states with feeling, "We work for long hours, we work with tension, even more so because of the steep rise in prices. Everything is becoming more and more expensive. The costs of raw materials are increasing, gas cylinder shortage has become a common place and we require at least 4 cylinders per day. We have problem of diesel which we require for running of ovens", he moans. "With the increasing competition in the market, it is virtually impossible to keep increasing our rates. Otherwise we will face flak from our customers", he adds. Moreover they have their share of labour problems from time to time. Most of the boys are from South India and go directly to cafes seeking jobs. "We have to turn away at least 4 – 5 boys daily", says Abdul Quadir. He too agrees that running a restaurant means heavy working hours and is very tedious, something which is not easily acceptable to the younger generation. Therefore, the number of restaurants which was formerly in vicinity of around 150 has come down to about 30, he adds. However, he feels business is not bad. In fact it always gets better. An interesting fact he mentions is that 90% of his customers are men. With eating out becoming more popular with Puneites, there is no doubt that despite rising costs, people will continue to frequent these places. After all where else can a cup of hot tea and Khari be tastier than at a familiar and homely Irani Café?

14. Pune Millennium Spectrum

Article by Sanjay Pendse and Sanjay Mukherjee – Source – *Pune Times* (*Times of India* Publication)

The melting pot of Pune's food culture begins to simmer in the wee hours of day as the tea comes to boil in countless flavours at its numerous tea stalls, restaurants and cafes. Its coffee shops, pubs and Five Star kitchens in the meanwhile pause for breath, and set off into suburban sunrise in their newly acquired sedans. A brief mention of the historical past is essential for a backdrop in order to understand the present trends. As Schlesinger puts it "The past is not behind us but within us". Hence a brief mention (description) of Pune's past – It is hard to imagine today, but at the turn of the nineteenth century eating out was not a respectable thing to do for people in the old part of the city.

A great grandmother recollects her daring in 1919 in Pune when she was shocked to look at bread for the first time in 'England returned aunt's kitchen'. This great grandmom was brought up in Deccan Gymkhana area. "They put eggs in it, you become a Christian if you eat it", she was warned. It was a taboo even to touch bread and biscuits, leave aside eating one, due to the ingredients viz. eggs, (non-veg. food).

But today Punekar is as proud as a Parisian of his favourite Boulanger, though eating food cooked outside the home was regarded as decadent, unhygienic and lazy.

So the sprawling Sadashiv Peth had just one family restaurant – Sujata, till the mid 80's. As an old timer recollects, there were violent protests against opening a non.veg. restaurant in the Peths, whereas today, opposite S.P. College (labeled as a Brahmin dominated college), there is a Durga Biryani House which sells Kheema-Pav, Cutlet, etc. So most success stories in this part of the city began roughly 60 years ago. For example, Bedekar or Shri Krishna Bhuvan Missal, Janaseva Arogya Bhavan, Chitale sweets and Savories', Hindustan Bakery owned by Mehendale, Appa's Canteen at Deccan Gymkhana. Being the first generation entrepreneurs moving on from traditional Brahminical, puritanical professions of teaching and preaching, most of them had a very modest beginning e.g. Shri Vaidyas Upahargriha which started way back in 1921, in Raviwar Peth. B.G. Chitales Milk Enterprise was started by Mr. B.G. Chitale, a migrant from Sangli, in Bhilawadi way back in 1950-51 on a modest scale. Today their turnover itself is roughly Rs. 5 – 10 Crores. In sharp contract 'Pune Cantonment' however, presented an entirely different picture. It always had fewer hang-ups about eating out. Possibly because it was home to British Sahib who loved going out in the evenings to a club or an officers' mess. The Sahib clearly taught the Punekars how to eat in style. (Merton's concept of Reference Group behaviour coupled with the impact of westernization, for eating out was clearly and entirely a western concept). Early adaptors like the Parsees, who were close to the Sahib, joined him at the club or restaurant. An old citizen journalist commented, "I remember everyone looked forward to eating at least once at Murat with its Italian connection, on East Street, which is now popular Punjabi Kwality Restaurant owned by Ghias. The brown Sahibs and the officers took over from where the Sahib had left off (Westernization). In the Cantonment Kayani, Café Naaz, Royal Bakery etc. all were mostly started by Iranis, Parsees or Muslims. As cultures and cuisines mixed, the camp quickly acquired a cosmopolitan flavour and became an irresistible attraction for the foodies. It was a great escape for the conservative Punekar. Going to an Iranian Restaurant in Camp or Deccan Gymkhana was a great adventure (e.g. as narrated by Shri. S.J. Joshi in *'Puneri'*, his great bold adventures at Lucky Restaurant with his school friend. "The egg omelette was the forbidden fruit. In fact we had no clue about using forks and knives. So we quietly copied army officers sitting at the other table", confesses a city professor.

But the first real boost to the city's food business came with the industrial boom and rapid urbanization of the 70's and the 80s. The period when Shetty owned Udipi joints like Vaishali and Roopali which flourished because of reasonable prices and cleanliness. But irrespective of cuisine and culture, Pune had already acquired a unique set of ingredients for success, finding and fastidiously preserving traditional recipes e.g. Shri Sarpotdar of Poona Guest House served typical Maharashtrian Brahmin food fare consisting of 'aluchi Pattal bhaji', 'puran poli' etc. For the days of fast, there was Upavasachi special khichadi, thalipeeth (special food item).

There was a whole load of pride and eccentricity in both customers and such proprietors related to concept of quantity, e.g. dal and rice, *varan bhat* served with flow of ghee – called 'Tupachi dhar' or mainly concepts of purity and pollution further steeped in taboos – socially controlled with fears / phobia of ex-communication. "When we used to cook biryani at Dorabjees 30 years ago, I could smell the aroma right here" commented a newspaper vendor outside coffee house. Coffee house itself fostered an almost club – like atmosphere. with regulars congregating here with clock work regularity for a yarn and a coffee. But then "as Punekar, you ought to have a flaming pride about some thing – anything", humourist Shri P.L. Deshpande once wrote. So Punekars thronged to their favourite joints – at Kayani for the biscuits which melt in your mouth, Perfect Sandwich at Marzorin, Zingy Bakarwadi and Mango Burfee at Chitale's, idli dosas and coffee at Vaishali, Roopali, a *missal pav* stall here, a *bhel puri* Walla there. And this despite the fact that these restaurants, like, the Pune shopkeepers, were not known for their service. "If you are in a hurry we are sorry". This was a rude attitude of a typical Puneri shopkeeper. Today quite a bit of that attitude has changed, inevitably because of the competition and growing 'eating out' culture. While in 70s, the only well run restaurant in the camp area was 'Latif' on East Street, today one is hard out to choose from a whole crop of them. At present, the once elite isolated area Koregaon Park has radically transformed into a food hub especially after Rajneesh in the late 70s – Osho Commune. One gets a variety of food stuffs right from Italian Pizza, Le Pizzeria to Mexican, Thai even Swiss. Particularly on North main road of Koregaon Park, there has been a virtual food revolution. In the 4 kms odd stretch there are more than 15 restaurants, serving Swiss, French, Mexican, Italian, Chinese, Vietanamese, Hyderabadi, and Thai, and Indian, Malaysian food. The recent addition is a Japanese restaurant run by Oshoites. The International make up of the population here in the heart land of the Osho Commune with its foreign visitors has much to do with this e.g. The German Bakery run by German Oshoite couple. Mr. Chandawarkar runs a South East Asian Restaurant here, 'Malaika Spice'. Today it is Pune's clientele which is supporting these eateries.

The Five Star hotels too have played their part by setting high food standards in the city. They host food festivals, e.g. In Holiday Inn 'Chinese food Shezuan', festival providing gastronomic delights and introducing new exotic flavours to Puneri palate. Along with the food, the décor and service has improved, from functional to positively classy. The ambience and atmosphere in fact, are now becoming as important as the food itself. So at Malaika Spice, Mr. Chandawarkar has made a point of hanging paintings on the walls, that are for sale (Pioneer in this was the much more modest 'Sunrise Café' in Deccan Gymkhana area). Jazz Garden has made an event of its musical drawings e.g. Rain Dance festival. River View dwells on its eating beside the river and the rustic, eco friendly atmosphere and experience; and Sanskruti on its cultural experience e.g. lac bangle making, garba dance, mehendi drawing- music food and dance, the trio together, far from the maddening crowd in serene tranquility with ethnic flavour. Markets and Supermarkets too echo changing food tastes and culture. The city has grown and attracted people from other cities, immigrants. So Haradayal Maurya's Lucknowi Chaat is a heartthrob amongst collegians, especially of Fergusson College. As the clientele has become more traveled and more cosmopolitan, sauces and dressings now figure on the shelves. Avocados, Zucchinis, Chinese cabbage and a variety of lettuces and broccoli jostle for space with beans and brinjals. The fast food culture is fast catching up – the good old vada pav is unbeatable, but pizzas are the new kid on the block with their speedy home delivery system. E.g. Dominos Pizza, Pizza Hut, and endless adaptations e.g. paneer, capsicum, or chicken tikka toppings. Poona Coffee House has now expanded its menu from simple South Indian Delight to Indian continental and Chinese. Pizza Hut with smoking atmosphere – singing waiters, glass and chrome décor, and loud music is indeed a big place for a mixed clientele in the once conservative Jangali Maharaj Road e.g. In 1999 they launched Usha Uthup song night – song for the World cup.

15. Pune News line – Tea Lounge – by Vinita Deshmukh, source Indian Express – February 28th 2000

Today city weddings very often are not only lavish and pompous but still some of them follow their community panchayat diktats of not holding an evening reception since eating after sunset adversely affects the digestive system and it is still believed that the consumption of food during night is lesser than the day and thus amounts to more wastage. Therefore, at lunch, a lavish spread of lip smashing pure vegetarian food sans onion, garlic, potatoes and brinjals is laid out. But weddings would go on past midnight with fresh pineapple juice kept at corner for evening, besides tea and coffee.

In the cacophony of wedding season and in this age of mindless food consumption, when food is generally outstandingly served, gorged and wasted, here is a segment of the society which still respects food as the fuel of our body, which in turn enhances the minds and soul. The host still clings on to this noble tradition ensured that food was honoured and so were the guest's tummies. Tradition Vs Modernity, the dilemma still persists. But this segment too is slowly shrinking as fast lifestyles catch up – invading practically every caste and community – viz. due to impact of modernization and westernization coupled with at times Sanskritisation especially amongst so called lower castes reference group behaviour.

Every single day has become an occasion to tantalize one's taste buds. Indeed, Puneites are magnificently obsessed with it. Pune seems to be on the forefront of food fads, indulgence No. 1 today for most of them being 'Food Food and more Food'. It has become stylish, up marketwise and helps to indulge in culinary delights, undoubtedly delightful too, as all kinds of food from different parts of the country and world present to teasingly tempt you. There is fusion of ethnic cuisine, coastal cuisine, continental, Chinese, and Thai. Sometimes such a gamut of variety confuses one. You name it and it is there.

Till the late 1970s the passion for eating out was negligible among Puneites. Restaurants then were sparsely scattered in the city and camp (cantonment) serving Indian, Chinese and Continental foods besides Maharashtrian and Gujarati Thalis. Family visits to these restaurants were only occasional, quite rare actually. Udipi joints did brisk business, but there was no accent on making a family outing a regular feature. It was largely confined to student population and bachelors. Suddenly, the complexion changed since the mid 1980s and besides Fergusson College Road, J.M. Road and Karve Road choked with eating houses. Now we find roadside vendors and fancy restaurants in practically every locality. Marathi plays (e.g. Balgandharva Ranga Mandir) and cinema halls might still draw large crowds, but quite clearly eating out and experimenting with new cuisine is the No 1 entertainment in Pune. Hence, as earlier mentioned, it is often the supply that generates demand and vice versa (according to the Economic theory of demand and supply). As Mr. Kanakraj Shetty, President of Hotels and Restaurants Association put it, "Since the last five years Puneites have become immensely passionate about visiting restaurants, particularly on the outskirts e.g. near Pirangut – The Dhaba, or Banjara Hills (ethnic outfit / joint) near Bavadhan. Puneites love to celebrate in a restaurant and taste fancy cuisine e.g. birthday bash at Pizza Hut or New Year Ball at Holiday Inn. They are more traditional in this respect – he adds. It is modernity accompanied by convenience, mainly generated due to paucity of living space and privacy. Imagine, even in the heart of the city where diehard Maharashtrian Brahmin swear by home food that is purely vegetarian, several beer bars and non-veg. cuisine restaurants have sprouted and are doing brisk business. In fact, a couple of them which served typical Maharashtrian snacks like *poha, sabudana khichadi, missal* and the likes have also transformed into full fledged permit rooms which serve non-veg. food. Hotel Poonam which was started by Nilubhau Limaye way back in the 50s today has a bar and non-veg. food. Now the waiters' co-operatives own it. Cooperative movement had attracted Mr. Limaye's attraction; hence a share of the Hotel ownership went to waiters and cooks. But now Pune no more remains only pensioner's haunt, economic prosperity is showing. Observe any restaurant and you will find that visitors comprise of all ages, and come from varied strata of society the conventional and the cosmopolitan, feeble old and fiery young, the little ones (from 3 months onwards), the rich, middle class and poor – they are all here. Birthdays, weddings, anniversaries, success in examination, and family reunions or fed up of mother's cooking – There can be any reason good enough to make a beeline to restaurants. E.g. Hotel Shreyas. Not only have the majority of Puneites become indulgent, but have turned adventurous too. Distance poses no problem as restaurants on the outskirts of Pune are drawing large patrons in fancy cars – affluent couples with expensive indulgence, especially amongst the neo-rich community where money seems to be in copious amount. In many families restaurant bills form a good part of their monthly expenditure. Many times they keep bills for tax purposes. Very often business and pleasure are combined, and they do not seem to be repenting it. Cashing on this opportunity, food entrepreneurs add new temptations with food festivals and special cuisine spreads to satiate our hunger, as we get hungry for innovation to gourmet fare e.g. Pune Food Festival – or better known as Khavaiya (festival). In short, Pune celebrates food festival practically all 12 months of the year barring the Shravan months when many Puneites are still wary about consuming non-veg. food even onion garlic is banned – strict taboo. But apart from rituals, it is also climate-wise bad, as eating such food during rainy season is bad for health. Still popular restaurants during weekends are packed to capacity and people are willing to wait outside for an hour or more e.g. Mudra Veg Restautant on L.B. Shastri Road where people wait in the queue even on footpaths outside. Honestly eating out is the very in thing to do. Many people have turned into *'Khanvaiyas'* in the bargain – They have become connoisseurs, able to enjoy the goodness of all cuisines. Quality of the food served is equally important, but people are almost getting addicted to food. Very often young children demand hotel food – Pizzas, burgers or at times even Maggie 2 minutes instant noodles. Today even in traditional families, children demand noodles. Very often we find kids eating junk food and avoiding roti, dal and rice, etc. Very often young mothers try fancying gourmet food at home e.g. Tarla Dalal's exotic recipes. Young restless teenagers, often tired of mom cooked food prefer to spend their pocket money on outside food. They feel home food is unpalatable, insipid, boring and monotonous. Very often young mothers crib about their children refusing to eat *sabji*, and instead gorging on jam and maggi noodles. Today a fast food revolution has ruthlessly overshadowed home made *dal chawal* (healthy simple meal) instead Pizzas, Burgers, Sizzlers, Noodles, Butter Chicken, Kacchi Dabeli rule.

Today's lifestyles have changed. It is often almost impossible to have dinner before sunset except for fastidious puritanical Jains (i.e. mainly senior old citizens) Nights out, disco-dancing, pub culture, which is a counter culture is fast on the rise in Pune city.

In short, changing the mosaic of the city are various trends – eating out being the most prominent among them.

16. Citadel January 1991 – Article by Pradeep Rodriguez

Changing Scenario of Pune's Culture

Today's booming restaurants indicate how the social crowd is. Most people prefer to have drinks with dinner. Pune is getting more perceptive of night life. A favourite way to pass time for collegians who hang out at cafes restaurants watching neon signs and pretty girls. For example at Venky's outlet at Cantonment off Mole Dina Road, often youngsters drink espresso coffee, milkshake, and non-veg food. Near the University fountain there are lots of street food vendors – better known as *Chowpatty*. Many families with old grannies and small babies in arms come here. This *Chowpatty* brightens at night or late evening. Many University / College hostelites also come here to eat vadapav, kulfi, etc. Young people, groups, couples – car loads of young people screech to a halt – here to eat right from dosas, idlis, bhel, missal, ice-cream to tandoori chicken as well as Chinese and non-veg. food. The night life is fast catching up with young folks here. Amazing number of girls and boys come here as it is a popular night-time pass time with roller skating night dhabas, picnic outings. Royal Connaught Boat Club often has dance, dinner and drink programmes. Yet a lot of people prefer home drinks with no prying eyes on them. Club culture is fast becoming very popular. In the club / hotels very often twenty plus age group comes. Most of them attend parties 2 to 3 times a week – they however prefer smaller parties, invite 2 – 3 couples for dinner and drive out of town for picnic. Each friend brings a dish / an item. Large number of hotels of city plan a number of parties e.g. Sports – Cricket event, e.g. World Cup 96, Soccer - Bash at Hotel Blue Diamond – most of such parties go on till wee hours in the morning – 3 a.m.

As forty plus Priya, mother of a twenty plus says during her young days girls were not allowed to go to parties. It was strict taboo, whereas today she is more liberal with her children. Changing cultural norms are giving way to popular culture. Though, parents are still suspicious about girls and boys going out more. A young girl of twenty plus was grounded for a month at home because she came home late after midnight from a dance party. The youngsters of twenty plus often booze (drink) at a party. Drinks are free flowing. People often get tipsy and drunk. In sharp contrast parents do not object to girls attending an NDA Ball. The cadets are respected gentlemen and all parties wind up by 10 at night. It is today not just partying. Turf club also organizes Tuesday, Wednesday Tambola. Royal Connaught Boat Club organizes dinner and dance accompanying Tambola show.

17. Bar Pub Culture – July 1921 (Citadel Article – By Herculus Mcdowell)

Cigarette smoke envelops the bar. Occupants are often found in semi-drunk state. A half-clad girl is singing tunes and dancing, somewhat like the yesteryears vamp of the film world, Helen. Noise level is jarring to the ears. Time is 9.30 – 10.30 at night. Clients are served with drinks – papads / chips, peanuts to eat, garbage bins are littered over. Some Pune bars have floated a cabaret bar. Bars and girls are inseparable. Prostitution and alcoholism go together – girls here appear to be no less than street walkers. Neon lights create dark cave like tavern type hazy atmosphere with cramped seating arrangement bar is full of men – women / girls soliciting prostitution. Clientele is regular. They have a few pegs and enjoy women like harem. Even on Pune-Satara Road – lots of bars are located. The men here drink by quarter and not peg. Every major street appears to sport a bar apart from five star hotels catering which relieves you of your wallet.

The other angle also creeps in at some places, a lodge is attached to a permit room e.g. a lodge at Laxmi Road sports bar. On the staircase one bumps into people from outside Pune. So called couples, not married, can book a room here by the hour. The clientele consists of even businessmen /executive, journalists, even college kids. (Sometimes rickshawala has to pack them home, totally drunk). At times people drink more than their wallet. Fights and arguments ensue between drinking patrons. Alcoholism and betting / gambling are equal partners. Today the trend has been set to go out and drive to a pub – mostly outskirts of Pune. The major advantage is you can even carryout your own drinks, as well as snacks. Pune police do not disturb them to shut down at 11 p.m. Those are the only places where one can drink throughout the night with no disturbance whatsoever.

18. Article, Sakal - A Marathi daily – Dated 8th April, 2000.

"Increasing number of Maharashtrian students being attracted towards hotel management courses". (By Deendayal Vaidya).

An anecdote is often told regarding hotel business. If one Marathi and one South Indian man (Shetty) both were to be given Rs. 5 lakh each, what would both of them do with it? The Marathi man will buy a land plot, build a house and rent it out for Rs. 10,000/- per month. He will rent out another place to a South Indian to run a hotel business. On the other hand a South Indian will pay a couple of lakhs to the Marathi man and buy the place and set up the hotel. The parable/humour/satire of the story cannot be missed. But this is the sad state of affairs of Maharashtrian men. The writer Deendayal was curious about finding out regarding as to how popular this profession of Hotel management was. He visited Bharati Vidyapeeth Hotel Management Department during "Summer Feast" – Ice cream Festival. He therefore had an opportunity to interview a couple of teaching faculty as well as a few students / past students. He interviewed Prof. Sachin Rairikar (faculty member). Mr. Rairikar stated that the outlook of looking at hotel management as a career / profession is gradually rising especially in field like airlines, shipping companies, big Five star hotels, private companies, Government canteens as well as in catering and marriage halls, and tourist agencies. Maharashtrian youth are not far behind as far as employment in these fields is concerned. In Bharati Vidyapeeth Hotel management course, more than 70% are Maharashtrian students. Prof. Sunita Sangle too endorsed the same opinion as Prof. Rairikar and further explained that though she has graduated from Maharashtra State Institute of Hotel management and Catering Technology – Pune, she at present conducts coaching for Bakery – baking. Hotel Management profession is no longer dominated by a certain caste/ community. Prof. Rairikar also explained the curriculum courses taught. Accordingly students learn Indian and Continental cuisine, Three star hotels food – cuisine – serving food as well as mixing cocktails and room service. Every morning students have to prepare complicated recipes (degree students). Every morning students have to prepare breakfast in 20 minutes at Government Canteen. To get used to five star hotels, these students have to learn how to set table, bar, bedroom arrangements. As most of the original recipes are in French, students are required to learn French e.g. a student Miss Parinita Bedekar was interested in studying hotel management in Std. 8th in school itself. Hence she decided to learn French in school itself. Principal Anthony De'Souza had obtained a degree in hotel management after having worked in different hotels in 1990 – he shifted over to academics – teaching line. From 1980 – 1990 was a very fruitful decade for the hotel industry. After completion of degree course, campus interviews are held by Hotel Oberoi, Taj etc. Principal D'Souza wanted his students to get good training in 5 star hotels. He said completion of course leads to a well groomed overall development of personality especially poise, grace and self-confidence. For this course students are required to learn a bit of engineering (Mechanical skills), law, food nutrition, health sciences, hence to pass a comment that hotel management is an inferior profession meant for people without brains is not true at all. During holidays students take apprenticeship at Taj or Oberoi. Abhijit Jagtap and his wife (both past students of the college) have recently opened a fast food joint at Karvenagar. He often has to cook if help is not available, his wife serves food herself – he says running a hotel is not an easy job at all. Mr. Swapnil Pradhan is a student. He is interested in cooking new continental type cuisine. After studies he, wants to try for a job in U.S.A. On Sundays he cooks at home. It is very difficult for a student to get a job in Five Star hotels or to start a hotel for himself. When he was asked about the lacunas among Marathi students in hotel industry, he said Marathi students should be ready to work in any type of job. There should be dignity of labour right from cook to waiter, anything. For studying hotel management for 'free seat' yearly expenses are 14,000/- whereas for 'payment seat' it is Rs. 30,000/- as told by Rahul Bhagwat and Milind Tamhankar, both students. Both agreed that after completion of course getting a job in a good hotel is very difficult. This was affirmed by Kunal Jhaveri. For apprenticeship we have to exert influence or take help from influential people e.g. to work in Oberoi Hotel from all over India there are 500 applications. Only 20 were selected (all probably with heavy influence or connections). The hotel management course is like a mirage at times. The glory, fame and glamour are only temporary – one has to work for 17 – 18 hours a day – sacrificing family life. But Mr. Nirmal Sarang who worked on an American Shipping Company is hopeful about a change in situation, Prof. Amitabh Bhopatkar is also hopeful that hotel management course/career will have bright days ahead.

Future Trends for Restaurants / Hoteliers

Most of the Restaurant Managers agree that one trend that is developing is that of people turning towards healthier food and lighter cuisine. People are becoming calorie conscious like European and Western clientele. Vegetarian food finds favour with such customers.

Today many restaurants are thinking of separate vegetarian sections with their own separate kitchen. Thanks to the pioneering efforts of Dr. Gangwal, which would be one of the reasons why even though Sanskruti is away from the city – near Loni, it has managed to create a flutter with its pure vegetarian food.

But Gul Anand of Jazz Garden thinks that restaurants in Pune still have an uphill task. "Right now we are just educating people about food. We are not even cooking one fourth of the food we can cook. Even on Christmas Eve if we cook mixed sea food platter with champagne and caviar sauce, some people want roti with it. At times pendulum oscillates between tradition and modernity, and modernity is still a penchant, for old stereo type food persists i.e. *subji* or chicken roti dal rice. Hence as Joseph Gus field (1966-*American Sociological Review*) has stated, tradition and modernity are not too polarities but are very much dependent upon each other. Nobody talks about how food habits can change the society, like they talk about art and music. Very often we find food habits and tastes being grafted on to an individual. To put it in Marxian terms, it is often a synthesis of thesis and antithesis – impact of westernization coupled with reference group behaviours, and synthesis, a blend of both. That is why as Mr. Anand comments even with sizzler and chicken, people want to eat roti, more of a hybrid. As Mr. Chandavarkar remarks a new breed of restaurateurs educated in food business (not just hotel management, but also those who have worked hands on) will come up and open their own restaurants in the first ten years of the new millennium. For example, Chef runs restaurants or specialty places which will be above competition. It is already happening in Pune. A new column by Anjali Mukerjee on food – elevates the mood when it comes to food. Pune has come a very long way in surprisingly short space of time, to the arrival of cuisines that are both traditional and global.

Lesser known Eateries of Pune

Maharashtrian fare – Vaidya Upahargriha was started by Shri. Raghunath Ram Chandra Vaidya in 1921 in Raviwar Peth. It has the best *missal* and *puri-bhaji* in town. Now it is run by his son Shankar Vaidya. He also sells Thalipeeth, Kanda-poha, and Shev-chiwda with grated coconut, coriander and onions. He also sells Kolhapur hot variety. This place is often frequented by Marathi filmstars. It is open from 7.30 to 11.30 a.m. and 3 to 7 p.m. In the old city, mobile food vendors with hand carts have on an average more than 150 customers a day. Ganapati season brings in lots of customers. On the pavement at Bund Garden is Bhelpuri sold by Ganesh Bhel – 60 years old. Now the sons Jagdish and Chandrasekhar continue the business. In Camp area Café Mahanaz owner sells vegetarian Irani Samosas as well as Falooda. Vrindavan Juice Bar (Near Harjivan Hospital) sells Pavbhaji, and sandwiches.

There is also one place called Litton Sweets opposite Gurudwara at Ganesh Peth which sells sweets and Namkeen. The owner migrated from Rawalpindi in 1947. He makes best *gulabjamun* and coconut milk burfi as well as *balushashi.* In the old city, Sadashiv Peth a congested area, Buwa Ice-cream, the best home made ice-cream is famous. We find reference to it in Marathi plays / books e.g. N.S. Phadke's hero of the novel takes his girl friend to have Buwa's ice-cream. Many Marathi film-stars patronize it even today. Mr. Sharad Talwalkar, 1st Chhota Gandharva, Late. Mr. P.L. Deshpande and even old Hindi film actors like Mr. Dev Anand still go there when they comes to Pune. Even Late Shri. Bhimsen Joshi, the most well known music-maestro used to frequent it.

Appendix - 3

Qualitative Material from Interviews

Interview Schedule – I

HOTELIERS / CLUBS

1. When was the hotel / restaurant started? Are you the Owner / Proprietor / or is it in Partnership.

2. What was the initial Investment?

3. Whether it is a family business or an independent enterprise?

4. Where are you originally from – Pune / Mumbai or some other city / state?

5. What is your educational qualification?

6. How big is your family, size, number of dependents, how many of them are helping in your hotel business?

7. What is your total earning? (approximately).

8. Do you accommodate some other relatives from your native place? (Funding for education or place to stay etc.)

9. What is the type of clientele / customers catered to?
   (a) Rich class / corporate clientele
   (b) Upper Class
   (c) Middle Class
   (d) Students / college students.

10. What type of employees are hired by you?
    (a) Skilled
    (b) Semi-skilled
    (c) Non-skilled / unskilled

11. Do you hire workers from Pune or your native place? Do you absorb local talent? Could you explain the caste / religion / and the sexwise composition?

12. What is the opinion of your customers about your restaurant?
    (a) Good food
    (b) Moderate price
    (c) Hospitality
    (d) Centrally located place

13. Are you a member of Hotel owners Association, if so why?
    (a) To manage problems – like high water tariff / electricity.
    (b) To manage surprise raids by Sales Tax / Income Tax officers

14. What are the problems faced by Hotel Owners Association?
    (a) Absenteeism
    (b) Lack of funds etc.

15. What is your contribution to social service?
    (a) Donations
    (b) Funds for Charitable Trusts

16. Do you feel that the service sector encourages migration / self employment / like minded caste fellows / relatives to come here?

17. Do you think that employment is above community level (Parochial level) or does it encourage migrants in general to Pune city in search of employment?

I POONA GUEST HOUSE

1. The owner is Social work oriented, believes in charity and old values. He is from Pune and started business way back in 1936. at present it is the 3rd generation. Initially his mother started it, later the owner's (grandfather) and at present his sons. It is family business. Way back in 1936 a full meal used to cost 2.1/2 annas, seating arrangement was on paat (wooden planks) placed on the floor.
2. The owner employs 75% people from outside Pune, e.g. Latur, Udgir, Konkan, Vidarbha, and sometimes even to the extent of getting them from Bengal. 23% are from outside Maharashtra. Most of the training is imparted at Poona Guest House itself. Some of his workers are even Muslims and Udipis. Most of his workers are non-skilled or semi-skilled. Workers from all castes, religions and sex are hired here.
3. He specializes in typical Maharashtrian Brahmani food (earlier the thali was for Rs 25/- only). Senior owner (the father) does not believe in trying out new types of dishes like pavbhaji, whereas his son believes in introducing new dishes. He even does outdoor catering business. The son is more practical / modern. There is a generation gap between himself and father. Senior owner believes in serving authentic Brahmin food alu patal bhaji (colocasia leaves – Arum gravy dish),Thalipeeth, Bajiro chivda (snacks).
4. Initial investment was Rs. 20,000 borrowed from Mr. Pendharkar (noted Marathi film personality). Old film / theatre personalities such as Shripad Joshi, Prabhakar Panashikar, Late Madhu Apte, Late Smt. Bhakti Barve used to frequent 'Poona Guest House'. As local laboUrers are not interested in working here, he has to hire migrant laboUrers.
5. Clientele include old Marathi theatre / film stars to lower middle class family members. Mostly Marathi middle class. There is nothing fashionable or jazzy about it. At present there are 28 rooms for staying.
6. He has lodging and boarding facilities and gives only to families; not to single men.
7. Owner's son does outdoor catering e.g even at outstation places like Kolhapur, Belgaum. He is also actively involved in food festivals. The owner has lamented the growing incidence of Marathi food losing in authenticity. He was very critical / skeptical of the new so called Maharashtrian joints (e.g like Hotel Shreyas,

selling Chola Bhatura, Pav Bhaji – who charge Rs. 75/- per Thali). He said that the Maharashtrian tradition has given way to other things like Punjabi, South Indian, and also due to heavy impact of Western culture to fast food etc.

II CAFÉ GOOD LUCK

1. The owner was an elderly man who started it in 1936. He has died in 2002.
2. The initial investment had been Rs 3000/- only in 1936.
3. He sells non-vegetarian Irani food + vegetarian food. He was an immigrant from Persia (Iran). (In the 1930s due to severe famine and drought he and his family had migrated to Pune).
4. He hired all local talent i.e. 10 – 12 people from Pune and trained them himself.
5. All sections of society are his clients – mostly college students / office goers frequent this place as it is reasonably priced.
6. The owner was very skeptical as to whether his sons and grandsons would ever be interested in running this family business.
7. He charges moderate prices for food here.
8. At present, full vegetarian thali is also available here at a moderate price to cater to the changing tastes and demands of the customers.

III HOTEL VAISHALI

1. The owner is from South Karnataka. It is a Udipi Hotel (famous for serving South Indian Snacks).
2. Initially it was known as 'Madras Café'. It was started in 1951 in a modest way. Initial investment was Rs. 2000/-. He was an immigrant from Udipi (South Canara) and came here to join his maternal uncle in the food business.
3. He hired most of the servants from his native place Udipi. Nearly 200 people are hired by him i.e cooks, helpers, waiters, sweepers.
4. He has himself imparted the training to them here. Sometimes labourers from Kolaba, Kolhapur district are also hired.
5. He has a mixed clientele mostly college students, Fergusson College, B.M.C.C College students throng this place. Office goers/ friends/ couples / families come here.
6. He believes that maintaining cleanliness / hygiene rendering quality food is more important than merely profit making.
7. The dosas available in the year 1951 have the same quality even in 1999 and that too at a moderate pricing. Even if the prices of essentia

goods like oil and onion have gone up. In the 1970s he changed the menu from purely South Indian to Vegetarian fast food – Veg. Burgers, Sandwiches, Ice-cream, pizza, milkshakes etc. He caters to changing demand of the public.

IV HOTEL PATHIK / HOTEL SUNFLOWER – 2 STAR HOTELS

1. The owner is a B.Sc. in Agriculture from Kopargaon (near Pune). He hails from an agricultural family.
2. He opened the hotel in 1972 with an initial investment of Rs. 8 lakhs.
3. He has close political connections with Congress Party.
4. He sells purely Veg. food and has recently launched fast food. Hotel Sunflower owned by wife.
5. His clientele includes business class, film and theatre personalities – due to proximity to Balgandharva Rangmandir). His clientele also includes tourists. He is one of the chief organizers of Pune Festival (during Ganpati).
6. During Pune Festival, he provides residential facilities for tourists, performers – dancers, singers etc. He has 18 rooms fully furnished out of which some are A.C.
7. He has hired local talent from Pune as well as from his native place Kopargaon. He has 25 workers involved in lodging. 30 workers involved in restaurant business; and 60 for newly started Sunflower Hotel.
8. He is also involved with MTDC tourism. He was critical of the functioning of MTDC. He lamented that Pune lacks in tourism activity and thereby has adverse effect on hotel industry. He worked with MTDC for 4 years.
9. He has recently started selling Chinese and Punjabi vegetarian dishes.

V JOSHI WADE-WALE

1. The enterprise was launched in 1989-90
2. The owner aims to serve / cater to the lower middle class people, vada-pav – was available in 1989 for Re. 1.50 p only.
3. The owner is a B.Com, helps his wife. Initial investment was Rs. 1.5 lakhs in 1989-90.
4. People employed here are mainly 10 – 15 trained young boys from Latur, as well as Pune. Local talent is also absorbed. Runaway

kids, 8-9th standard pass boys, eat here and stay here and learn about cooking.

5. The clientele includes people right from labourers, daily wage earners / college students / office goers to rich and four wheeler owners – couples, families and small kids. Thus, wide strata of society (economic / social class) come here.

6. In December 1998, Mastani – Milkshakes (Mango + Ice cream + Mango milk shakes) was launched in Gauri Mastani House which his wife manages. There are 5 outlets in Pune (1) Balgandharva (2) Kothrud (3) Nasik Phata (4) Wakdewadi (5) Hadapsar. The owner strictly believes in cleanliness – hygiene as well as quality of food. He believes in low pricing so that even the poorest can afford to buy it. It is a mini-meal by itself.

VI POONA COFFEE HOUSE (PCH)

1. The owner is a prominent (MP) from Pune. It was started in 1978. Earlier only South Indian snacks were served. But later Lunch, Dinner, Fast-food were also sold. But now all kinds of Vegetarian and Non-Vegetarian dishes are available.

2. It is 'A' grade hotel. Local talent is absorbed. 50-55 people both skilled as well as semi-skilled work here.

3. Clientele: They cater to all kinds of clients such as rich, upper middle class. College students, business executives, office goers / foreigners, cosmopolitan mixed crowd / young to middle age etc. They also have a bar and hence serve alcoholic drinks.

VII HOTEL SHREYAS – A GRADE – NON STAR HOTEL

1. The owner launched it in 1966.
2. At present 48 rooms are available here.
3. The initial investment was Rs. 10 lakhs. A new additional conference room has been constructed.
4. The clientele includes middle class, upper middle class as well as business class.
5. Local talent is absorbed from Pune.
6. Pure Maharashtrian vegetarian food (*thali*) – Rs. 60 /- per thali.
7. The hotel has homely atmosphere and they believe in personalized service. It is a family business.

VIII KOHINOOR EXECUTIVE – 4 STAR HOTEL

1. The owner started the hotel initially in partnership.

2. The initial investment was Rs. 20 – 22 lakhs in 1989.
3. The hotel has a capacity of 58 Rooms, Conference hall, Restaurant and Bar.
4. They serve both Vegetarian and Non-vegetarian food.
5. The customers are mainly company executives from local companies like Themax, Bajaj etc., as well as local neorich, upper middle class.
6. Out of the labourers hired 80% are skilled trained workers (Permanent one) and 20% are casual labourers. Local talent is absorbed. The owner believes that by maintaining quality and adding to a variety of cuisines, it contributes to the over all development of his personal staff.

IX HOTEL ASHIANA / ASHISH PLAZA – 3 STAR

1. The owner started Hotel Ashiana in 1977. Ashish Plaza was started in 1994. The initial investment was Rs. 6 -7 lakhs per room. There are 35 rooms with an occupancy of 80%. The clientele is mainly from Corporate Business class.
2. The hotel serves both Vegetarian and Non-vegetarian food.
3. Local talent is absorbed here. Out of 120, 1/3rd are skilled and the remaining are semi-skilled.
4. It is a family business – both the father and sons are involved in business.
5. It is essentially meant for corporate clientele. So Conference facilities are available.
6. The publicity of the hotel is by word of Mouth. The family mainly concentrates on hotel business.

X HOTELAMBROSIA – (Woman Entrepreneur) – Hotel Located on Outskirts of PUNE – BAVDHAN.

1. The owner is a lawyer and teaches at a well known college in Pune.
2. It was started in 1991 along with her husband who is also a practicing advocate. They had bought land initially for cultivation to build a farm house – 50 acres, Rs. 4 lakhs cost of the land. They later planned to develop it into a Holiday Resort.
3. The hotel serves vegetarian food. The owner (wife originally belonged to Bangalore, but had come to Pune 35 years ago to study Law and has since become a resident of Pune city).
4. The clientele is mainly from upper middle class, young couples or picnic goers.

5. The labourers are hired from Pune, whereas the cooks are hired from Punjab and South India. Out of which 10 – 15 are skilled workers. The total number of workers is 150.
6. The owner's wife is grooming daughter to pursue hotel management. She plans to develop it into A holiday resort.
7. The clientele include Industrial / Corporate. And big celebrations are held here such as Iyengar Yoga Institute – Anniversary Celebration.
8. They also serve Chinese Vegetarian food.

HOTELS COVERED IN CANTONMENT AREA

XI HOTELS – DORABJEES (OLD PARSEE TYPE FOOD EATERY)

1. The Restaurant was started by an immigrant from Navsari(Semi Urban town in Gujarat) in 1889. At present it is managed by 3rd / 4th generation.
2. They employ local talent. They have been trained here.- 7 apprentices.
3. It has a homely atmosphere and loyal customers for 50 – 60 years.
4. The clientele includes a wide spectrum of society, right from very poor to middle class to very rich people (mostly Parsees). They also do outdoor catering for Navjot, Wedding etc). They also provide dabba (tiffin) facility.
5. They believe in quality, hygiene and personalized touch for their valuable customers.
6. They believe in social service and they often give food to blind school children and orphans.

XII LATIF'S (MUGHALI NON-VEGETARIAN FOOD)

1. Latif was launched in 1963. The owner was initially a caterer. Later he bought it for Rs. 1.5 lakhs.
2. It is essentially a family business. At present 3rd generation runs it. The son and his mother as the father (initial owner) died. The son has studied at Food Craft Institute in Pune. The clientele includes upper middle, rich class, college students, come here for fast food – pizzas etc. Nowadays Chinese, Continental food is also available.
3. In 2010 May interview *(Indian Express*). The owner lamented about the ever increasing cost of mutton and fish as a result, they have now incorporated Punjabi Tandoori, Butter Chicken dishes

into their menu. However, traditional Parsee dish 'Fish Patra nu macchi' (Fish baked and served on a plantain leaf) is still sold here.

4. A total of 12 workers are hired.

XIII KAMLING–CHINESE AUTHENTIC FOOD

1. The present owner's grandfather started it in 1941.
2. It is a joint family business since 1952-60. The owner is from Mumbai (her parents immigrants from China). Initial investment Rs. 6000/- in 1941.
3. Clientele – mostly upper middle class, rich class, college students as well as foreigners.
4. Local talent hired.

XIV MANGALVIHAR (VEGETARIAN SOUTH INDIAN)

1. It was launched in 1963.
2. The owner's son manages it and has a diploma from Food Craft Institute, Pune.
3. About 20 people are employed here who are semi skilled, local talent is absorbed.
4. The customers are middle class, college students, working class, office goers, etc.

XV RITZ (OLDEST GUJARATI FOOD IN PUNE)

1. The hotel is 120 years old formerly owned by a different owner, later bought by others.
2. There are four partners in the hotel.
3. It has acquired four star status now. The owner hails from Mumbai.
4. Gujarati Thali costs Rs. 125/-
5. Clientele – Corporate, rich upper middle class families, business groups.
6. There are lodging, boarding facilities – 24 rooms booked all year round (Corporate business clientele).
7. There are about 50 – 60 people employed, local talent skilled 4 – 5 cooks trained, semi-skilled.
8. The owner also owns Hotel Rajadhani, opposite Pune Zilla Parishad.
9. It caters to quality client trained manpower (trained in food management) ethnicity along with sophistication – purely vegetarian food.

XVI SAHARA (VEGETARIAN DINING HALL 'B' GRADE HOTEL)

1. The owner is an Irani Muslim – started in 1993-94.
2. The clientele is middle class, office goers, and businessmen.
3. The staff hired is semi-skilled from Pune, local talent is absorbed 15-16 people trained in the hotel itself.
4. They serve Gujarati Thali for Rs. 60.

XVII HOTEL BLUE DIAMOD – FIVE STAR HOTEL

I had interviewed the then CEO of Blue Diamond (Corporate owned by the Poona Industrial Hotels Pvt. Ltd.), Now owned by the Taj Group of Hotels Pvt. Ltd.

1. The Hotel was started by Mr. S.L. Kirloskar in 1969, which was initially managed by his brother Mr. Ratnakar Kirloskar.
2. Initial investment was about 3 crores or so.
3. The Kirloskars originally from Karad (Satara) known as Kirloskar wadi after the great luminary Late Shri Laxmanrao Kashinath Kirloskar.
4. Previously 75 per cent of the shares were held by Kirloskars in Blue Diamond.
5. The clientele mainly belongs to the Corporate Business Executive class.
6. Local talent 99.9% is absorbed here.
7. Kirloskar's have an engineering background and not hotel business at all.
8. It was then managed by Mr. Atul Kirloskar and his aunt Mrs Shashitai Kirloskar (wife of late Shrikant Kirloskar – son of S.L. Kirloskar). Atul is son of late Chandrakant Kirloskar.
9. The menu includes Vegetarian and Non-vegetarian food, Punjabi, Continental, Chinese etc.
10. The hotel occupancy was 60 per cent.
11. There were 400 employed workers (skilled highly trained the CEO has a degree in Food Management as well as business management from abroad). There are also semi-skilled workers.
12. The Poona Hotels Pvt. Ltd. group was in the midst of handing over to Taj Group of Hotels.
13. The CEO has stated that there was a lot of competition, because 5-7 hotels which had been started recently such as Holiday Inn, Le Meridian. Hence the monopoly of Blue Diamond as a business hotel was being challenged by other new hotels.

CLUBS

I POONA CLUB

1. The Poona club is 113 years old. In 1941 the President was Mr. Claud Lynt. At present President is an Indian Businessman
2. After 1947 all presidents are Indian. I had interviewed one who was one of the Vice-Presidents of the Club.
3. It was initially a polo Gymkhana club owned by the British. Land owned by Poona club leased out to RSI club (Rajendra Singhviji Club – Army Armed Forces Club) one of the five best Golf courses in the country.
4. The clientele includes the elite of Pune (cream of society) upper middle class and 20 per cent service class – Government officials and about 70 per cent are corporate members many of whom are Rotarians.
5. Mainly local talent is absorbed here. Skilled 50 per cent, semi-skilled 50 per cent as well as casual workers.
6. The menu comprises of both Vegetarian and Non-vegetarian food and alcohol drinks are sold.
7. There were 21 rooms – 85 per cent occupancy. During racing season 120% occupancy.
8. Some of the distinguished members of this club are Baba Kalyani, Atul Kirloskar, Ram Jethmalani, Nana Chudasama, Suresh Kalmadi, etc.

II TURF CLUB

I Interviewed General Manager of the club.

1. The Turf Club is part of Royal Western India Company Ltd. Registered under Companies Act, started in 1990 –Bombay Soldiers Club in 1917 and was gradually given to Turf Club.
2. The Club had hired 100 permanent staff and had absorbed local talent out of which 70 were from Khed Taluka. And had also hired casual labour.
3. During the racing season there is 60 to 70 per cent occupancy.
4. Essentially non-vegetarian food served.
5. The Total workers hired were 200, out of which 120 are skilled. Unskilled are four, 100 are semi skilled.
6. The members of the club are from very rich / upper middle / neorich / business / industrialist / corporate class.
7. The room rate – tariff Rs. 850/- per single room (member) Rs. 1000/ - Double Room – for members.

8. The occupancy 50-60 per cent no check out time. 24 hours any time.
9. Due to recession in the Year 1999-2000 attendance for Racing club is only 40 – 60 per cent.
10. Many luminaries / members of the Club such as Air Comodore Vijapath Singhania (Raymond / J.K. Synthetics), Shri Vijay Mallya, Chairman U.B. Group, Dr. C.S. Poonawala (Serum Insititute), Mr. Sham Ruia (Rapatcast) Rapicut Carbide.
11. The membership 30 years ago was only Rs. 15,000 /- per year. In the year 1999 it was 1,50,000/-.
12. There are 8,500 members.
13. Many top industrialists like B.G. Shirke – son Vijay Shirke, Weikfield – Malhotras, Atul Kirloskar often sponsor races. Dr. Cyrus Poonawala gave Rs. 20 lakhs for sponsoring race, he also owns many horses.

MULTIPLIER EFFECT (QUESTIONNAIRE)

(Employment Related Sub-Contracting)

1. Name of the Hotel
2. Whether hotel / club served vegetarian – non-vegetarian food.
3. From where /whom do you get your supply of raw materials, e.g. rice, wheat, fruits vegs, dates, milk, cereals, pulses, meat, poultry, eggs, oil, ghee, cold drinks etc.
4. How much quantity do you require per day in kgs / quintals / litres etc.
5. Do you buy on monthly/ six monthly or yearly basis ?
6. Who are your suppliers, traders etc. ?
7. Do you buy from wholesale traders or retail traders ?
8. Does your trader give you a discount, if so, how much ?
9. Do you get a certain fixed amount of discount or does it vary from season to season or to be more specific the market situation ?
10. Do you hire outside services (maintenance facilities) e.g. gardening, cleaning, house keeping, front office management, income-tax consultants ?
11. Do you buy magazines / periodicals other than daily newspapers from outside ?
12. Do you rent out your hall / terrace /lawn etc., for marriages and parties ?
13. Do you yourself do all the decoration especially of flowers, electrical

bulbs – illumination / music / video shooting / cameras photos or do you sub-contract the services and get help from outside ?

14. In case of marriage / thread ceremony do you provide the Brahmin Priest for officiating the ceremony.
15. Do you have alcohol/beer permit (Sub-Contract) ?
16. Do you hire outside services for security reasons ?
17. Do you have a regular *paanwala* / florist etc. ?
18. Do you hire outside services of singers, musicians etc. ?
19. Do you do booking / travel agency ?
20. Do you have a 'T' Tourist taxi, car service, courier service, etc. at your hotel ? Do you do travel booking ?
21. Do you buy cold drinks, soda, ice cream ?
22. From whom do you buy your music cassettes / records /video tape ?
23. Do you have laundry service / dhobi / washing machine ?
24. Do you have shopping arcade / curios shop / shopping mall ?

EMPLOYMENT MULTIPLIER

I TURF CLUB

1. The Turf club buys fresh vegetables and fruits from Gultekdi (Market Yard Pune).
2. For the non-vegetarian they have an annual contract.
3. The club invites tenders (3 quotations – the lowest budget one they give order to).
4. They buy groceries from wholesale home delivery.
5. Under the catering department – production and service food and beverage managers – sub production – chef – Menu planning quality control, etc.
6. The kitchen – Chef is skilled, cook is skilled, pantryman, veg cutter and pot washing men, etc. are all semi-skilled.
7. They rent out their hall / ground for marriages – no religious ceremony is allowed. It is a universal / secular club.
8. They organize reception (marriage), they hire Bombay Decorators for supply of flowers plus light decoration. No press or photographers are allowed inside.
9. They organize May Queen Ball, Christmas and New Year Parties etc.
10. Turf Club does not allow its space to be used for commercial purposes. Due to the Racing seasons from July to October in

Pune, December to June in Mumbai (Mahalaxmi Club). The club is mainly unavailable during the above mentioned specific period.

II HOTELSHREYAS

1. The Hotel management buys fruits, vegetables from market yard. e.g. tomatoes 100 kg. per day; Milk 100 Ltrs. From Chitale Bandhu as well as 2 other local dairies.
2. They buy from wholesale traders – market yard – 'Nandkumar' Atul Trading Company at 5 – 10 per cent discount.
3. They buy flowers for decoration / wedding from Deccan Flower Merchant.
4. They rent out 'Ambar' Terrace hall for wedding etc.
5. The equipment is supplied by Nitin speakers, electricians and Bhalerao Neha Video Services.
6. The hotel also provides a Brahmin priest for wedding by the name ofShriyut Phadke Guruji.
7. The lift maintenance is done by OTIS, Pest control – Rido Pest
8. The soft drinks e.g. Thums up are supplied by Poona Bottling Company Pvt. Ltd.
9. The security guard is provided by Sai Management Services.
10. They buy Ice creams from Kaware Cold Drinks.
11. The music – audio / video tapes are supplied by Alurkar Music House. They also have cable TV and piped music facilities in their hotel rooms.
12. The hotel has a travel agency run by Neeraj Travels for 5 years in the hotel.
13. The magazines – newspapers – are brought from local book sellers
14. The laundry service is provided by Shabir Shaikh.
15. Mr. Shidore is hired as landscape gardening consultant.
16. The *paan wallas* are called as per the customer demand, they supply pan, supari, etc.
17. There are no florist or tourist taxi or courier services available here.

III HOTELVAISHALI

1. They buy vegetables, fruits from Mandai Phule Market etc., for e.g. daily requirement 400 kgs of potatoes per day for dosa, bhaji, batatawada etc. Milk 50 – 100 litres per day from 2 milkmen and Sane dairy.

2. They buy dal, rice, pulses, oil, etc. on a monthly basis from Dethalal Gopaldas – Mangalwar Peth Gultekadi.
3. The cold drinks are Pepsi, Coke, Thums up supplied by Poona Bottling.
4. They buy Ice cream from Kwality / Walls, etc
5. The pest control is done by Peecop.

IV HOTEL BLUE DIAMOND

1. They buy fresh fruit vegetable from Phule Sabji Mandai.
2. Hotel has appointed subcontractors as the daily requirement of milk is 150 - 200 litres.
3. They buy poultry – eggs, chicken from wholesale traders.
4. The contractual services include - service maintenance and engineers, consultants.
5. The Lift maintenance is provided by OTIS.
6. The florist and *paanwala* are in the hotel itself.
7. The security is provided by the hotel itself.
8. Alcohol – main distributors – e.g. Patel Mistry.
9. The illumination – sub contracting expert – Bombay decorators.
10. The hotel has two shops – one is of curios handicrafts and the other one is an emporium.
11. The hotel has a Music CD cassette shop.

SOFTWARE COMPANY EXECUTIVES INTERVIEW SCHEDULE - PROFORMA

1. Name of the Person.
2. Educational Qualification
   (a) Bachelor Degree / Diploma
   (b) Post graduate
   (c) Doctorate

3. Age of the person.
   (a) 25 – 35 years
   (b) 35 – 45 years
   (c) 45 – 55 years
   (d) 55 – 60 years and above

4. Do you put up your clients / foreign counterparts / collaborator in a hotel? Do you volunteer to make arrangements for their stay in Pune? Which hotel and why?

5. Why do you choose a particular hotel in Pune?
   (a) Do you get discount – how much?
   (b) Do you host quite a few lunch or executive banquets etc.
   (c) Company expense account.
   (d) The hotel owner is a relative or a friend of yours.

6. How often do you go abroad on company assignments, etc.?

7. How often do you take your clients business partners, etc., to a restaurant?
   (a) Once a week
   (b) Twice a week
   (c) Thrice a week
   (d) Once everyday
   (e) Once every fortnight.
   (f) Once every month
   (g) Twice every month
   (h) Occasionally
   (i) Very rarely

8. When you eat out with your clients / business partners which particular restaurant do you visit and why?
   (a) Proximity to your office.
   (b) Moderate pricing
   (c) Variety of food available
   (d) Good hospitality / service prompt
   (e) Continental / western type (Bland food)

9. What type of food does your client / partner prefer
   (a) Vegetarian / Non-vegetarian
   (b) Continental
   (c) Italian (Pizza)
   (d) Chinese
   (e) Indian – Gujarati, Punjabi, Maharashtrian, South Indian, Snacks – Western, Indian
   (f) Fast food.

10. Does your client/yourself take an appetizer / drink
    (a) Chilled beer
    (b) Glass of wine

(c) A Peg of whisky
(d) Gin and lime
(e) Vodka / cocktail or a mere mock tail or just an aerated soft drink e.g. Pepsi, fruit juice.

11. How many dishes do you order
(a) One main dish
(b) Two dishes with side dish
(c) Three dishes
(d) Full thali meal and snacks
(e) Fast food

12. How much do you spend on eating at one time?
(a) Rs 50 – 100
(b) Rs. 100 – 500
(c) Rs. 500 – 1000
(d) Rs 1000 and above

13. Do you have any expense account? Any chance of reimbursement (Y/N)

14. Do you keep record (Xerox) of the bills ?

15. Do you use your credit card to pay bill?
(a) Visa
(b) Master card
(c) Citibank
(d) Cash

16. Do you get invited to a hotel / restaurant often (Y/N)

17. Do you think that by your hospitality it has generated a lot of goodwill amongst your clients?
(a) Your wife is a good hostess / an asset
(b) She is a sleeping partner in your business
(c) She is a good listener / communicator
(d) Knows foreign languages which is very useful for foreign collaborations such as Japanese, German etc.

18. Do you feel that by your hospitality it has enhanced your business in any way ?
(a) Your company gets more contracts from them

(b) You have earned more profits due to sales.
(c) Your client is now a good friend and not just a partner
(d) You often mix pleasure with business.

SOFTWARE EXECUTIVES IN PUNE

I Cirrus Logic (American Company Collaboration – San Jose California – CEO

I had interviewed a senior executive as the CEO of the company was out of the country.

1. He is an M.Tech (IIT Bombay)
2. Age Group – 35 to 45 years
3. He / his company puts up clients in Pride Executive i.e. 4 star hotel (near Rahul Cinema Theatre, Pune University Road)
4. He has a Company expense account – 10 – 20% discount is offered by the hotel.
5. He stated that as Cirrus Logic is a marketing firm, eating out with clients is very rare.
6. He as well 1 -2 engineers go to San Jose once / twice a year.
7. Hotel preferred to – proximity to office and home.
8. His partners / clients prefer to eat non-vegetarian / vegetarian Punjabi food (e.g. Chicken tandoori, dal rice, roti etc).
9. Normally, clients are taken out for lunch hence no appetizers are ordered.
10. There are 3 dishes ordered for 4 persons.
11. The client's are foreigners, NRI's who prefer to take ice-cream, fruit salads for dessert.
12. At one time he spends Rs 100/- to 500/- if on company expense – he uses Citibank or else by cash.
13. He often gets invited by Hotels like Aurora Towers (because of their association with Deltas Air Lines he had gone to Holiday Inn recently).
14. He does not take his wife out with clients (she is a school teacher at Loyola High School and is not a business / sleeping partner).

II Veritas Systems Pvt. Ltd. (Software Company Head Office Sillicon Valley – California – USA).

1. Lady Executive
2. Age – 35 to 45 years
3. B.E. (Electrical Engineering M.S. from University, Baroda) M S. from Rutgers University U.S.A. New Jersey, U.S.A.

4. She puts up her foreign partners clients in Holiday Inn and Pride Executive – proximity of office. They get 10 – 15% discount.
5. She does have a Company Expense Account.
6. She goes abroad twice a year to California, Silicon Valley.
7. Company meetings held at Holiday Inn – 130 people had come from California, Silicon Valley.
8. She gets invited to hotels once in 6 months.
9. She and her husband prefer ethnic food – places like Zaika, Banjara Hills, Garden Court (Bavdhan).
10. The clients prefer Punjabi Non-Vegetarian Tandoori.
11. The clients take appetizers – Beer or soft drinks
12. The clients are often taken to Coffee House Camp for fast food or full thali.
13. Her clients / partners like to eat Indian sweet dishes like gulabjamun etc.
14. She spends Rs. 100 – Rs. 500 at one time.
15. She orders 1 – 2 dishes per person. Approximately Rs. 250 per person.
16. She gets complete reimbursement by company.
17. She uses Mastercard.
18. She is very career minded and is classified under DINK (Double Income No Kids) category.

III Persistent Systems Pvt.Ltd.

I had interviewed the owner of the enterprise

1. Owner / Proprietor.
2. He is a M.Tech (IIT).
3. Age 35 – 45 years.
4. He puts up his clients in Hotel Pride Executive due to its proximity.
5. Discount 10 – 20%.
6. He goes thrice a year to USA / Europe along with other company executives.
7. He takes his clients out 10 times a year.
8. When he takes his clients out he chooses a hotel for variety of food, cozy atmosphere, as well as trying out new ones every time.
9. Type of food client prefers – Non-Vegetarian Indian food.
10. The client takes an appetizer depending upon the climate e.g. Chilled Beer during summers.
11. The clients order one dish per person, generally 5 people order 5 dishes.

12. The owner's wife does not go out with him but loves to entertain at home (Indian hospitality) (*Atithi Devo Bhava*).
13. His clients prefer Indian Sweet dishes instead of ice- cream e.g Kheer, Gulabjamun.
14. At one time she spends 100 – 500.
15. He gets company reimbursement.
16. The payment is made by cash.
17. He gives tip to waiter 5 – 10%.
18. The record of the bill is kept for tax purposes.

BUSINESS EXECUTVES ENTREPRENEURS INTERVIEW SCHEDULE

1. Name of the Person.

2. Educational Qualification
   (a) Bachelor Degree / Diploma
   (b) Post graduate
   (c) Doctorate

3. Age of the person.
   (a) 25 – 35 years
   (b) 35 – 45 years
   (c) 45 – 55 years
   (d) 55 – 60 years and above

4. Type of Business
   (a) Employed in a company
   (b) Self employed
   (c) Freelancer
   (d) Partnership
   (e) Consultants

5. How often do you get invited to a restaurant?
   (a) Once a week
   (b) Twice a week
   (c) Thrice a week
   (d) Once everyday
   (e) Once every fortnight.
   (f) Once every month

(g) Twice every month
(h) Occasionally
(i) Very rarely

6. Do you eat out with your
(a) Wife
(b) Wife and kids
(c) Associates
(d) Business partners
(e) Colleagues
(f) Close friends
(g) Relatives other than wife /kids
(h) Neighbours
(i) Clients

7. What type of food do you prefer ?
(a) Vegetarian / Non-vegetarian
(b) Continental
(c) Italian (Pizza)
(d) Chinese
(e) Indian – Gujarati, Punjabi, Maharashtrian, South Indian, Snacks – Western, Indian
(f) Fast food.

8. Any specific restaurant you like to visit or do you like to try out a new one every time. If so why?
(a) Moderate pricing.
(b) Proximity to your house / office.
(c) Good food variety.
(d) Good service / hospitality
(e) Waiters are prompt serve hot food.
(f) Location – Centrally located.
(g) Quiet and peaceful surrounding
(h) Cozy comfortable place

9. How many dishes do you order ?
(a) One main dish
(b) Two dishes with side dish
(c) Three dishes
(d) Full thali meal and snacks
(e) Fast food

10. How much do you spend on eating at one time?
    Rs. 50 – 100
    Rs. 100 – 500
    Rs. 500 – 1000
    Rs. 1000 and above

11. Do you get discount at a certain hotel?
    (a) You organize executive lunches / dinner
    (b) Company account.
    (c) Hotel owner is your friend.
    (d) Hotel owner is your relative.
    (e) Do you often hold conferences over there?

12. Do you keep a record (Xerox) of the bills ?

13. Do you use your credit card to pay bill?
    Visa
    Master card
    Citibank
    Cash

14. Do you take any appetizer before food?
    (a) Beer
    (b) Whisky
    (c) Wine
    (d) Gin with lime tit bits
    (e) Soft drink
    (f) Pepsi or fruit juice.

15. Purpose of going to a hotel other than eating
    (a) Live single new city – Pune.
    (b) Couple working wife hence eating out.
    (c) DINK – double income no kids.
    (d) Couple and children – leisure – Sunday – holiday
    (e) Meeting clients / partners business negotiation
    (f) Combine eating out with watching movie / play / recreation – leisure + convenience.
    (g) Meeting old friends.
    (h) Get together

(i) Only on Sunday / Thursday a change from daily routine of cooking and eating at home.
(j) Dating girls.
(k) Company expense account in cash or kind.
(l) Privacy – paucity space at home.
(m) After busy shopping / an excuse for chatting latest gossiping news.
(n) Hobby / past time of trying out new places / dishes every time.

16. How often you tip waiter ?
    (a) Good prompt service / hospitality. Even if service charge is levied still do you tip him what is the percentage or is it a fixed amount.

17. What do you think about changing scenario of development of hotels in Pune in terms of employment, income revenue generation and changing tastes and habit ?
18. Going down the memory lane (nostalgia) if you were to relive your college days, carefree days, and today more responsibility at home as well as business – hogging dishes/ competition, admiring / eyeing young girls and eating delicacies.

19. Do you get invited to a hotel / restaurant get- to gether ?

20. Do your sons / daughters have two wheelers? How much pocket money do you give them?

INTERVIEWS OF BUSINESS EXECUTIVES IN PUNE

I FORMER VICE-PRESIDENT, KALYANI STEEL, NOW CONSULTANT

1. B.E., M.B.A.
2. Freelance consultancy
3. Goes to a hotel once a month now.
4. He goes out to a hotel with wife, sons and relatives, other than wife as well as clients.
5. He eats both vegetarian and non-vegetarian food but prefers non-veg food.
6. He eats Chinese as well as Indian
7. He visits hotels for good food and vicinity to a house (lives on Senapati Bapat Road).

8. No reimbursement as he has retired from company, hence gets no discount.
9. He pays by cash (keeps record for tax reasons).
10. He enjoys eating with wife, kids also luxurious – leisure recreation as well as meeting clients.
11. He orders 2 dishes and a side dish.
12. He prefers to take whisky (drink)
13. Spends Rs. 500 – 1000 one time.
14. He tips the waiter for good service etc.
15. He often gets invited to hotels as well as goes for get-togethers.
16. Going down memory lane (Pune Engineering College student – went to Modern Café close to the college or Café Delight – dosas). Studious student not much of running around like today.

II BUSINESS EXECUTIVE – SYNERGY ADVERTISING AGENCY

1. Lady owner / proprietor
2. Graduate and an MBA
3. Self employed (owns an agency – partnership)
4. She gets invited once a year.
5. She visits thrice a week – dinner friends DINK –Double income no kids. Once a week with husband and business associates.
6. Prefers non-veg. In veg – South Indian.
7. Snacks – at Vaishali - Dinner new place every time.
8. Gets discounts 10% accommodates clients etc. in a hotel – Pride Executive.
9. Pays by cash for small amount - Big hotel by credit card - Keeps the record of the bill – entertainment expense.
10. She likes to socialize as well as invite friends – busy working couple.
11. Dishes – 2 dishes.
12. At one time spends 100 – 500.
13. Tip the waiter always.
14. Get together socially once in 15 days.

III SYNERGY – JUNIORS THEY WERE ALSO INTERVIEWED

1. Mr. X and Mr. Y.
2. They both work and eat out together.
3. Go out twice a week.

4. Go out with friends etc.
5. Both are vegetarians – eat Punjabi food.
6. Eat for good food, vicinity to office and home.
7. Pay by cash.
8. Eat out of necessity (New in Pune city single).
9. They do not tip the waiter.
10. They would certainly love to relive college carefree days again.

IV SYNERGY – JUNIOR (Manager)

1. B. Com. 25 – 35 years.
2. Copywriter in Synergy Employed.
3. Attends hotel parties, press conference on behalf on company.
4. Very rarely gets invited to hotel.
5. Eats out twice a week with husband DINK.
6. Eats both veg. Non.Veg.
7. Indian, Punjabi, South Indian, continental, Mexican.
8. Likes to eat out due toproximity to office, home good food variety – cozy environment.
9. Discount at Pride Executive – 10 – 15% hold meeting and conference at Pride Executive.
10. She prefers to pay by cash.
11. No record is kept.
12. DINK – working couple/old friends.
13. Eats 2 dishes + starter.
14. Rs. 100 – 500 at one time.
15. Tips the waiter – feels habits and tastes have changed would certainly love to relive college days.

V SYNERGY

I had interviewed a junior staff member

1. Age 25 to 35 years.
2. Employed in Synergy.
3. Visits hotels once a month.
4. Unmarried – prefers to eat out with friends.
5. Strict Vegetarian – prefers to eat Punjabi food.
6. Goes to hotels proximity to house stays Kothrud e.g. Hotel Sweekar.
7. Variety of Veg. food.
8. Pays by Cash.

9. Orders two dishes.
10. Pay Rs. 100 – 500 at one time. Does no tip waiter.
11. Would love to relive college carefree days.
12. Feels today eating out has become a status symbol.

VI ARCHITECT

I had interviewed the proprietor of the firm

1. Proprietor
2. 25 – 35 years
3. B. Arch (Architecture).
4. Business – Proprietor
5. Goes out 2 – 3 times a week average.
6. Once a week eats with his friends circles. He is a strict vegetarian (unlike his wife).
7. He likes to eat veg. low fatty, low calorie food – continental. He is a very health conscious person.
8. Loves to try out a new hotel every time even on recommendation.
9. He likes to go out proximity to office / house like to go out prefers privacy not crowded places.
10. For him discount is applicable.
11. He uses credit card (Diners club).
12. He keeps records of bills (business expenses etc.).
13. He goes out with wife / business partner / clients as well as meeting old friends.
14. He orders 1 main dish and 1 side dish.
15. He occasionally takes beer depending on climate.
16. He spends Rs. 500 – 700 one time.
17. The waiter is tipped 5% service charge.
18. He gets invited from companies / twice a week for presentation. He drinks cocktails single or with wife.

VII ROTARIAN BUSINESSMAN – EX GOVERNOR OF ROTARY

1. Age group 55 – 60 years.
2. Owns an Engineering firm.
3. Double BE ACE + Ph.D. in Management.
4. Gets invited by Rotary or friends and by clients.
5. He is a vegetarian – prefers Buffet, Punjabi as well as Maharashtrian.
6. He chooses hotel for its atmosphere, decorum, cleanliness and hygiene.

7. Gets discount e.g. member of Poona Club (chain ex-man of Indo-American Chamber of Commerce roughly 10 – 30%).
8. For star hotels he uses credit cards – diners Citibank, American Express card.
9. He keeps record of bill (tax etc.).
10. He likes to go out with family i.e. wife and son every Sunday.
11. He orders 3 - 4 dishes e.g. Veg. Dal, Curry, salad. He is a strict vegetarian.
12. He takes whisky / gin depending upon the occasion or beer depending on climate and company.
13. His family consists of 4 members and he spends 500 – 1000 one time.
14. If service charge then no tip to waiter otherwise 10%.
15. College carefree days – Poona Engineering College (COEP now) used to visit hotel Poonam / Jeevan, Badshahi, Tilak Road, Today nostalgic (Santosh Hotel) would certainly love to relive it. Today he says eating / tasting food have changed a lot. Today people eat out a lot. He being an ex-governor of Rotary International. He goes to Holiday Inn e.g. Rotary convention, also Le Meridian – and also goes to Poona Club member, but at the same time likes to go to Subji Mandai (old time sake – *missal pav.* He mentioned about University Foundation Chowpatty – eating Bhel etc.

VIII ROTARIAN AND PRESIDENT – (CANTONMENT AREA) BUSINESSMAN / EXECUTIVE

1. Owner / Proprietor
2. Age 55 – 60 years.
3. Educational Qualifications – B.Sc. (Hon) L.L.B DBM.
4. He is self employed – own business Fire Conveyor Fan Belt and Industrial Equipment. Family business – Industrial supplier.
5. He very often gets invited atleast 5 – 6 times a year being a Rotarian.
6. He gets invited once or twice a year by Bhojwani (Holiday Inn).
7. He goes out 4 times a month / week, with his wife, son or his close friends.
8. He prefers non-veg. food i.e. Chinese food on camp (near Lal Temple), Eddies Kitchen.
9. He often goes to Blue Diamond / Le Meredian with other fellow Rotarians / meeting – Poona Club etc.
10. He likes to try out new places every time e.g. Sarjah – on Baner Road and Banjara Hills etc.

11. He selects the restaurant / hotels due to its moderate pricing and good quality and variety of foods.
12. He does not get discount at hotels except if it is sponsored by a company e.g. Eureka Forbes etc.
13. He prefers to pay by cash or if it is a large sum by credit card – Citibank card.
14. If 3 - 4 people go out e.g. Chinese food, it is soup (starter), noodles/ fish dish + Ice cream.
15. At one time he spends say Rs. 500 - 1000.
16. He keeps a record of the bills – company account.
17. If service charge is levied i.e. 10% then he does not tip the waiter.
18. He being a cricketer (Ranji Trophy player) from Bombay, member of P.J. Hindu Gymkhana (nostalgic memories of eating out with friends, players – He would certainly love to relive college days). His college was Jamshed College of Law.
19. He is a resident of Pune since 1962 – feels that Pune has become more cosmopolitan as compared to earlier times. He loves to watch cricket, he is a member of Cantonment Rotary Board. His wife is an M.Sc in Chemistry and was a lecturer at Wadia and Fergusson College. She is a member of the Inner Wheel of Rotary. His son is B.Com. M.B.A. and has joined his father's business.

IX MEDICAL DOCTOR – FORMER PRINCIPAL (HOMEOPATHY COLLEGE) NOW RETIRED

1. Age of the person 60 – 70 years.
2. He is Self Employed – owns Clinic on Karve Road, (Oberoi House).
3. He is not much invited to a restaurant.
4. He goes once a week to a restaurant with his wife. Once a month with his family and once a month with his fellow Rotarians as well as some medical colleagues.
5. He and his son eat non.veg, whereas wife is a strict vegetarian.
6. He prefers Punjabi food as well as all types of Western food.
7. He lives on Law College Road, hence selects a hotel for proximity to his clinic and residence.
8. He prefers Chinese food too. He often goes to Chinese room (Oriental – Karve Road). He believes in a quiet cozy surrounding.
9. As he is a frequent visitor to Chinese room the owner gives him 15 -17% discount.
10. He pays by cash or Citibank card if the amount is big, and he keeps record of bills for tax reasons.

11. As both of them are busy doctors, husband, wife and son, it is convenient eating out on Sundays with family friends / colleagues.
12. He orders 2 Veg. dishes and 1 Non.Veg. and 1 rice / roti. He loves to eat ice-cream / pudding as dessert and not Indian sweet dishes.
13. At one time he spends Rs. 500 – 1000 roughly.
14. Nostalgic memories of Bombay college days – he used to visit Udipi joints at Kings circle, Matunga, a place called Mysorewalla. His childhood / youth was spent in Delhi, where he relished Kathi Kabab.
15. He does not get his bills reimbursed but keeps the record of them for tax purposes.
16. He has Citibank Card and uses it for paying large amount of hotel bills. For small amount he pays by cash.

X INTERVIEW ROTARIAN

1. Owner / Proprietor.
2. Educational Qualifications – B.E. (Mechanical) from Karad Engineering College, Shivaji University, Kolhapur.
3. Age Group – 45 to 55 years.
4. Private Limited Company – Relcon Engineering, along with one more Director/ Partner.
5. He gets invited 1 – 2 times in a year (couple – hotels). There are total 35 clubs of Rotary. One meeting is held every month.
6. He goes to a restaurant / hotel – once a fortnight.
7. He goes for business / Rotarians 2 – 3 times a year.
8. He goes with family / Rotarian for Dinner once a fortnight.
9. He mostly prefers vegetarian food. Non-Veg occasionally.
10. He and his family like all types of food, Chinese, Punjabi, Mexican.
11. He and his family (son and daughter, wife) like to visit Shangrilla on Karve Road or for dinner Ashish Plaza (F.C. Road).
12. He does not get his bills reimbursed but keeps the record of them for tax reasons.
13. He pays by cash if amount is small or by credit card, Bank of India, Record of bills for tax reasons is kept.
14. He attends dinners where 5 – 19 per cent discount is offered.
15. He believes that by attending dinners of Rotarians there is assimilation of fellow Rotarian.
16. He enjoys weekend – outing with family and old college friends.
17. He often eats at Shreyas – Veg. Thali of family of four, 1 dish per person. He very occasionally takes drinks with friends / Rotarians.

18. He spends Rs. 100 – 500 on vegetarian food.
19. He pays / tips to waiter on services rendered i.e. 3 -4 per cent as well as 10% service charge, if he frequents the place.
20. Memory lane – As a young college student he ate at Alu Canteen (Karad Engineering College) e.g. Sunday – Mess feast. There was no fast food at than time. The night time was for studies. He used to enjoy after study omlette / and pav bread.
21. He gives his daughter Rs. 200 – 300 per month. He has given her a two wheeler. Son is still 17 years of age and studying in 12th standard in Fergusson College. He does not own a 2 wheeler but he goes by bus.
22. He belongs to upper / middle class family and does not believe in extravagant living.

CONTENT ANALYSIS OF THE INTERVIEWS TAKEN – MAIN POINTS

- Eating out of necessity (single new to Pune city).
- Software executives often do a lot of entertaining outside. Two of the interviewees preferred to entertain their guests at home instead of hotel. They believed in Indian hospitality. 'Atithi Devo Bhava'.
- It is a status Symbol – entertaining guests.
- DINK – Working couple find it more convenient to eat out at hotels with their guests.
- NRIs foreigners like to go to ethnic Indian Food joint.
- The discount – depends on how often you take guests out for going to hotel.
- The Foreign partners / purely personal reasons / NRIs.
- It is convenient eating out especially for working couple.
- People love different types (variety of food) etc. often like to try out new places etc.
- People often prefer a place – proximity to office or house.
- They choose a hotel due to its ambience, cozy quiet atmosphere, privacy.
- Often, eating out of pleasure with wife, children, family or have an old friends get together.

ROTARIANS INTERVIEW – MAIN POINTS

- The Rotarians often have to go out for Rotarian dinners / meetings – a lot of socializing for assimilating different fellow Rotarians.

- They are all invited by different hotels / restaurants and also often get discount.
- Out of 4 Rotarians interviewed 2 were strict vegetarians.
- They often spend Rs. 500 – 1000 at one time.
- All are busy professionals – out of them 3 have own engineering firms whereas one is a doctor.
- They all keep record of bills for tax purposes.
- All of them use credit cards for large amounts / for small snacks etc. pay by cash.
- All of them being very busy they love / enjoy to go out with their families, old friends etc.
- They often tip the waiters and often get discount at hotels etc.
- They prefer outings often for long drives / picnic type with their family members old friends etc.
- They are very conscious citizens. Often they talk about the growing traffic menace / youngsters loafing around – loosing respect for elders, etc., the growing number of street hawkers – food vending. Problems of drug abuse / drug addicts etc.

Appendix - 4

[Listed at the turn of the century; many more have come up since then]

Important Large Industrial Units in and Around Pune

1. Advani Oerlikon Ltd. (welding rods)
2. Alfa Laval Ltd. (Dairy Machinery)
3. Atlas Copco (India) Ltd. (Air compressors).
4. Ayurved Rashashala (Ayurvedic medicines).
5. Bajaj Auto Limited (Scooters and three wheelers).
6. Bajaj Tempo Limited (Tempo vehicles)
7. Bajaj Electricals Pvt. Ltd. (Fans)
8. Bharat Forge Ltd. (Industrial forgings).
9. Bharat Electronics Ltd.
10. Buckau Wolf India Ltd. (Sugar Machinery)
11. Century Enka Ltd. (Nylon yarn).
12. Chloride India Ltd. (Car Batteries)
13. Cummins Diesel and Services (India) Ltd. (Car Batteries).
14. Cummins Diesel and Services (India) Ltd.
15. Dr. Beck & Co. (India) Ltd. (Wire enamels, impregnating varnishes and synthetic resins for electrical industry).

During the last few years, Pune, has not only witnessed setting up of some major industries with initial investment of crores of rupees around Pune city, but also outside PMR area. Among these important industries are:

1. Ispat Profiles Ltd (Steel Mill)
2. Sulzer India Piston (Compressors)
3. Multistage Pulzer (Centrifuges)
4. Kalyani Sharp Ltd. (TV And VCR)

5. Tata Honeywell (Computers)
6. Fiskar Ltd (Scissors)
7. Mahindra & Mahindra Ltd; Automotive Division (Pressed Components)
8. Shirke Paper Mills Ltd (Paper)
9. Western India Enterprises

TABLE - 1

Total Number of Establishment in Greater Pune

PUNE MUNICIPAL CORPORATION

No.	*Types of Establishments*	*1973*	*1981*	*1984*	*1985*	*1987*	*1988*
1	Shops	25,507	34,101	38,754	32,376	38,607	41,000
2	Commercial Establishments	6,310	10,899	13,705	13,481	17,651	19,000
3	Hotels	2,173	2,610	3,929	2,583	2,830	3,000
4	Theaters	28	38	37	34	34	
	Total	34,018	47,648	56,425	48,474	59,122	63,000

TABLE - 2

PIMPRI – CHINCHWAD MUNICIPAL CORPORATION

No.	*Types of Establishments*	*1983*	*1984*	*1985*	*1987*	*1988*
1.	Shops	2,365	3,565	6,220	6,923	8,000
2.	Commercial Establishments	1,831	2,158	2,556	3,136	3,000
3.	Hotels	334	370	410	593	
4.	Theaters	5	5	5		
	Total	3,887	6,098	9,191	11,870	12,000

TABLE - 3

PUNE, KHADKI AND DEHU ROAD CANTONMENT, PUNE

No.	*Types of Establishments*	*1985*	*1987*	*1988*
1.	Shops	3904	3136	2959
2.	Commercial Establishments	820	611	880
3.	Hotels	262	221	291
4.	Theaters	21	11	11
	Total	5007	3979	4141

Appendix - 5

(Listed at the turn of the century; many more have come up since then)

LIST OF COLLEGES AND INSTITUTIONS IN THE AREA OF ELECTRONICS

Army Institute of Technology
College of Engineering
Dighi, Pune 411015

Bharati Vidyapeeth's College
of Engineering, Katraj
Dhankawadi, Pune Satara Road
Pune 411 043

Government College of Engg.
Shivajinagar, Pune 411 005

D.Y. Patil College of Engg.
Pimpri, Pune 411 018

Maharashtra Institute of
Technology, S.No. 24,
Behind L.I.C Colony,
Paud Road, Kothrud,
Pune 411 029.

Maharshi Karve Stree Shikshan
Sanstha's Cummins College of
Engineering for Women
Karvenagar, Pune 411029.

P.V.G's College of Engg and
Technology, 44, Vidyanagar,
Parvati Darshan,
Pune 411 009

Pune Institute of Computer
Technology, S.No.27,
Dhankawadi, Pune Satara Road,
Pune 411 043

Vishwakarma Institute of
Technology, 666 Upper Indiranagar,
Bibwewadi, Pune 411 037.

Appendix - 6

[Listed at the turn of the century; many more have come up since then]

MULTINATIONAL COMPANIES HAVING PRODUCTION FACILITIES IN PUNE

Amphenol Amphetronix Ltd.
105, Bhosari Industrial Area
Pune 411 026

Be-delft Electronics Ltd.
EL-30 'J' Block MIDC
Bhosari, Indl. Area
Pune 411 026

BHA Group
6th Floor, Mutha Chambers,
Senapati Bapat Road,
Pune 411 016

Daewoo Anchor Electronics
(Proposed Office in Pune)
Bake House, 1st Floor
Bombay 400 001

GE Elpro Medical System Ltd.
Chinchwadgaon
Pune 411 033

Godrej G.E. Appliances Ltd.,
229/230 M.G. Road,
Pune 411 001

Mahindra British Telecom Ltd.
148 Mumbai Pune Road,
P.O. Box No. 1119, Pimpri
Pune 411 018

Mitsubishi Washing Machine
315, Ashoka Mall, Bund Garden
Road, Opp. Hotel Holiday Inn.
Pune 411 001.

Philips India Ltd.
Loni Kalbhor
Pune 412 201

Whirlpool of India Ltd.,
Shankar Parvati Chamber
Dhole Patil Road
Pune 411 001.

Appendix - 7

[Listed at the turn of the century; many more have come up since then]

MULTINATIONAL COMPANIES HAVING OFFICE IN PUNE

B&R Industrial Automation
Pvt. Ltd., 312 Aurora Towers,
East Wing, M.G. Road,
Pune 411001

Birla AT&T Communications
Ltd.
11/1 Sharada Centre, Off Karve
Road, Pune 411 004

BPL US WEST Cellular Ltd.
BPL Centre, 42/A, Hirabaug
Services,
Shukrawar Peth
Pune 411 002

CG Powerware Ltd.
(Exide Electronics USA)
3rd Floor Bldg, No.1, Mutha
Chambers, S.B. Road,
Pune 411016
Siemens Nixdort Information
Systems Ltd., 1 Lunkad Villa
Law College Road,
Pune 411 004.

CG-Core EI Logic System Ltd.,
Surya Bhavan, 1181, F.C. Road,
Pune 411 005

Global Wireless Technology Ltd.
Global House, Prabhat Road,
Lane No. 5, Erandawane,
Pune 411 004.

Pagepoint Service (I) Pvt. Ltd.
Motorola's Paging
Ashoka Pabillion, 1st floor,
Dr. Ambedkar Road,
Pune 411 001

Samsung India Electronics Ltd.,
204/205, Bldg., No II, Gera
Gardens, Koregaon Park,
Pune 411 001

Appendix - 8

[Listed at the turn of the century; many more have come up since then]

LIST OF FOREIGN COLLABORATIONS IN ELECTRONICS SECTOR

Name of Company	Collaboration with
1. AAR-EM Electronics Pvt. Ltd.,	A.GD.E
2. Ador Powerton Industries Energiestechnik Germany.	Elproleit Und, Ltd.
3. BE-DELFT Electronics Ltd. Holland	Delft Instruments International
4. DGP Hinoday Industries	Hitachi Metals, Japan
5. Forbes Zellwager Analytics	Zellweger SA, France
6. Hi-REL Components (I)	Corona S.G., Italy
7. Jaya Hind Sciaky Ltd. Switzerland	Schiaky Intertechnique
8. Kalyani Sharp India Ltd. Japan.	Sharp Corporation,
9. KAT Controls Pvt. Ltd USA	Target Systems Inc.
10. KLAPP heating Tools Pvt. Ltd. Japan.	Hakko Corporation,
11. Kronhe Marshall Pvt. Ltd. Gmbh, Germany	Karonhe Marshall
12. Philips India Ltd. Netherland	N.V. Philips,

13.	SVAM Electronics Pvt. Ltd. GMbh Germany.	Allfen Burger
14.	Tata Honeywell USA.	Honeywell Inc.
15.	The Arvind Mills Ltd. USA	E.F. Johnson Co.
16.	U.B. Engineering Ltd. USA	Eagle Aerospace Inc.
17.	Ultramatix Computer Support Sys Pvt. Ltd.	RC Condizionatori SPA Italy

Appendix - 9

[Listed at the turn of the century; many more have come up since then]

RESEARCH AND DEVELOPMENT INSTITUTIONS

Armament Research & Development
Establishment, Pashan
Pune 411 021.

Electronic Testing & Development
Centre (ETDC) Meltron,
Agriculture College Compound,
Pune 411 005

Centre Water & Power Research
Station Khadakwasala
Pune 411 024

College of Engineering
Electronics Department,
Shivajinagar, Pune 411 005

Centre for Information
Technology, Pune University Campus
Pune 411 007

Industrial Training Insttute
Aundh, ITI Road,
Shivajinagar, Pune
411 007

Centre for Materials & Electronics
Merado Compound, NDA Road
Pashan, Pune 411 008

Industrial Training Institute
Pimpri Chinchwad Sector
27/A, Pradhikaran Nigdi,
Pune 411 044.

Institute of Armament Technology
Girinagar, Pune 411 025

Institute of Electronic & Telecom
Raghuraj, Erandawane,
Pune 411 004

Missile System Quality Assurance
Agency, Khadki, Pune 411 003

National Chemical Laboratory
Pashan Road, Pune 411 008

National Informatics Centre
(WR) Ganeshkhind Road,
Pune 411 007

Naval Armament Inspectorate
Ammunition Factory,
Khadki, Pune 411 003

Research and Development
Establishment, (Engineers)
Dighi, Pune 411 015

Senior Quality Assurance
Establishment (Electronics)
Wing, CQAE Complex, Aundh,
Pune 411 005

Vocational Education
& Training Regional Office,
Ghole Road, Pune
411 005.

Appendix - 10

[Listed at the turn of the century; many more have come up since then]

CENTRAL MINISTRIES / ASSOCIATION CONCERNED WITH ELECTRONIC INDUSTRY

CENTRAL MINISTRIES

Principal Secretary to the
Prime Minister,
Government of India
South Block, New Delhi 110 011

Foreign Secreatry,
Ministry of External Affairs,
Government of India,
South Block,
New Delhi 110 011

Secretary,
Ministry of Commerce,
Government of India
Udyog Bhavan Maulana AzadRoad,
New Delhi 110 001

Secretary,
Ministry of Finance,
Government of India
North Block,
New Delhi 110 001

Secretary
Ministry of Communications
Government of India
Sanchar Bhavan, Ashoka Road,

Secretary
Ministry of Industry
Government of India
Udyog Bhavan, Rafi Marg

New Delhi 110 001
Secretary,
Ministry of Electronics,
Government of India,
Electronics Niketan, 6 CGO
Complex, New Delhi 110 003

New Delhi 110 001
Secretary,
Ministry of Information and
Broadcasting, Government of India
Shastri Bhavan, Dr. Rajendra
Prasad Road New Delhi 110 001

Appendix (Material from magazines newspaper Pune Plus 3rd March, Times of India.

The Malwani take away and home delivery centre is for the coastal food fanatic which is run by a poultry owner Mr. Chanakya Ma selling chicken to literally counting who wanted to give some value additions to his customers. Hence the launch of Malwani coastal food (Malwalis a coastal area of Konkan region of Maharashtrawhich) is famous for its tasty non-veg food such as fish mutton chicken along with sol-curry a preparation made from Kokum (a berry fruit grown in Konkan) used for culinary purposes as a sweet-sour flavour a preparation made with it along with coconut milk, ballemilk and spices used as a cooling agent after spicy food as well as an appetizer as digestive aid.

The enterprise is owned by Mr. Chanakya Malvin Kurve and his wife who are originally natives of Malwan. Hence the sojourn from counting chickens to literally cooking them in Aundh (Pune).

Appendix - 11

BIBILIOGRAPHY – A

1. Atre, P.K. 1953. 'Karheche Pani' 'The water from the river Karha' (Autobiography) published by Parchure Publishing House Mumbai, India.

2. Atre, P.K. 1963 'Mee Kassa Jhalo' ' My Growing Years' published by Parchure Publishing House, Mumbai, India.

3. Bell, Daniel. 1974. 'The Coming of the Post-Industrial Society – A Venture in Social Forecasting!'. Arnold Heinemann publications, published by Gulab Vazirani New Delhi, India.

4. Bourdieu, Pierre. 1977. 'Outline of a Theory of Practice' Oxford University Press, Oxford, U.K.

5. Bourdieu, Pierre. 1987. 'Distinction: A Social critique of the judgment of taste'. Harvard University Press, Cambridge, USA. 1986 edition Rout ledge Publications, London, UK.

6. Bhagwati, Jagdish. 1982. 'The World Economy in the Emerging Service Economy' (Ed) by Orio Giarinni, 1987, for Services World Forum Geneva, Switzerland. Published by Perganon Press, Oxford U.K.

7. Bhurke, Shyam. 1994. 'Pune ek Sathavan'. 'My memories about Pune City'. Published by Sun Publications, Pune, India

8. Campbell, C. 1987. 'The Romantic Ethic and the spirit of Modern Consumerism' Basil, Blackwell Publications, Oxford, U.K

9. Clark 1940 'The Conditions of Economic Progress' Mac Milan Publications, London U.K. (Revised edition 1957).

10. Dearborn, Fitzroy. 1997. 'International Encyclopedia of Economics' (ed) by Frank Mac gill, WIPIDE Publication, London, U.K

11. Eat well, John. 1987. 'The New Palgrave Dictionary of Economics' (ed) by Murray Milgate and Peter Newman. Macmillan Press Ltd. U.K

12. Edwards, Tim. 2000. 'Contradictions of Consumption, Concepts, Practices and politics in Consumer Society'. Open University Press, Buckingham, Philadelphia, U.S.A.

13. Ezekiel, Hannan and Pavaskar Madhoo. 1976. 'Second India Studies – Services'. Macmillan Publications, New Delhi, India.

14. Fisher, A.G.B. 1939. 'Production, Primary Secondary and Tertiary'. Economic Record no 15, June 24 – 28th 1939.

15. Finklestein, J. 1989. 'Dinning Out – A Sociology of Modern Manners'. New York University Press New York, USA.

16. Fourashe, J. 1949. 'Le grand espoir du Xeme Siècle. PUF. Paris. 4th edition 1958.

17. Fuchs, Victor R. 1968. 'The Service Economy' Series no 87, Columbia University Press, New York, USA. (National Bureau of Economic Research).

18. Gadgil, D.R. 1945. 'Poona – A Socio-Economic Survey' Part I and II. Gokhale Institute of Economics and Politics, publication no 25. Published by Arya Bhushan Press, Pune, India.

19. Gershuny, J. 1978. 'The New Service Economy' Columbia University Press, New York, USA.

20. Giarini, Orio. 1987 (Ed). 'The Emerging Service Economy'. For services World Forum, Geneva Switzerland. Published by Pergamon Press, Great Britain (by Wheaton and Co. Ltd).

21. Ghurye, G.S. 1950. 'Caste and Race in India' Popular Publication, Mumbai, India.

22. Gronow, J. 1991. 'Need, Taste and Pleasure, Understanding Food and Consumption' in EL. Furist, R, Pratalla, M. Ellerstorm, L Holm and U, Kjaerned (Ed) 'Palatable words – Socio-Cultural Food Studies'. Solum – Vorlag publication Oslo, Norway, Europe.

23. Gus field, Joseph R. 1967 (Jan), Vol 72, No, 4 'Tradition and Modernity, misplaced Polarities in the study of social change' in American Journal of Sociology, USA.

24. Hagen, Everett H. E. 1962. 'On the theory of Social change'. Porsey Press, INC, Honey wood, IL, USA.

25. Hill, T.P. 1977. 'On Goods and Services' Review of Income and Wealth. pp : 315 – 318

26. Joshi, Jayashree Gajanan 1985. 'Differential Residential patterns and Social Interactions with specific reference to Pune city. PhD thesis SNDT Women's University Mumbai, thesis under guidance of Prof. Y.B. Damle (Professor Emeritus University of Pune) (Unpublished Thesis)

27. Joshi, Narayan, Vishnu. 1868. 'Pune Shaharache Varnan' 'The Description of Pune City'. Published by Oriental Press, Mumbai.

28. Joshi, S.J. 1978. 'Puneri' 'The Puneite' Vidya Publications, Pune, India.

29. Karve Iravati, Dinkar. 1953. 'Kinship Organization in India', Published by Deccan College (Monograph Series) Poona, India.

30. Keynes, John. Maynard. 1936. 'Income savings, Investment'. Chapter No. 6 in 'The General theory of Employment, Interest and Money' Published by MacMillan Publication Cambridge. Press, U.K. (For Royal Economic Society).

31. Kapadia, K.M. 1981. 'Marriage and Family in India' Oxford University Press Publications Mumbai, India.

32. Khandge Neela. 1999 'Directory of Software Industry in Pune'. Secretary - General, Mahratta Chamber of Commerce and Industries and Agriculture, Pune, India.

33. Khandge Neela. 1999. 'Directory of Electronics Industries in Pune'. Secretary-General, Mahratta Chamber of Commerce and Industries and Agriculture, Pune, India.

34. Knight, Frank. 1921 'Risk, Uncertainty and Profit' Part II, Chapter IX. Houghton, Miff in Publication Co, Boston, New York, USA.

35. Kuhn, Thomas. 1962 (1970, enlarged edition) 'The Structure of Scientific Revolutions' – University of Chicago Press Publications, USA

36. Kulkarni, A.P. 1991 'Employment Multiplier in Pune – Industrial and Economic growth of an Indian city since 1950'. Published by centre for studies in Social Sciences, Pune, India.

37. Kuznet, Simon and Chenery Hollis 1960. (September). 'Economic growth and structural change' in Economic Review, New York, USA.

38. Lamont, M 1992. 'Money, Morals and Manners – The Culture of French and American Upper-middle class'. University of Chicago press publications, Chicago, USA.

39. Lash. S and Urry. J. 1994. 'Economies of Signs and Space'. Sage publications, London, U.K.

40. Marshall, Alfred. 1890. 'Principles of Economics' Macmillan and Co. Ltd, London, UK.

41. Mc Cracken, Grand David. 1988 'Culture and Consumption'; 'New Approaches to the Symbolic character of Consumer goods and Activities'. Indiana University Press, Bloomington, USA.

42. McIntosh, Win. Alex. 1996 'Sociologies of Food and Nutrition'. Plenum Press, New York, USA.

43. Mukherji.C. 1983. 'From graven images: Patterns of modern materialism' Columbia University Press, New York, USA.

44. Natu V.N. 1995. 'Adhich Pune Gulzar' 'Pune – A city of Blossom' Published by Varda Books, Pune India.

45. Marx, Karl. 1884/1981. 'Capital' Volume 2 Vintage publications, New York, USA

46. Marx, Karl. 1884/1981. 'Capital' a critique of Political Economy Volume No 1. International publishers, New York, USA

47. Parsons, Talcott. 1951. 'The Social System' Free press publications, Glencoe, Illinois, USA.

48. Ray, Larry and Sayer, Andrew (Ed) 1999. 'Culture and Economy: After the cultural turn' Sage Publications, London U.K.

49. Ritzer, George 2001 'Explorations in the Sociology of Consumption: Fast Food, Credit Cards and Casinos'. Sage publications, London U.K.

50. Schumpeter, Joseph. Alois. 1932 'The Theory of Economic Development'. McGraw Hill Book Co. New York, USA.

51. Schumpeter, Joseph. Alois. 1954 'History of Economic Analysis'. Allen and Unwin Publications, London, U.K.

52. Schumpeter, Joseph. Alois. 1950 'Capitalism, Socialism and Democracy' 3rd edition; Harper and Brothers Publication. New York, USA.

53. Rostow, W.W. 1953. 'The Process of Economic Growth' Oxford University Press, Oxford, U.K

54. Singh, Rashmi Uday. 2000 'Midday Good Food Guide to Pune' Times of India Publication Mumbai, India.

55. Singh, Yogendra. 2000 'Culture Change in India: Identity and Globalization'. Rawat Publication Jaipur, India.

56. Smith, Adams. 1776. 'An Inquiry into the nature and causes of Wealth of Nations'. Volume II. MDCCLXXVI, strand, printed for W. Stratchman and T. Cad ell London, U.K.

57. Merton, Robert. King. 1949 (1957 enlarged edition) 'Social Theory and Social Structure'. Free Press Publication, Glencoe, Illinois, USA.

58. Sovani N.V, Apte D.P and Pendse R.G. 1956. 'Poona' Re-survey. Gokhale Institute of Economics and Politics, publication no 34. Published by Sangam Press, Pune, India.

59. Varanasikar, Vrushali. 1992. 'Pune Shaharatil Hotel Vyavasayache Vyavasthapan'. 'The Management of Hotel Industry in Pune City'. PhD Thesis under guidance of Dr. S.B. Bapat. Department of Commerce SNDT Women's University Press. India (Unpublished Thesis).

60. Veblen, Thorn stein 1949. 'The Theory of Leisure class'. Published by George Allen and Unwin Ltd. Great Britain (first Published in 1925, second impression 1949).

61. Weber Max. 1958. 'The Protestant Ethic and Spirit of Capitalism'. (Translated into English by Talcott Parsons – original German title was 'Die Protestanhische Ethik und-der Geist des Kapitalismus – Charles Srichness Sons publication New York USA.

62. 'Capitalism' 1950 in Encyclopedia of Social Sciences' Volume III, New York, USA.

63. Hotel and Restaurant Association. 1985. 'Productivity Passport to Prosperity. Western Region' Published by United Agency Mumbai.

64. MATERIAL FROM MAGAZINES REFERRED TO: 1. Citadel 1990, 1991, 1992, 1993, 1994, 1997, 1998, 1999, 2001 for articles on Immigrants to Pune City. Published by Magna Publications Pune, India (1990 – 2000-2001). 2. Citizen, Weekly Magazine (Years 1989-1994) published by Indian Express group, Pune India.

65. For Appendix Section (Articles about restaurants, hotels around Pune) Newspapers referred to were Times of India, Indian Express, Sakal (Morning in Marathi).

BIBLIOGRAPHY – B

References: for Street Food vending in Pune.

1. Bapat Meera 1992: 'Street Food vending in Pune', Centre for studies in Social Sciences. Pune (India) C.S.S.S published by CSSSS Pune (India).
2. Pierre Bourdieu. 1984. 'Distinction: A social critique of judgment of taste'. Cambridge. Harvard University Press, USA.
3. Charmes Jacques. 1990. 'A Critical Review of Concepts, Definition, and Studies in the Informal Sector' in David Turnham et al (eds), The Informal Sector Revisited, O E C D Development Centre, Paris, France.
4. Keskar Anupama. 1990. 'Adjustment to the changing status of the Role of Old Age, A study of aged persons'. For Nehru Institute of Social Studies, Tilak Maharashtra Vidyapeeth, (TMV), Pune, Published by T.M.V. Pune 4110037.
5. Lubell Harold. 1991. 'The Informal Sector in the 1980s and 1990s'. OECD Development Centre Studies, OECD publication Paris, France.
6. Mazumdar Dipak. 1976. 'The Urban Informal Sector. World Development Volume 4 No 8.
7. Sethuraman. S.V. 1981. 'Concepts, methodology and Scope. Chapter 2 of Sethuraman. S.V. (Ed). 'The Urban Informal Sector in Developing Countries: Employment, Poverty and Environment, ILO – Geneva Switzerland.
8. Singh Yogendra. 2000. 'Culture Change in India' – Identity and Globalization: Rawat Publications, Jaipur India.
9. Tokmann Victor E 1990. 'The Informal Sector in Latin America: 15 years later in David Tumham et al (eds) The Informal Sector Revisited, OECD Development Centre, Paris, France.
10. Census Survey of Hawkers on BMC Lands. March 1998. Report by Tata Institute of Social Sciences (unit for Urban Studies, Deonar Mumbai, 400088, and Youth for unity and voluntary Action. YUVA – Mumbai. Study conducted for Brihan Mumbai Municipal Corporation, Mumbai.

11. Lever, W.F.1996. 'Summing Up' in Nigel Harris and Ida Fabric us(Ed) Cities and Structural Adjustment. (UCL)
12. Papola, T.S.1994. "The Informal Sector: Concept and policy in M.K. Rao (Ed) Growth of urban informal sector and economic development.'Kanishka publications, New Delhi.
13. Singer, Hans.1990.in David Turnham et.al (eds). 'The Informal Sector Revisited ed' OECD, Development Center, Paris, France.
14. Tokmann, Victor E.1990. 'The Informal Sector in Latin America: 15 years later in David Turnham et al (Eds)' The Informal sector revisited OECD Development Centre, Paris, France.
15. Townroe, P.M .1996 'Thechanging structure of the city economy' in Nigel Horrks and Ida Fabric us (Ed) Cities and Structural Adjustment. (UCL)
16. UNDP.1996. 'Human Development'. Oxford University Press, New York U S A.
17. Lever, W.F.1996 'Summing Up' in Nigel Harris and Ida Fabric us(Ed) Cities and Structural Adjustment'. (UCL)
18. Keith, Hart.1973. Internal income opportunities in urban employment Ghana, in 'The Journal of Modern African Studies' Vol. 11 no1.
19. ILO 1972. Employment, Income equality a strategy for increasing productive employment in Kenya, Geneva, Switzerland.

References

(FOR INDUSTRIES & PROFILE OF PUNE):

1. Neela Khandge (1978, 1985, 1990, 1995 editions), Industrial and Commercial Directory of Pune, Secretary General, Maharatta Chambers of Commerce and Industries and Agriculture, Tilak Road, Pune 411 002

2. Neela Khandge (1999 edition), Directory of Software Industry in Pune, Secretary General, Maharatta Chambers of Commerce and Industries and Agriculture, Tilak Road, Pune 411 002

3. Neela Khandge (1999 edition), Directory of Electronics Industry in Pune, Secretary General, Maharatta Chambers of Commerce and Industries and Agriculture, Tilak Road, Pune 411 002.

Index

R

T

U

V

W